Undergraduate Topics in Computer Science

Undergraduate Topics in Computer Science (UTiCS) delivers high-quality instructional content for undergraduates studying in all areas of computing and information science. From core foundational and theoretical material to final-year topics and applications, UTiCS books take a fresh, concise, and modern approach and are ideal for self-study or for a one- or two-semester course. The texts are all authored by established experts in their fields, reviewed by an international advisory board, and contain numerous examples and problems. Many include fully worked solutions.

More information about this series at http://www.springer.com/series/7592

Gerard O'Regan

Concise Guide to Software Engineering

From Fundamentals to Application Methods

 Springer

Gerard O'Regan
SQC Consulting
Cork
Ireland

ISSN 1863-7310   ISSN 2197-1781   (electronic)
Undergraduate Topics in Computer Science
ISBN 978-3-319-57749-4   ISBN 978-3-319-57750-0   (eBook)
DOI 10.1007/978-3-319-57750-0

Library of Congress Control Number: 2017939621

Printed on acid-free paper

This Springer imprint is published by Springer Nature
The registered company is Springer International Publishing AG
The registered company address is: Gewerbestrasse 11, 6330 Cham, Switzerland

In memory of my dear godmother

Mrs. Maureen Barry

Preface

Overview

The objective of this book was to provide a concise introduction to the software engineering field to students and practitioners. The principles of software engineering are discussed, and the goal is to give the reader a grasp of the fundamentals of the software engineering field, as well as guidance on how to apply the theory in an industrial environment.

Organization and Features

Chapter 1 presents a broad overview of software engineering, and discusses various software lifecycles and the phases in software development. We discuss requirements gathering and specification, software design, implementation, testing and maintenance. The lightweight Agile methodology is introduced, and it has become very popular in industry.

Chapter 2 provides an introduction to project management for traditional software engineering, and we discuss project estimation, project planning and scheduling, project monitoring and control, risk management, managing communication and change, and managing project quality.

Chapter 3 discusses requirements engineering and discusses activities such as requirements gathering, requirements elicitation, requirements analysis, requirements management, and requirements verification and validation.

Chapter 4 discusses design and development, and software design is the blueprint of the solution to be developed. It is concerned with the high-level architecture of the system, as well as the detailed design that describes the algorithms and functionality of the individual programmes. The detailed design is then implemented in a programming language such as C++ or Java. We discuss software development topics such as software reuse, customized-off-the-shelf software (COTS) and open-source software development.

Chapter 5 discusses software configuration management and discusses the fundamental concept of a baseline. Configuration management is concerned with identifying those deliverables that must be subject to change control, and controlling changes to them.

Chapter 6 discusses software inspections, which play an important role in building quality into a product. The well-known Fagan inspection process that was developed at IBM in the 1970s is discussed, as well as lighter review and walk-through methodologies.

Chapter 7 is concerned with software testing, and discusses the various types of testing that may be carried out during the project. We discuss test planning, test case definition, test environment set-up, test execution, test tracking, test metrics, test reporting and testing in an e-commerce environment.

Chapter 8 is concerned with the selection and management of a software supplier. It discusses how candidate suppliers may be identified, formally evaluated against defined selection criteria, and how the appropriate supplier is selected. We discuss how the selected supplier is managed during the project.

Chapter 9 discusses software quality assurance and the importance of process quality. It is a premise in the quality field that good processes and conformance to them is essential for the delivery of high-quality product, and this chapter discusses audits and describes how they are carried out.

Chapter 10 is concerned with software metrics and problem-solving, and this includes a discussion of the balanced score card which assists in identifying appropriate metrics for the organization. The Goal Question Metric (GQM) approach is discussed, and this allows appropriate metrics related to the organization goals to be defined. A selection of sample metrics for an organization is presented, and problem-solving tools such as fishbone diagrams, pareto charts and trend charts are discussed.

Chapter 11 discusses software reliability and dependability, and covers topics such as software reliability and software reliability models; the Cleanroom methodology, system availability; safety and security critical systems; and dependability engineering.

Chapter 12 discusses formal methods, which consist of a set of mathematical techniques to specify and derive a programme from its specification. Formal methods may be employed to rigorously state the requirements of the proposed system. They may be employed to derive a programme from its mathematical specification, and they may be used to provide a rigorous proof that the implemented programme satisfies its specification. They have been mainly applied to the safety critical field.

Chapter 13 presents the Z specification language, which is one of the more popular formal methods. It was developed at the Programming Research Group at Oxford University in the early 1980s. Z specifications are mathematical, and the use of mathematics ensures precision and allows inconsistencies and gaps in the specification to be identified. Theorem provers may be employed to demonstrate that the software implementation meets its specification.

Chapter 14 presents the unified modelling language (UML), which is a visual modelling language for software systems, and I used to present several views of the system architecture. It was developed at Rational Corporation as a notation for modelling object-oriented systems. We present various UML diagrams such as use case diagrams, sequence diagrams and activity diagrams.

Chapter 15 discusses software process improvement. It begins with a discussion of a software process, and discusses the benefits that may be gained from a software process improvement initiative. Various models that support software process improvement are discussed, and these include the Capability Maturity Model Integration (CMMI), ISO 9000, Personal Software Process (PSP) and Team Software Process (TSP).

Chapter 16 gives an overview of the CMMI model and discusses its five maturity levels and their constituent process areas. We discuss both the staged and continuous representations of the CMMI, and SCAMPI appraisals that indicate the extent to which the CMMI has been implemented in the organization, as well as identifying opportunities for improvement.

Chapter 17 discusses various tools to support the various software engineering activities. The focus is first to define the process and then to find tools to support the process. Tools to support project management are discussed as well as tools to support requirements engineering, configuration management, design and development activities and software testing.

Chapter 18 discusses the Agile methodology which is a popular lightweight approach to software development. Agile provides opportunities to assess the direction of a project throughout the development lifecycle, and ongoing changes to requirements are considered normal in the Agile world. It has a strong collaborative style of working, and it advocates adaptive planning and evolutionary development,

Chapter 19 discusses innovation in the software field including miscellaneous topics such as distributed systems, service-oriented architecture, software as a service, cloud computing and embedded systems. We discuss the need for innovation in software engineering, and discuss some recent innovations such as aspect-oriented software engineering.

Chapter 20 is the concluding chapter in which we summarize the journey that we have travelled in this book.

Audience

The main audience of this book are computer science students who are interested in learning about software engineering and in learning on how to build high-quality and reliable software on time and on budget. It will also be of interest to industrialists including software engineers, quality professionals and software managers, as well as the motivated general reader.

Acknowledgements

I am deeply indebted to family and friends who supported my efforts in this endeavour, and my thanks, as always, to the team at Springer. This book is dedicated to my late godmother (Mrs. Maureen Barry), who I always enjoyed visiting in Ringaskiddy, Co. Cork.

Cork, Ireland   Gerard O'Regan

Contents

List of Figures

List of Tables

Background

1

Abstract

This chapter presents a broad overview of software engineering and discusses various software lifecycles and the phases in software development. We discuss requirements gathering and specification, software design, implementation, testing and maintenance. The lightweight Agile methodology is introduced, and it has become very popular in industry. Mathematics may potentially assist software engineers in delivering high-quality software products that are safe to use and the extent to which mathematics should be employed remains a topic of active debate.

Keywords

Standish chaos report · Software lifecycles · Waterfall model · Spiral model · Rational Unified Process · Agile development · Software inspections · Software testing · Project management

1.1 Introduction

The approach to software development in the 1950s and 1960s has been described as the *"Mongolian Hordes Approach"* by Brooks [1].[1] The "method" or lack of method was applied to projects that were running late, and it involved adding a large number of inexperienced programmers to the project, with the expectation that this would allow the project schedule to be recovered. However, this approach was deeply flawed as it led to inexperienced programmers with inadequate knowledge

---

[1]The "Mongolian Hordes" management myth is the belief that adding more programmers to a software project that is running late will allow catch-up. In fact, as Brooks says adding people to a late software project actually makes it later.

© Springer International Publishing AG 2017
G. O'Regan, *Concise Guide to Software Engineering*, Undergraduate Topics in Computer Science, DOI 10.1007/978-3-319-57750-0_1

of the project attempting to solve problems, and they inevitably required significant time from the other project team members.

This resulted in the project being delivered even later, as well as subsequent problems with quality (i.e. the approach of throwing people at a problem does not work). The philosophy of software development back in the 1950/1960s was characterized by:

> The completed code will always be full of defects.
> The coding should be finished quickly to correct these defects.
> Design as you code approach.

This philosophy accepted defeat in software development and suggested that irrespective of a solid engineering approach, the completed software would always contain lots of defects and that it therefore made sense to code as quickly as possible and to then identify the defects that were present, so as to correct them as quickly as possible to solve a problem.

In the late 1960s, it was clear that the existing approaches to software development were deeply flawed and that there was an urgent need for change. The NATO Science Committee organized two famous conferences to discuss critical issues in software development [2]. The first conference was held at Garmisch, Germany, in 1968, and it was followed by a second conference in Rome in 1969. Over fifty people from eleven countries attended the Garmisch conference, including Edsger Dijkstra, who did important theoretical work on formal specification and verification. The NATO conferences highlighted problems that existed in the software sector in the late 1960s, and the term *"software crisis"* was coined to refer to these. There were problems with budget and schedule overruns, as well as the quality and reliability of the delivered software.

The conference led to the birth of *software engineering* as a discipline in its own right and the realization that programming is quite distinct from science and mathematics. Programmers are like engineers in that they build software products, and they therefore need education in traditional engineering as well as the latest technologies. The education of a classical engineer includes product design and mathematics. However, often computer science education places an emphasis on the latest technologies, rather than on the important engineering foundations of designing and building high-quality products that are safe for the public to use.

Programmers therefore need to learn the key engineering skills to enable them to build products that are safe for the public to use. This includes a solid foundation on design and on the mathematics required for building safe software products. Mathematics plays a key role in classical engineering, and in some situations, it may also assist software engineers in the delivery of high-quality software products. Several mathematical approaches to assist software engineers are described in [3].

There are parallels between the software crisis in the late 1960s and serious problems with bridge construction in the nineteenth century. Several bridges collapsed or were delivered late or overbudget, due to the fact that people involved in their design and construction did not have the required engineering knowledge.

Fig. 1.1 Standish report—
results of 1995 and 2009
survey

This led to bridges that were poorly designed and constructed, leading to their collapse and loss of life, as well as endangering the lives of the public.

This led to legislation requiring engineers to be licensed by the Professional Engineering Association prior to practicing as engineers. This organization specified a core body of knowledge that the engineer is required to possess, and the licensing body verifies that the engineer has the required qualifications and experience. This helps to ensure that only personnel competent to design and build products actually do so. Engineers have a professional responsibility to ensure that the products are properly built and are safe for the public to use.

The Standish group has conducted research (Fig. 1.1) on the extent of problems with IT projects since the mid-1990s. These studies were conducted in the USA, but there is no reason to believe that European or Asian companies perform any better. The results indicate serious problems with on-time delivery of projects and projects being cancelled prior to completion.[2] However, the comparison between 1995 and 2009 suggests that there have been some improvements with a greater percentage of projects being delivered successfully and a reduction in the percentage of projects being cancelled.

Fred Brooks argues that software is inherently complex and that there is no *silver bullet* that will resolve all of the problems associated with software development such as schedule or budget overruns [1, 4]. Poor software quality can lead to defects in the software that may adversely impact the customer and even lead to loss of life. It is therefore essential that software development organizations place sufficient emphasis on quality throughout the software development lifecycle.

The Y2K problem was caused by a two-digit representation of dates, and it required major rework to enable legacy software to function for the new millennium. Clearly, well-designed programs would have hidden the representation of the date, which would have required minimal changes for year 2000 compliance. Instead, companies spent vast sums of money to rectify the problem.

---

[2]These are IT projects covering diverse sectors including banking and telecommunications, rather than pure software companies. Software companies following maturity frameworks such as the CMMI generally achieve more consistent results.

The quality of software produced by some companies is impressive.[3] These companies employ mature software processes and are committed to continuous improvement. There is a lot of industrial interest in software process maturity models for software organizations, and various approaches to assess and mature software companies are described in [5, 6].[4] These models focus on improving the effectiveness of the management, engineering and organization practices related to software engineering and in introducing best practice in software engineering. The disciplined use of the mature software processes by the software engineers enables high-quality software to be consistently produced.

1.2 What Is Software Engineering?

Software engineering involves the multi-person construction of multi-version programs. The IEEE 610.12 definition of software engineering is:

> Software engineering is the application of a systematic, disciplined, quantifiable approach to the development, operation, and maintenance of software; that is, the application of engineering to software, and the study of such approaches.

Software engineering includes the following:

1. Methodologies to design, develop and test software to meet customers' needs.
2. Software is engineered. That is, the software products are properly designed, developed and tested in accordance with engineering principles.
3. Quality and safety are properly addressed.
4. Mathematics may be employed to assist with the design and verification of software products. The level of mathematics employed will depend on the *safety critical* nature of the product. Systematic peer reviews and rigorous testing will often be sufficient to build quality into the software, with heavy *mathematical techniques reserved for safety and security critical software.*
5. Sound project management and quality management practices are employed.
6. Support and maintenance of the software is properly addressed.

Software engineering is not just programming. It requires the engineer to state precisely the requirements that the software product is to satisfy and then to produce designs that will meet these requirements. The project needs to be planned and

---

[3]I recall projects at Motorola that regularly achieved 5.6σ-quality in a L4 CMM environment (i.e. approx. 20 defects per million lines of code. This represents very high quality).

[4]Approaches such as the CMM or SPICE (ISO 15504) focus mainly on the management and organizational practices required in software engineering. The emphasis is on defining software processes that are fit for purpose and consistently following them. The process maturity models focus on what needs to be done rather how it should be done. This gives the organization the freedom to choose the appropriate implementation to meet its needs. The models provide useful information on practices to consider in the implementation.

delivered on time and budget. The requirements must provide a precise description of the problem to be solved, i.e. *it should be evident from the requirements what is and what is not required.*

The requirements need to be rigorously reviewed to ensure that they are stated clearly and unambiguously and reflect the customer's needs. The next step is then to create the design that will solve the problem, and it is essential to validate the correctness of the design. Next, the software code to implement the design is written, and peer reviews and software testing are employed to verify and validate the correctness of the software.

The verification and validation of the design is rigorously performed for safety critical systems, and it is sometimes appropriate to employ mathematical techniques for these systems. However, it will usually be sufficient to employ peer reviews or software inspections as these methodologies provide a high degree of rigour. This may include approaches such as Fagan inspections [7], Gilb's inspections [8] or Prince 2's approach to quality reviews [9].

The term *"engineer"* is a title that is awarded on merit in classical engineering. It is generally applied only to people who have attained the necessary education and competence to be called engineers and who base their practice on classical engineering principles. The title places responsibilities on its holder to behave professionally and ethically. Often, in computer science, the term *"software engineer"* is employed loosely to refer to anyone who builds things, rather than to an individual with a core set of knowledge, experience and competence.

Several computer scientists (such as Parnas[5]) have argued that computer scientists should be educated as engineers to enable them to apply appropriate scientific principles to their work. They argue that computer scientists should receive a solid foundation in mathematics and design, to enable them to have the professional competence to perform as engineers in building high-quality products that are safe for the public to use. The use of mathematics is an integral part of the engineer's work in other engineering disciplines, and so the *software engineer* should be able to use mathematics to assist in the modelling or understanding of the behaviour or properties of the proposed software system.

Software engineers need education[6] on specification, design, turning designs into programs, software inspections and testing. The education should enable the software engineer to produce well-structured programs that are fit for purpose.

---

[5]Parnas has made important contributions to computer science. He advocates a solid engineering approach with the extensive use of classical mathematical techniques in software development. He also introduced information hiding in the 1970s, which is now a part of object-oriented design.

[6]Software companies that are following approaches such as the CMM or ISO 9001 consider the education and qualification of staff prior to assigning staff to performing specific tasks. The appropriate qualifications and experience for the specific role are considered prior to appointing a person to carry out the role. Many companies are committed to the education and continuous development of their staff and on introducing best practice in software engineering into their organization.

Parnas has argued that software engineers have responsibilities as professional engineers.[7] They are responsible for designing and implementing high-quality and reliable software that is safe to use. They are also accountable for their decisions and actions[8] and have a responsibility to object to decisions that violate professional standards. Engineers are required to behave professionally and ethically with their clients. The membership of the professional engineering body requires the member to adhere to the code of ethics[9] of the profession. Engineers in other professions are licensed, and therefore, Parnas argues a similar licensing approach be adopted for professional software engineers[10] to provide confidence that they are competent for the particular assignment. Professional software engineers are required to follow best practice in software engineering and the defined software processes.[11]

Many software companies invest heavily in training, as the education and knowledge of its staff are essential to delivering high-quality products and services. Employees receive professional training related to the roles that they are performing, such as project management, software design and development, software testing and service management. The fact that the employees are professionally qualified increases confidence in the ability of the company to deliver high-quality products and services. A company that pays little attention to the competence and continuous development of its staff will obtain poor results and suffer a loss of reputation and market share.

---

[7]The ancient Babylonians used the concept of accountability, and they employed a code of laws (known as the Hammurabi Code) c. 1750 B.C. It included a law that stated that if a house collapsed and killed the owner, then the builder of the house would be executed.

[8]However, it is unlikely that an individual programmer would be subject to litigation in the case of a flaw in a program causing damage or loss of life. A comprehensive disclaimer of responsibility for problems rather than a guarantee of quality accompanies most software products. Software engineering is a team-based activity involving many engineers in various parts of the project, and it would be potentially difficult for an outside party to prove that the cause of a particular problem is due to the professional negligence of a particular software engineer, as there are many others involved in the process such as reviewers of documentation and code and the various test groups. Companies are more likely to be subject to litigation, as a company is legally responsible for the actions of their employees in the workplace, and a company is a wealthier entity than one of its employees. The legal aspects of licensing software may protect software companies from litigation. However, greater legal protection for the customer can be built into the contract between the supplier and the customer for bespoke software development.

[9]Many software companies have a defined code of ethics that employees are expected to adhere. Larger companies will wish to project a good corporate image and to be respected worldwide.

[10]The British Computer Society (BCS) has introduced a qualification system for computer science professionals that it used to show that professionals are properly qualified. The most important of these is the BCS Information System Examination Board (ISEB) which allows IT professionals to be qualified in service management, project management, software testing and so on.

[11]Software companies that are following the CMMI or ISO 9001 standards will employ audits to verify that the processes and procedures have been followed. Auditors report their findings to management, and the findings are addressed appropriately by the project team and affected individuals.

1.3 Challenges in Software Engineering

The challenge in software engineering is to deliver high-quality software on time and on budget to customers. The research done by the Standish group was discussed earlier in this chapter, and the results of their 1998 research (Fig. 1.2) on project cost overruns in the US indicated that 33% of projects are between 21 and 50% overestimate, 18% are between 51 and 100% overestimate and 11% of projects are between 101 and 200% overestimate.

The accurate estimation of project cost, effort and schedule is a challenge in software engineering. Therefore, project managers need to determine how good their estimation process actually is and to make appropriate improvements. The use of software metrics is an objective way to do this, and improvements in estimation will be evident from a reduced variance between estimated and actual effort. The project manager will determine and report the actual versus estimated effort and schedule for the project.

Risk management is an important part of project management, and the objective is to identify potential risks early and throughout the project and to manage them appropriately. The probability of each risk occurring and its impact is determined, and the risks are managed during project execution.

Software quality needs to be properly planned to enable the project to deliver a quality product. Flaws with poor quality software lead to a negative perception of the company and may potentially lead to damage to the customer relationship with a subsequent loss of market share.

There is a strong economic case to building quality into the software, as less time is spent in reworking defective software. The cost of poor quality (COPQ) should be measured and targets set for its reductions. It is important that lessons are learned during the project and acted upon appropriately. This helps to promote a culture of continuous improvement.

A number of high-profile software failures are discussed in [6]. These include the millennium bug (Y2K) problem; the floating-point bug in the Intel microprocessor; the European Space Agency Ariane-5 disaster; and so on. These failures led to embarrassment for the organizations, as well as the associated cost of replacement and correction.

Fig. 1.2 Standish 1998 report—estimation accuracy

The millennium bug was due to the use of two digits to represent dates rather than four digits. The solution involved finding and analysing all code that had a Y2K impact; planning and making the necessary changes; and verifying the correctness of the changes. The worldwide cost of correcting the millennium bug is estimated to have been in billions of dollars.

The Intel Corporation was slow to acknowledge the floating-point problem in its Pentium microprocessor and in providing adequate information on its impact to its customers. It incurred a large financial cost in replacing microprocessors for its customers. The Ariane-5 failure caused major embarrassment and damage to the credibility of the European Space Agency (ESA). Its maiden flight ended in failure on 4 June 1996, after a flight time of just 40 s.

These failures indicate that quality needs to be carefully considered when designing and developing software. The effect of software failure may be large costs to correct the software, loss of credibility of the company or even loss of life.

1.4   Software Processes and Lifecycles

Organizations vary by size and complexity, and the processes employed will reflect the nature of their business. The development of software involves many processes such as those for defining requirements; processes for project estimation and planning; and processes for design, implementation, testing, and so on.

It is important that the processes employed are fit for purpose, and a key premise in the software quality field is that the quality of the resulting software is influenced by the quality and maturity of the underlying processes and compliance to them. Therefore, it is necessary to focus on the quality of the processes as well as the quality of the resulting software.

There is, of course, little point in having high-quality processes unless their use is institutionalized in the organization. That is, all employees need to follow the processes consistently. This requires that the employees are trained on the processes and that process discipline is instilled with an appropriate audit strategy that ensures compliance to them. Data will be collected to improve the process. The software process assets in an organization generally consist of:

- A software development policy for the organization,
- Process maps that describe the flow of activities,
- Procedures and guidelines that describe the processes in more detail,
- Checklists to assist with the performance of the process,
- Templates for the performance of specific activities (e.g. design, testing),
- Training materials.

The processes employed to develop high-quality software generally include the following:

– Project management process,
– Requirements process,
– Design process,
– Coding process,
– Peer review process,
– Testing process,
– Supplier selection and management processes,
– Configuration management process,
– Audit process,
– Measurement process,
– Improvement process,
– Customer support and maintenance processes.

The software development process has an associated lifecycle that consists of various phases. There are several well-known lifecycles employed such as the waterfall model [10], the spiral model [11], the Rational Unified Process [12] and the Agile methodology [13] which have become popular in recent years. The choice of a particular software development lifecycle is determined from the particular needs of the specific project. The various lifecycles are described in more detail in the following sections.

1.4.1 Waterfall Lifecycle

The waterfall model (Fig. 1.3) starts with requirements gathering and definition. It is followed by the system specification (with the functional and non-functional requirements), the design and implementation of the software, and comprehensive testing. The testing generally includes unit, system and user acceptance testing.

The waterfall model is employed for projects where the requirements can be identified early in the project lifecycle or are known in advance. We are treating the waterfall model as the "V" life cycle model, with the left-hand side of the "V"

Fig. 1.3 Waterfall V lifecycle model

detailing requirements, specification, design and coding and the right-hand side detailing unit tests, integration tests, system tests and acceptance testing. Each phase has entry and exit criteria that must be satisfied before the next phase commences. There are several variations to the waterfall model.

Many companies employ a set of templates to enable the activities in the various phases to be consistently performed. Templates may be employed for project planning and reporting; requirements definition; design; testing; and so on. These templates may be based on the IEEE standards or industrial best practice.

1.4.2   Spiral Lifecycles

The spiral model (Fig. 1.4) was developed by Barry Boehm in the 1980s [11], and it is useful for projects where the requirements are not fully known at project initiation, or where the requirements evolve as a part of the development lifecycle. The development proceeds in a number of spirals, where each spiral typically involves objectives and an analysis of the risks, updates to the requirements, design, code, testing and a user review of the particular iteration or spiral.

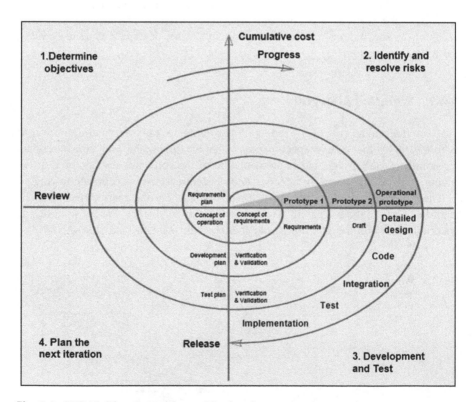

Fig. 1.4 SPIRAL lifecycle model … public domain

The spiral is, in effect, a reusable prototype with the business analysts and the customer reviewing the current iteration and providing feedback to the development team. The feedback is analysed and used to plan the next iteration. This approach is often used in joint application development, where the usability and look and feel of the application are a key concern. This is important in Web-based development and in the development of a graphical user interface (GUI). The implementation of part of the system helps in gaining a better understanding of the requirements of the system, and this feeds into subsequent development cycles. The process repeats until the requirements and the software product are fully complete.

There are several variations of the spiral model including rapid application development (RAD); joint application development (JAD) models; and the dynamic systems development method (DSDM) model. The Agile methodology (discussed in Chap. 18) has become popular in recent years, and it employs sprints (or iterations) of 2- to 4-week duration to implement a number of user stories. A sample spiral model is shown in Fig. 1.4.

There are other life-cycle models such as the iterative development process that combines the waterfall and spiral lifecycle model. An overview of Cleanroom is presented in Chap. 11, and the methodology was developed by Harlan Mills at IBM. It includes a phase for formal specification, and its approach to software testing is based on the predicted usage of the software product, which allows a software reliability measure to be calculated. The Rational Unified Process (RUP) was developed by Rational, and it is discussed in the next section.

1.4.3   Rational Unified Process

The *Rational Unified Process* [12] was developed at the Rational Corporation (now part of IBM) in the late 1990s. It uses the unified modelling language (UML) as a tool for specification and design, where UML is a visual modelling language for software systems that provides a means of specifying, constructing and documenting the object-oriented system. It was developed by James Rumbaugh, Grady Booch and Ivar Jacobson, and it facilitates the understanding of the architecture and complexity of the system.

RUP is *use case driven, architecture centric, iterative* and *incremental* and includes cycles, phases, workflows, risk mitigation, quality control, project management and configuration control (Fig. 1.5). Software projects may be very complex, and there are risks that requirements may be incomplete or that the interpretation of a requirement may differ between the customer and the project team. RUP is a way to reduce risk in software engineering.

Requirements are gathered as use cases, where the *use cases describe the functional requirements from the point of view of the user of the system.* They describe what the system will do at a high level and ensure that there is an appropriate focus on the user when defining the scope of the project. *Use cases also drive the development process*, as the developers create a series of design and implementation models that realize the use cases. The developers review each

Fig. 1.5 Rational Unified Process

successive model for conformance to the use case model, and the test team verifies that the implementation correctly implements the use cases.

The software architecture concept embodies the most significant static and dynamic aspects of the system. The architecture grows out of the use cases and factors such as the platform that the software is to run on, deployment considerations, legacy systems and the non-functional requirements.

RUP decomposes the work of a large project into smaller slices or mini-projects, and *each mini-project is an iteration that results in an increment to the product.* The iteration consists of one or more steps in the workflow and generally leads to the growth of the product. If there is a need to repeat an iteration, then all that is lost is the misdirected effort of one iteration, rather than the entire product. In other words, RUP is a way to mitigate risk in software engineering.

1.4.4   Agile Development

There has been a massive growth of popularity among software developers in lightweight methodologies such as *Agile*. This is a software development methodology that is more responsive to customer needs than traditional methods such as the waterfall model. *The waterfall development model is similar to a wide and slow moving value stream*, and halfway through the project, 100% of the requirements are typically 50% done. *However, for agile development, 50% of requirements are typically 100% done halfway through the project.*

This methodology has a strong collaborative style of working, and its approach includes the following:

- Aims to achieve a narrow fast flowing value stream,
- Feedback and adaptation employed in decision-making,
- User stories and sprints are employed,
- Stories are either done or not done (no such thing as 50% done),
- Iterative and incremental development is employed,
- A project is divided into iterations,
- An iteration has a fixed length (i.e. time boxing is employed),
- Entire software development lifecycle is employed for the implementation of each story,
- Change is accepted as a normal part of life in the Agile world,
- Delivery is made as early as possible,
- Maintenance is seen as part of the development process,
- Refactoring and evolutionary design employed,
- Continuous integration is employed,
- Short cycle times,
- Emphasis on quality,
- Stand-up meetings,
- Plan regularly,
- Direct interaction preferred over documentation,
- Rapid conversion of requirements into working functionality,
- Demonstrate value early,
- Early decision-making.

Ongoing changes to requirements are considered normal in the Agile world, and it is believed to be more realistic to change requirements regularly throughout the project rather than attempting to define all of the requirements at the start of the project. The methodology includes controls to manage changes to the requirements, and good communication and early regular feedback are an essential part of the process.

A story may be a new feature or a modification to an existing feature. It is reduced to the minimum scope that can deliver business value, and a feature may give rise to several stories. Stories often build upon other stories, and the entire software development lifecycle is employed for the implementation of each story. *Stories are either done or not done*, i.e. *there is such thing as a story being 80% done*. The story is complete only when it passes its acceptance tests. Stories are prioritized based on a number of factors including:

- Business value of story,
- Mitigation of risk,
- Dependencies on other stories.

The Scrum approach is an Agile method for managing iterative development, and it consists of an outline planning phase for the project followed by a set of sprint cycles (where each cycle develops an increment). *Sprint planning* is performed before the start of the iteration, and stories are assigned to the iteration to fill the available time. Each Scrum sprint is of a fixed length (usually 2–4 weeks), and it develops an increment of the system. The estimates for each story and their priority are determined, and the prioritized stories are assigned to the iteration. *A short morning stand-up meeting is held daily* during the iteration and attended by the Scrum master, the project manager[12] and the project team. It discusses the progress made the previous day, problem reporting and tracking, and the work planned for the day ahead. A separate meeting is held for issues that require more detailed discussion.

Once the iteration is complete, the latest product increment is demonstrated to an audience including the product owner. This is to receive feedback and to identify new requirements. The team also conducts a retrospective meeting to identify what went well and what went poorly during the iteration. This is for continuous improvement of the future iterations. Planning for the next sprint then commences. The Scrum master is a facilitator who arranges the daily meetings and ensures that the Scrum process is followed. The role involves removing roadblocks so that the team can achieve their goals and communicating with other stakeholders.

Agile employs pair programming and a collaborative style of working with the philosophy that two heads are better than one. This allows multiple perspectives in decision-making and a broader understanding of the issues.

Software testing is very important, and Agile generally employs automated testing for unit, acceptance, performance and integration testing. Tests are run frequently with the goal of catching programming errors early. They are generally run on a separate build server to ensure that all dependencies are checked. Tests are rerun before making a release. *Agile employs test-driven development with tests written before the code.* The developers write code to make a test pass with ideally developers only coding against failing tests. This approach forces the developer to write testable code.

Refactoring is employed in Agile as a design and coding practice. The objective is to change how the software is written without changing what it does. Refactoring is a tool for evolutionary design where the design is regularly evaluated, and improvements are implemented as they are identified. It helps in improving the maintainability and readability of the code and in reducing complexity. The automated test suite is essential in showing that the integrity of the software is maintained following refactoring.

Continuous integration allows the system to be built with every change. Early and regular integration allows early feedback to be provided. It also allows all of the automated tests to be run, thereby identifying problems earlier. Agile is discussed in more detail in Chap. 18.

---

[12]Agile teams are self-organizing and the project manager role is generally not employed for small projects (<20 staff).

1.5 Activities in Waterfall Lifecycle

The waterfall software development lifecycle consists of various activities including the following:

- User (Business) requirements definition,
- Specification of system requirements,
- Design,
- Implementation,
- Unit testing,
- System testing,
- UAT testing,
- Support and maintenance.

These activities are discussed in the following sections, and the description is specific to the non-Agile world.

1.5.1 User Requirements Definition

The user (business) requirements specify what the customer wants and define what the software system is required to do (*as distinct from how this is to be done*). The requirements are the foundation for the system, and if they are incorrect, then the implemented system will be incorrect. *Prototyping may be employed* to assist in the definition and validation of the requirements. The process of determining the requirements, analysing and validating them and managing them throughout the project lifecycle is termed *requirements engineering*.

The *user requirements* are determined from discussions with the customer to determine their actual needs, and they are then refined into the *system requirements*, which state the *functional* and *non-functional* requirements of the system. The specification of the user requirements needs to be unambiguous to ensure that all parties involved in the development of the system share a common understanding of what is to be developed and tested.

Requirements gathering involves meetings with the stakeholders to gather all relevant information for the proposed product. The stakeholders are interviewed, and requirements workshops are conducted to elicit the requirements from them. An early working system (prototype) is often used to identify gaps and misunderstandings between developers and users. The prototype may serve as a basis for writing the specification.

The requirements workshops are used to discuss and prioritize the requirements, as well as identifying and resolving any conflicting requirements. The collected information is consolidated into a coherent set of requirements. Changes to the requirements may occur during the project, and these need to be controlled. It is essential to understand the impacts (e.g. schedule, budget and technical) of a proposed change to the requirements prior to its approval.

Requirements verification is concerned with ensuring that the requirements are properly implemented (i.e. building it right) in the design and implementation. *Requirements validation* is concerned with ensuring that the right requirements are defined (building the right system) and that they are precise, complete and reflect the actual needs of the customer.

The requirements are validated by the stakeholders to ensure that they are actually those desired and to establish their feasibility. This may involve several reviews of the requirements until all stakeholders are ready to approve the requirements document. Other validation activities include reviews of the prototype and the design, and user acceptance testing.

The requirements for a system are generally documented in a natural language such as "English". Other notations that are employed include the visual modelling language UML [14] and formal specification languages such as VDM or Z for the safety critical field.

The Agile software development methodology argues that as requirements change so quickly that a requirements document is unnecessary, since such a document would be out of date as soon as it was written.

1.5.2 Specification of System Requirements

The specification of the system requirements of the product is essentially a statement of what the software development organization will provide to meet the business (user) requirements. That is, the detailed business requirements are a statement of what the customer wants, whereas the specification of the system requirements is a statement of what will be delivered by the software development organization.

It is essential that the system requirements are valid with respect to the user requirements, and they are reviewed by the stakeholders to ensure their validity. Traceability may be employed to show that the business requirements are addressed by the system requirements.

There are two categories of system requirements, namely functional and non-functional requirements. The *functional requirements* define the functionality that is required of the system, and it may include screenshots, report layouts or desired functionality specified as use cases. The *non-functional requirements* will generally include security, reliability, availability, performance and portability requirements, as well as usability and maintainability requirements.

1.5.3 Design

The design of the system consists of engineering activities to describe the architecture or structure of the system, as well as activities to describe the algorithms and functions required to implement the system requirements. It is a creative process concerned with how the system will be implemented, and its activities include architecture design, interface design and data structure design. There are often several possible design solutions for a particular system, and the designer will need to decide on the most appropriate solution.

The design may be specified in various ways such as graphical notations that display the relationships between the components making up the design. The notation may include flow charts, or various UML diagrams such as sequence diagrams, state charts and so on. Program description languages or pseudocode may be employed to define the algorithms and data structures that are the basis for implementation.

Function-oriented design is mainly historical, and it involves starting with a high-level view of the system and refining it into a more detailed design. The system state is centralized and shared between the functions operating on that state.

Object-oriented design has become popular, and it is based on the concept of *information hiding* developed by Parnas [15]. The system is viewed as a collection of objects rather than functions, with each object managing its own state information. The system state is decentralized, and an object is a member of a class. The definition of a class includes attributes and operations on class members, and these may be inherited from superclasses. Objects communicate by exchanging messages.

It is essential to verify and validate the design with respect to the system requirements, and this will be done by traceability of the design to the system requirements and design reviews.

1.5.4 Implementation

This phase is concerned with implementing the design in the target language and environment (e.g. C++ or Java), and it involves writing or generating the actual code. The development team divides up the work to be done, with each programmer responsible for one or more modules. The coding activities often include code reviews or walk-throughs to ensure that quality code is produced and to verify its correctness. The code reviews will verify that the source code conforms to the coding standards and that maintainability issues are addressed. They will also verify that the code produced is a valid implementation of the software design.

Software reuse provides a way to speed up the development process. Components or objects that may be reused need to be identified and handled accordingly. The implemented code may use software components that have either being developed internally or purchased off the shelf. Open-source software has become popular in recent years, and it allows software developed by others to be used (*under an open-source licence*) in the development of applications.

The benefits of software reuse include increased productivity and a faster time to market. There are inherent risks with customized-off-the shelf (COTS) software, as the supplier may decide to no longer support the software, or there is no guarantee that software that has worked successfully in one domain will work correctly in a different domain. It is therefore important to consider the risks as well as the benefits of software reuse and open-source software.

1.5.5   Software Testing

Software testing is employed to verify that the requirements have been correctly implemented and that the software is fit for purpose, as well as identifying defects present in the software. There are various types of testing that may be conducted including *unit testing, integration testing, system testing, performance testing and user acceptance testing*. These are described below:

Unit Testing

Unit testing is performed by the programmer on the completed unit (or module) and prior to its integration with other modules. The programmer writes these tests, and the objective is to show that the code satisfies the design. The unit test case is generally documented, and it should include the test objective and the expected results.

Code coverage and branch coverage metrics are often generated to give an indication of how comprehensive the unit testing has been. These metrics provide visibility into the number of lines of code executed, as well as the branches covered during unit testing.

The developer executes the unit tests; records the results; corrects any identified defects; and retests the software. *Test-driven development* (TDD) has become popular (e.g. in the Agile world) this involves writing the unit test cases (and possibly other test cases) before the code, and the code is then written to pass the defined test cases.

Integration Test

The development team performs this type of testing on the integrated system, once all of the individual units work correctly in isolation. The objective is to verify that all of the modules and their interfaces work correctly together and to identify and resolve any issues. Modules that work correctly in isolation may fail when integrated with other modules. The developers generally perform this type of testing.

System Test

The purpose of system testing is to verify that the implementation is valid with respect to the system requirements. It involves the specification of system test cases, and the execution of the test cases will verify that the system requirements have been correctly implemented. An independent test group generally conducts this type of testing, and the system tests are traceable to the system requirements.

Any system requirements that have been incorrectly implemented will be identified and defects logged and reported to the developers. The test group will verify that the new version of the software is correct, and regression testing is conducted to verify system integrity. System testing may include security testing, usability testing and performance testing.

The preparation of the test environment requires detailed planning, and it may involve ordering special hardware and tools. It is important that the test environment is set up early to allow the timely execution of the test cases.

Performance Test

The purpose of performance testing is to ensure that the performance of the system is within the bounds specified by the non-functional requirements. It may include *load performance testing*, where the system is subjected to heavy loads over a long period of time, and *stress testing*, where the system is subjected to heavy loads during a short time interval.

Performance testing often involves the simulation of many users using the system and involves measuring the response times for various activities. Test tools are employed to simulate a large number of users and heavy loads. It is also employed to determine whether the system is scalable to support future growth.

User Acceptance Test

UAT testing is usually performed under controlled conditions at the customer site, and its operation will closely resemble the real-life behaviour of the system. The customer will see the product in operation and will judge whether or not the system is fit for purpose.

The objective is to demonstrate that the product satisfies the business requirements and meets the customer expectations. Upon its successful completion, the customer is happy to accept the product.

1.5.6   Support and Maintenance

This phase continues after the release of the software product to the customer. Software systems often have a long lifetime, and the software needs to be continuously enhanced over its lifetime to meet the evolving needs of the customers. This may involve regular new releases with new functionality and corrections to known defects.

Any problems that the customer identifies with the software are reported as per the customer support and maintenance agreement. The support issues will require investigation, and the issue may be *a defect in the software, an enhancement to the software* or *due to a misunderstanding*. The support and maintenance team will identify the causes of any identified defects and will implement an appropriate solution to resolve. Testing is conducted to verify that the solution is correct and that the changes made have not adversely affected other parts of the system. Mature organizations will conduct post-mortems to learn lessons from the defect[13] and will take corrective action to prevent a reoccurrence.

The presence of a maintenance phase suggests an acceptance of the reality that problems with the software will be identified post-release. The goal of building a correct and reliable software product the first time is very difficult to achieve, and the customer is always likely to find some issues with the released software product. It is accepted today that quality needs to be built into each step in the development process, with the role of software inspections and testing to identify as many defects as possible prior to release and minimize the risk that serious defects will be found post-release.

The effective in-phase inspections of the deliverables will influence the quality of the resulting software and lead to a corresponding reduction in the number of defects. The testing group plays a key role in verifying that the system is correct and in providing confidence that the software is fit for purpose and ready to be released. The approach to software correctness involves testing and retesting, until the testing group believes that all defects have been eliminated. Dijkstra [16] comments on testing are well known:

> Testing a program demonstrates that it contains errors, never that it is correct.

That is, irrespective of the amount of time spent testing, it can never be said with absolute confidence that all defects have been found in the software. Testing provides increased confidence that the program is correct, and statistical techniques may be employed to give a measure of the software reliability.

Many software companies may consider one defect per thousand lines of code (KLOC) to be reasonable quality. However, if the system contains one million lines of code, this is equivalent to a thousand post-release defects, which is unacceptable.

Some mature organizations have a quality objective of three defects per million lines of code, which was introduced by Motorola as part of its Six-Sigma (6σ) program. It was originally applied it to its manufacturing businesses and subsequently applied to its software organizations. The goal is to reduce variability in manufacturing processes and to ensure that the processes performed within strict process control limits.

1.6   Software Inspections

Software inspections are used to build quality into software products. There are a number of well-known approaches such as the Fagan methodology [17]; Gilb's approach [8]; and Prince 2's approach.

---

[13]This is essential for serious defects that have caused significant inconvenience to customers (e.g. a major telecoms outage). The software development organization will wish to learn lessons to determine what went wrong in its processes that prevented the defect from been identified during peer reviews and testing. Actions to prevent a reoccurrence will be identified and implemented.

Fagan inspections were developed by Michael Fagan of IBM. It is a seven-step process that identifies and removes errors in work products. The process mandates that requirement documents, design documents, source code and test plans are all formally inspected by experts independent of the author of the deliverable to ensure quality.

There are various *roles* defined in the process including the *moderator* who chairs the inspection. The *reader's* responsibility is to read or paraphrase the particular deliverable, and *the author* is the creator of the deliverable and has a special interest in ensuring that it is correct. The *tester* role is concerned with the test viewpoint.

The inspection process will consider whether the design is correct with respect to the requirements, and whether the source code is correct with respect to the design. Software inspections play an important role in building quality into software and in reducing the cost of poor quality in the organization.

1.7 Software Project Management

The timely delivery of quality software requires good management and engineering processes. Software projects have a history of being delivered late or overbudget, and good project management practices include the following activities:

- Estimation of cost, effort and schedule for the project,
- Identifying and managing risks,
- Preparing the project plan,
- Preparing the initial project schedule and key milestones,
- Obtaining approval for the project plan and schedule,
- Staffing the project,
- Monitoring progress, budget, schedule, effort, risks, issues, change requests and quality,
- Taking corrective action,
- Replanning and rescheduling,
- Communicating progress to affected stakeholders,
- Preparing status reports and presentations.

The project plan will contain or reference several other plans such as the project quality plan; the communication plan; the configuration management plan; and the test plan.

Project estimation and scheduling are difficult as often software projects are breaking new ground and may differ from previous projects. That is, previous estimates may often not be a good basis for estimation for the current project. Often, unanticipated problems can arise for technically advanced projects, and the estimates may often be optimistic. Gantt charts are often employed for project scheduling, and these show the work breakdown for the project, as well as task dependencies and allocation of staff to the various tasks.

The effective management of risk during a project is essential to project success. Risks arise due to uncertainty, and the risk management cycle involves[14] risk identification; risk analysis and evaluation; identifying responses to risks; selecting and planning a response to the risk; and risk monitoring. The risks are logged, and the likelihood of each risk arising and its impact is then determined. The risk is assigned an owner and an appropriate response to the risk determined.

1.8 CMMI Maturity Model

The CMMI is a framework to assist an organization in the implementation of best practice in software and systems engineering. It is an internationally recognized model for software process improvement and assessment and is used worldwide by thousands of organizations. It provides a solid engineering approach to the development of software, and it supports the definition of high-quality processes for the various software engineering and management activities.

It was developed by the Software Engineering Institute (SEI) who adapted the process improvement principles used in the manufacturing field to the software field. They developed the original CMM model and its successor CMMI. The CMMI states *what the organization needs to do* to mature its processes rather than *how this should be done*.

The CMMI consists of five maturity levels with each maturity level consisting of several process areas. Each process area consists of a set of goals, and these goals are implemented by practices related to that process area. Level two is focused on management practices; level three is focused on engineering and organization practices; level four is concerned with ensuring that key processes are performing within strict quantitative limits; and level five is concerned with continuous process improvement. Maturity levels may not be skipped in the staged representation of the CMMI, as each maturity level is the foundation for the next level. The CMMI and Agile are compatible, and CMMI v1.3 supports Agile software development.

The CMMI allows organizations to benchmark themselves against other organizations. This is done by a formal SCAMPI appraisal conducted by an authorized lead appraiser. The results of the appraisal are generally reported back to the SEI, and there is a strict qualification process to become an *authorized lead appraiser*. An appraisal is useful in verifying that an organization has improved, and it enables the organization to prioritize improvements for the next improvement cycle. The CMMI is discussed in more detail in Chap. 16.

---

[14]These are the risk management activities in the Prince 2 methodology.

1.9   Formal Methods

Dijkstra and Hoare have argued that the way to develop correct software is to derive the program from its specifications using mathematics and to employ *mathematical proof* to demonstrate its correctness with respect to the specification. This offers a rigorous framework to develop programs adhering to the highest quality constraints. However, in practice, mathematical techniques have proved to be cumbersome to use, and their widespread use in industry is unlikely at this time.

The *safety-critical area* is one domain to which mathematical techniques have been successfully applied. There is a need for extra rigour in the safety and security critical fields, and mathematical techniques can demonstrate the presence or absence of certain desirable or undesirable properties (e.g. *"when a train is in a level crossing, then the gate is closed"*).

Spivey [18] defines a *"formal specification"* as the use of mathematical notation to describe in a precise way the properties which an information system must have, without unduly constraining the way in which these properties are achieved. It describes *what* the system must do, as distinct from *how* it is to be done. This abstraction away from implementation enables questions about what the system does to be answered, independently of the detailed code. Further, the unambiguous nature of mathematical notation avoids the problem of ambiguity in an imprecisely worded natural language description of a system.

The formal specification thus becomes the key reference point for the different parties concerned with the construction of the system and is a useful way of promoting a common understanding for all those concerned with the system. The term *"formal methods"* is used to describe a formal specification language and a method for the design and implementation of computer systems.

The specification is written precisely in a mathematical language. The derivation of an implementation from the specification may be achieved via *stepwise refinement*. Each refinement step makes the specification more concrete and closer to the actual implementation. There is an associated *proof obligation* that the refinement be valid and that the concrete state preserves the properties of the more abstract state. Thus, assuming the original specification is correct, and the proofs of correctness of each refinement step are valid; then, there is a very high degree of confidence in the correctness of the implemented software.

Formal methods have been applied to a diverse range of applications, including circuit design, artificial intelligence, specification of standards, specification and verification of programs. They are described in more detail in Chap. 12.

1.10   Review Questions

1. Discuss the research results of the Standish group the current state of IT project delivery?
2. What are the main challenges in software engineering?
3. Describe various software lifecycles such as the waterfall model and the spiral model.
4. Discuss the benefits of Agile over conventional approaches. List any risks and disadvantages?
5. Describe the purpose of the CMMI? What are the benefits?
6. Describe the main activities in software inspections.
7. Describe the main activities in software testing.
8. Describe the main activities in project management?
9. What are the advantages and disadvantages of formal methods?

1.11   Summary

The birth of software engineering was at the NATO conference held in 1968 in Germany. This conference highlighted the problems that existed in the software sector in the late 1960s, and the term "*software crisis*" was coined to refer to these. The conference led to the realization that programming is quite distinct from science and mathematics and that software engineers need to be properly trained to enable them to build high-quality products that are safe to use.

The Standish group conducts research on the extent of problems with the delivery of projects on time and budget. Their research indicates that it remains a challenge to deliver projects on time, on budget and with the right quality.

Programmers are like engineers in the sense that they build products. Therefore, programmers need to receive an appropriate education in engineering as part of their training. The education of traditional engineers includes training on product design and an appropriate level of mathematics.

Software engineering involves multi-person construction of multi-version programs. It is a systematic approach to the development and maintenance of the software, and it requires a precise statement of the requirements of the software product and then the design and development of a solution to meet these requirements. It includes methodologies to design, develop, implement and test software as well as sound project management, quality management and configuration management practices. Support and maintenance of the software needs to be properly addressed.

Software process maturity models such as the CMMI have become popular in recent years. They place an emphasis on understanding and improving the software process to enable software engineers to be more effective in their work.

References

1. F. Brooks, *The Mythical Man Month* (Addison Wesley, Boston, 1975)
2. Petrocelli, in *Software Engineering*, eds. by IN. Buxton, P. Naur, B. Randell. Report on two NATO Conferences held in Garmisch, Germany (October 1968) and Rome, Italy (October 1969) (1975)
3. G. O'Regan, *Mathematical Approaches to Software Quality* (Springer, London, 2006)
4. F. Brooks, *No Silver Bullet. Essence and Accidents of Software Engineering. Information Processing* (Elsevier, Amsterdam, 1986)
5. G. O'Regan, *Introduction to Software Process Improvement* (Springer, London 2010)
6. G. O'Regan, *Introduction to Software Quality* (Springer, Switzerland, 2014)
7. M. Fagan, design and code inspections to reduce errors in software development. IBM Syst. J. **15**(3) (1976)
8. T. Gilb, D. Graham, *Software Inspections*. (Addison Wesley, Boston, 1994)
9. Office of Government Commerce, *Managing Successful Projects with PRINCE2* (2004)
10. W. Royce, in *The Software Lifecycle Model* (Waterfall Model). Proceedings of WESTCON, August, 1970
11. B. Boehm, A spiral model for software development and enhancement. Computer **21**(5), 61–72 (1988)
12. J. Rumbaugh et al., *The Unified Software Development Process* (Addison Wesley, Boston, 1999)
13. K. Beck, *Extreme Programming Explained. Embrace Change* (Addison Wesley, Boston, 2000)
14. I. Jacobson, G. Booch, J. Rumbaugh, *The Unified Software Modelling Language User Guide* (Addison-Wesley, Boston, 1999)
15. D. Parnas, On the criteria to be used in decomposing systems into modules. Commun. ACM **15**(12), 1053–1058 (1972)
16. E.W. Dijkstra, *Structured Programming* (Academic Press, Cambridge, 1972)
17. M. Fagan, Design and code inspections to reduce errors in software development. IBM Syst. J. **15**(3) (1976)
18. J.M. Spivey, *The Z Notation*. A Reference Manual. Prentice Hall International Series in Computer Science, 1992

Software Project Management

2

Abstract

This chapter provides an introduction to project management for traditional software engineering, and we discuss project estimation, project planning and scheduling, project monitoring and control, risk management, managing communication and change and managing project quality.

Keywords

Business case · Project planning · Estimation · Scheduling · Risk management · Project board · Project governance · Project reports · Project metrics · Project monitoring and control · Quality management · Prince 2 · PMP and PMBOK

2.1 Introduction

Software projects have a history of being delivered late or over budget, and software project management is concerned with the effective management of software projects to ensure the successful delivery of a high-quality product, on time and on budget, to the customer. *A project is a temporary group activity designed to accomplish a specific goal such as the delivery of a product to a customer. It has a clearly defined beginning and end in time.*

Project management involves good project planning and estimation; the management of resources; the management of issues and change requests that arise during the project; managing quality; managing risks; managing the budget; monitoring progress; taking appropriate action when progress deviates from expectations; communicating progress to the various stakeholders; and delivering a high-quality product to the customer. It involves the following:

© Springer International Publishing AG 2017
G. O'Regan, *Concise Guide to Software Engineering*, Undergraduate Topics in Computer Science, DOI 10.1007/978-3-319-57750-0_2

- Defining the business case for the project,
- Defining the scope of the project and what it is to achieve,
- Estimation of the cost, effort and schedule,
- Determining the start and end dates for the project,
- Determining the resources required,
- Assigning resources to the various tasks and activities,
- Determining the project lifecycle and phases of the project,
- Staffing the project,
- Preparing the project plan,
- Scheduling the various tasks and activities in the schedule,
- Preparing the initial project schedule and key milestones,
- Obtaining approval for the project plan and schedule,
- Identifying and managing risks,
- Monitoring progress, budget, schedule, effort, risks, issues, change requests and quality,
- Taking corrective action,
- Replanning and rescheduling,
- Communicating progress to affected stakeholders,
- Preparing status reports and presentations.

The scope of the project needs to be determined, and the estimated effort for the various tasks and activities established. The project plan and schedule will then be developed and approved by the stakeholders, and these are maintained during the project. The project plan will contain or reference several other plans such as the project quality plan; the communication plan; the configuration management plan; and the test plan.

Project estimation and scheduling are difficult as software projects are often breaking new ground and differ from previous projects. That is, historical estimates may often not be a good basis for estimation for the current project. Often, unanticipated problems may arise for technically advanced projects, and the estimates may be overly optimistic.

Gantt charts are generally employed for project scheduling, and these show the work breakdown for the project as well as task dependencies and allocation of staff to the various tasks.

The effective management of risk during a project is essential to project success. Risks arise due to uncertainty, and the risk management cycle involves[1] risk identification; risk analysis and evaluation; identifying responses to risks; selecting and planning a response to the risk; and risk monitoring.

Once the risks have been identified, they are logged (e.g. in the risk log). The likelihood of each risk arising and its impact is then determined. The risk is assigned an owner and an appropriate response to the risk determined.

---

[1]These are the risk management activities in the Prince2 methodology.

Once the planning is complete, the project execution commences, and the focus moves to monitoring progress, managing risks and issues, replanning as appropriate, providing regular progress reports to the project board and so on.

Two popular project management methodologies are the *Prince* 2 methodology, which was developed in the UK, and *Project Management Professional (*PMP*)* and its associated project management body of knowledge (PMBOK) from the *Project Management Institute* (PMI) in the USA.

2.2 Project Start-up and Initiation

There are many ways in which a project may arise, but it is always essential that there is a clear rationale (*business case*) for the project. A telecoms company may wish to develop a new version of its software with attractive features to gain market share. An internal IT department may receive a request from its business users to alter its business software in order to satisfy new legal or regulatory requirements. A software development company may be contacted by a business to develop a bespoke solution to meet its needs and so on.

All parties must be clear on what the project is to achieve, and how it will be achieved. It is fundamental that there is a *business case* for the project (this is the reason for the project), as it clearly does not make sense for the organization to spend a large amount of money without a sound rationale for the project. In other words, the project must make business sense (e.g. it may have a financial return on the investment or it may be to satisfy some business or regulatory requirement).

At the project start-up, the initial scope and costing for the project are determined, and the feasibility of the project is determined.[2] The project is authorized,[3] and a project board is set up for project governance. The project board verifies that there is a sound business case for the project, and a *project manager* is appointed to manage the project.

The *project board* (or steering group) includes the key stakeholders and is accountable for the success of the project. The project manager provides regular status reports to the project board during the project, and the project board is consulted when key project decisions need to be made.

The project manager is responsible for the day-to-day management of the project, and good planning is essential to its success. The approach to the project is decided,[4] and the project manager *kicks off the project* and mobilizes the project team. The detailed requirements and estimates for the project are determined, the

---

[2]This refers to whether the project is technically and financially feasible.

[3]Organizations have limited resources, and as many projects may be proposed it will not be possible to authorise every project, and so several projects with weak business cases may be rejected.

[4]For example, it may be decided to outsource the development to a third party provider, purchase an off-the-shelf solution, or develop the solution internally.

schedule of activities and tasks established, and resources are assigned for the various tasks and activities.[5] The project manager prepares the project plan, which is subject to the approval of the key stakeholders. The initial risks are identified and managed, and a risk log (or repository) is set up for the project. Once the planning is complete, project execution commences.

2.3   Estimation

Estimation is an important part of project management, and the accurate estimates of effort, cost and schedule are essential to delivering a project on time and on budget, and with the right quality.[6] Estimation is employed in the planning process to determine the resources and effort required, and it feeds into the scheduling of the project. The problems with over- or underestimation of projects are well known, and good estimates allow the following:

- Accurate calculation of the project cost and its feasibility,
- Accurate scheduling of the project,
- Measurement of progress and costs against the estimates,
- Determining the resources required for the project.

  Poor estimation leads to:

- Projects being over- or underestimated,
- Projects being over or under-resourced (impacting staff morale),
- Negative impression of the project manager.

  Consequently, estimation needs to be rigorous, and there are several well-known techniques available (e.g. work-breakdown structures, function points and so on). Estimation applies to both the early and later parts of the project, with the later phases of the project refining the initial estimates, as a more detailed understanding of the project activities is then available. The new estimates are used to reschedule and to predict the eventual effort, delivery date and cost of the project. The following are guidelines for estimation:

- Sufficient time needs to be allowed to do estimation,
- Estimates are produced for each phase of software development,
- The initial estimates are high level,

---

[5]The project scheduling is usually done with the Microsoft Project tool.

[6]The consequences of under estimating a project include the project being delivered late, with the project team working late nights and weekends to recover the schedule, quality being compromised with steps in the process omitted, and so on.

- The estimates for the next phase should be solid, whereas estimates for the later phases may be high level,
- The estimates should be conservative rather than optimistic,
- Estimates will usually include contingency,
- Estimates should be reviewed to ensure their adequacy,
- Estimates from independent experts may be useful,
- It may be useful to prepare estimates using various methods and to compare.

Project metrics may be employed to measure the accuracy of the estimates. These metrics are reported during the project and include the following:

- Effort Estimation Accuracy,
- Budget Estimation Accuracy,
- Schedule Estimation Accuracy.

Next, we discuss various estimation techniques including the work-breakdown structure, the analogy method and the Delphi method.

2.3.1   Estimation Techniques

Estimates need to be produced consistently, and it would be inappropriate to have an estimation procedure such as *"Go ask Fred"*,[7] as this clearly relies on an individual and is not a repeatable process. The estimates may be based on a work-breakdown structure, function points or another appropriate methodology. There are several approaches to project estimation (Table 2.1) including the following:

2.3.2   Work-Breakdown Structure

This is a popular approach to project estimation (*it is also known as decomposition*) and involves the following:

- Identify the project deliverables to be produced during the project,
- Estimate the size of each deliverable (in pages or LOC),
- Estimate the effort (number of days) required to complete the deliverable based on its complexity and size, and experience of team,
- Estimate the cost of the completed deliverable,
- The estimate for the project is the sum of the individual estimates.

---

[7]Unless "Go Ask Fred" is the name of the estimation methodology or the estimation tool employed.

Table 2.1 Estimation techniques

Technique	Description
Work-breakdown structure	Identify the project deliverables to be produced during the project. Estimate the size of each deliverable (in pages or LOC). Estimate the effort (number of days) required to complete the deliverable based on its size and complexity. Estimate the cost of the completed deliverable
Analogy method	This involves comparing the proposed project with a previously completed project (i.e. similar to the proposed project). The historical data and metrics for schedule, effort and budget estimation accuracy are considered, as well as similarities and differences between the projects to provide effort, schedule and budget estimates
Expert judgement	This involves consultation with experienced personnel to derive the estimate. The expert(s) can factor in differences between past project experiences, knowledge of existing systems and the specific requirements of the project
Delphi method	The *Delphi method* is a consensus method used to produce accurate schedules and estimates. It was developed by the Rand Corporation and improved by Barry Boehm and others. It provides extra confidence in the project estimates by using experts independent of the project manager or third party supplier
Cost predictor models	These include various cost prediction models such as *Cocomo* and Slim. The Costar tool supports Cocomo, and the Qsm tool supports Slim
Function points	*Function points* were developed by Allan Albrecht at IBM in the late 1970s and involve analysing each functional requirement and assigning a number of function points based on its size and complexity. This total number of function points is a measure of the estimate for the project

The approach often uses productivity data that is available from previously completed projects. The effort required for a complex deliverable is higher than that of a simple deliverable (where both are of the same size). The project planning section in the project plan (or a separate estimation plan) will include the lifecycle phases and the deliverables/tasks to be carried out in each phase. It may include a table along the following lines (Table 2.2).

2.4   Project Planning and Scheduling

A well-managed project has an increased chance of success, and good planning is an essential part of project management. There is the well-known adage that states, "*Fail to plan, plan to fail*".[8] The project manager and the relevant stakeholders will consider the appropriate approach for the project and determine whether a solution should be purchased off the shelf, whether to outsource the software development to

---

[8]This quotation is adapted from Benjamin Franklin (an inventor and signatory to the American declaration of independence).

Table 2.2 Example work-breakdown structure

Lifecycle phase	Project deliverable or task description	Est. size	Est. effort	Est. cost
Planning and requirements	Project plan	40	10 days	$5000
	Project schedule	20	5 days	$2500
	Business requirements	20	10 days	$5000
	Test plan	15	5 days	$2500
	Issue/risk log	3	2 days	$1000
	Lessons learned log	1	1 day	$500
Design	System requirements	15	5 days	$2500
	Technical/DB design	30	10 days	$5000
Coding	Source code	5000 (LOC)	10 days	$5000
	Unit tests/results	200	2 days	$1000
Testing	ST specs	30	10 days	$5000
	System testing		10 days	$5000
	UAT specs	30	10 days	$5000
	UAT testing		10 days	$5000
Deployment	Release notes/procedures	20	5 days	$2500
	User manuals	50	10 days	$5000
	Support procedures	15	10 days	$5000
	Training plan	25	5 days	$2500
Project closure	End project report	10	2 days	$1000
	Lessons learned report	5	2 days	$1000
Contingency	10%		13.4	$6700
Total			147.4	$73,700

a third party supplier or whether to develop the solution internally. A simple process map for project planning is presented in Fig. 2.1.

Estimation is a key part of project planning, and the effort estimates are used for scheduling of the tasks and activities in a project-scheduling tool such as *Microsoft Project* (Fig. 2.2).

The schedule will detail the phases in the project, the key project milestones, the activities and tasks to be performed in each phase as well as their associated timescales, and the resources required to carry out each task. The project manager will update the project schedule regularly during the project.

Projects vary in size and complexity, and the formality of the software development process employed needs to reflect this. The project plan defines how the project will be carried out, and it generally includes sections such as:

– Business case,
– Project scope,
– Project goals and objectives,
– Key milestones,

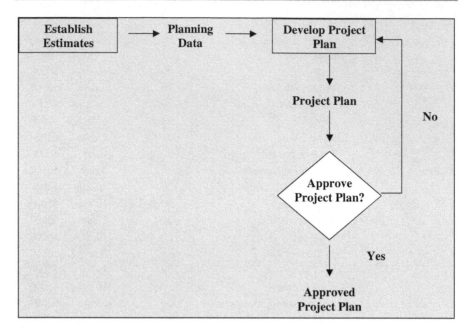

Fig. 2.1 Simple process map for project planning

Fig. 2.2 Sample Microsoft project schedule

- Project planning and estimates,
- Key stakeholders,
- Project team and responsibilities,
- Knowledge and skills required,
- Communication planning,
- Financial planning,
- Quality and test planning,
- Configuration management.

Communication planning describes how communication will be carried out during the project, and it includes the various project meetings and reports that will be produced; financial planning is concerned with budget planning for the project; quality and test planning is concerned with the planning required to ensure that a high-quality product is delivered; and configuration management is concerned with identifying the configuration items to be controlled and systematically controlling changes to them throughout the lifecycle. It ensures that all deliverables are kept consistent following approved changes.

The project plan is a key project document, and it needs to be approved by all stakeholders. The project manager needs to ensure that the project plan, schedule and technical work products are kept consistent with the requirements. Another words, if there are changes to the requirement, then the project plan and schedule will need to be updated accordingly.

Checklists are useful in verifying that the tasks have been completed. The sample project management checklist below (Table 2.3) verifies that project planning has been appropriately performed and that controls are in place.

Table 2.3 Sample project management checklist

No.	Item to check
1.	Is the project plan complete and approved by the stakeholders?
2.	Does the project have a sound business case?
3.	Are the risk log, issue log and lessons learned log set up?
4.	Are the responses to the risks and issues appropriate?
5.	Is the Microsoft Schedule available for the project?
6.	Is the project schedule up to date?
7.	Is the project appropriately resourced?
8.	Are estimates available for the project? Are they realistic?
9.	Has quality planning been completed for the project?
10.	Has the change control mechanism been set up for the project?
11.	Are all deliverables under configuration management control?
12.	Has project communication been appropriately planned?
13.	Is the project directory set up for the project?
14.	Are the key milestones defined in the project plan?

2.5 Risk Management

Risks arise due to uncertainty, and *risk management is concerned with managing uncertainty*, and especially the management of any undesired events. Risks need to be identified, analysed and controlled in order for the project to be successful, and risk management activities take place throughout the project lifecycle.

Once the initial set of risks to the project has been identified, they are analysed to determine their *likelihood of occurrence* and their *impact* (e.g. on cost, schedule or quality). These two parameters determine the *risk category*, and the most serious risk category refers to a risk with a high probability of occurrence and a high impact on occurrence.

Countermeasures are defined to reduce the likelihood of occurrence and impact of the risks, and contingency plans are prepared to deal with the situation of the risk actually occurring. Additional risks may arise during the project, and the project manager needs to be proactive in their identification and management.

Risks need to be reviewed regularly especially following changes to the project. These could be changes to the business case or the business requirements, loss of key personnel and so on. Events that occur may affect existing risks (including the probability of their occurrence and their impact) and may lead to new risks. Countermeasures need to be kept up to date during the project. Risks are reported regularly throughout the project.

The risk management cycle is concerned with identifying and managing risks throughout the project lifecycle. It involves identifying risks; determining their probability of occurrence and impact should they occur; identifying responses to the risks; and monitoring and reporting. Table 2.4 describes these activities in greater detail:

The project manager will maintain a risk repository (this may be a tool or a risk log) to record details of each risk, including its type and description; its likelihood and its impact (yielding the risk category); and the response to the risk.

2.6 Quality Management in Projects

There are various definitions of "quality" such as Juran's definition that quality is "*fitness for purpose*", and Crosby's definition of quality as "*conformance to the requirements*". The Crosby's definition is useful when asking whether we are building it right, whereas the Juran's definition is useful when asking whether we are building the right system. Crosby's definition is useful in requirements verification, where software inspections and testing verify that the requirements have been correctly implemented. Juran's definition is useful in requirements validation.

It is a fundamental premise in the quality field that it is more cost effective to build quality into the product, rather than adding it later during the testing phase. Therefore, quality needs to be considered at every step during the project, and every

Table 2.4 Risk management activities

Activity	Description
Risk management strategy	This defines how the risks will be identified, monitored, reviewed and reported during the project, as well as the frequency of monitoring and reporting
Risk identification	This involves identifying the risks to the project and recording them in a risk repository (e.g. risk log). It continues throughout the project lifecycle. Prince 2 classifies risks into: – *Business* (e.g. collapse of subcontractors) – *Legal and regulatory* – *Organizational* (e.g. skilled resources/management) – *Technical* (e.g. scope creep, architecture, design) – *Environmental* (e.g. flooding or fires)
Evaluating the risks	This involves assessing the likelihood of occurrence of a particular risk and its impact (on cost, schedule, etc.) should it materialize. These two parameters result in the risk category.
Identifying risk responses	The project manager (and stakeholders) will determine the appropriate response to a risk such as reducing the probability of its occurrence or its impact should it occur. These include the following: – *Prevention* which aims to prevent it from occurring – *Reduction* aims to reduce the probability of occurrence or impact should it occur – *Transfer* aims to transfer the risk to a third party – *Acceptance* is when nothing can be done about it – *Contingency* is actions that are carried out should the risk materialize
Risk monitoring and reporting	This involves monitoring existing risks to verify that the actions taken to manage the risks are effective, as well as identifying new risks. This provides an early warning that an identified risk is going to materialize, and *a risk that materializes is a new project issue* that needs to be dealt with
Lessons learned	This is concerned with determining the effectiveness of risk management during the project and to learn any lessons for future projects

deliverable needs to be reviewed to ensure its fitness for purpose. The review may be similar to a *software inspection*, a *structured walk-through* or another appropriate methodology.

The project plan will include a section on quality planning for the project (this may be a reference to a separate plan). The quality plan will define how the project plans to deliver a high-quality project, as well as the quality controls and quality assurance activities that will take place during project execution. The quality planning for the project needs to ensure that the customer's quality expectations will be achieved.

The project manager has overall responsibility for project quality, and the quality department (if one exists) will assign a quality engineer to the project, and the quality engineer will promote quality and its importance to the project team, as well as facilitating quality improvement. The project manager needs to ensure that sound software engineering processes are employed, as well as ensuring that the defined standards and templates are followed.

It is an accepted principle in the quality field that good processes and conformance to them are essential for the delivery of a high-quality product. The quality engineer will conduct process audits to ensure that the processes and standards are followed consistently during the project. An audit report is published, and any audit actions are tracked to closure.

Software testing is conducted to verify that the software correctly implements the requirements, and a separate project test plan will define the various types of testing to be performed during the project. These will typically include unit, integration, system, performance and acceptance testing and the results from the various test activities enable the fitness for purpose of the software to be determined, as well as judging whether it is ready to be released or not.

The project manager will report the various project metrics (including the quality metrics) in the regular project status reports, and the quality metrics provide an objective indication of the quality of the product at that moment in time.

The cost of poor quality may be determined at the end of the project, and this may require a time recording system for the various project activities. The effort involved in detecting and correcting defects may be recorded, and a COPQ chart similar to Fig. 10.28 presented.

Poor quality may arise due to several reasons. For example, it may be caused by inadequate reviews or testing of the software; inadequate skills or experience of the project team; or poorly defined or understood requirements.

The project manager will conduct a lessons learned meeting at the end of the project to identify and record all of the lessons learned from the project. These are then published as a lessons learned report and shared with relevant stakeholders as part of continuous improvement.

2.7 Project Monitoring and Control

Project monitoring and control are concerned with monitoring project execution and taking corrective action when project performance deviates from expectations. The progress of the project should be monitored against the plan and corrective actions taken as appropriate. The key project parameters such as budget, effort and schedule as well as risks and issues are monitored, and the status of the project communicated regularly to the affected stakeholders.

The project manager will conduct progress and milestone reviews to determine the actual progress, with new issues identified and monitored. The appropriate corrective actions are identified and are tracked to closure. The main focus of project monitoring and control is as follows:

– Monitor the project plan and schedule and keep on track,
– Monitor the key project parameters,

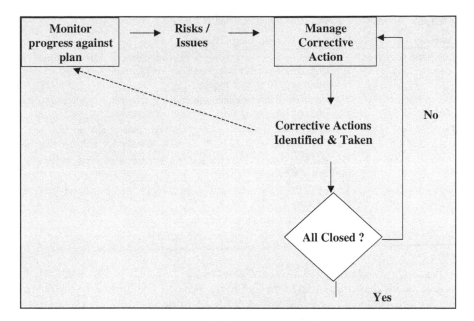

Fig. 2.3 Simple process map for project monitoring and control

- Conduct progress and milestone reviews to determine the actual status,
- Replan as appropriate,
- Monitor risks and take appropriate action,
- Analyse issues and change requests and take appropriate action,
- Track corrective action to closure,
- Monitor resources and manage any resource issues,
- Report the project status to management and project board.

A sample process map is presented in Fig. 2.3.

The project manager will monitor progress, risks and issues during the project, and take appropriate corrective action. The status of the project will be reported in the regular status reports sent to management and the project board, with the status reviewed with management regularly during the project.

2.8 Managing Issues and Change Requests

The management of issues and change requests is a normal part of project management. An *issue* can arise at any time during the project (e.g. a supplier to the project may go out of business, an employee may resign, specialized hardware for testing may not arrive in time and so on), and an issue refers to a problem that has occurred which may have a negative impact on the project. The severity of the issue is an indication of its impact on the project, and the project manager needs to manage it appropriately.

Table 2.5 Activities in managing issues and change requests

Activity	Description of issue/change request
Log issue or change request	The project manager logs the issue or change request. It is assigned to a unique reference number and priority (severity), and categorized into an issue (problem) or change request
Assess impact	This involves analysis to determine the impacts such as technical, cost, schedule and quality. The risks need to be identified
Decision on implementation	A decision is made on how to deal with the issue or change request. The CCB is often involved in the decision to authorize a change request
Implement solution	The affected project documents and software modules are identified and modified accordingly
Verify solution	Testing (Unit, System and UAT) is employed to verify the correctness of the solution
Close issue/CR	The issue or change request is closed

A *change request* is a stakeholder request for a change to the scope of the project, and it may arise at any time during the project. The impacts of the change request (e.g. technical, cost and schedule) need to be carefully considered, as a change introduces new risks to the project that may adversely affect cost, schedule and quality. It is therefore essential to fully understand the impacts in order to make an informed decision on whether to authorize or reject the change request. The project manager may directly approve small change requests, with the impacts of a larger change request considered by the project *change control board* (CCB).

The activities involved in managing issues and change requests are summarized in Table 2.5.

2.9 Project Board and Governance

The *project board*[9] (or steering group) is responsible for directing the project, and it is directly accountable for the success of the project. It consists of senior managers and staff in the organization who have the authority to make resources available, to remove roadblocks and to get things done.

It is consulted whenever key project decisions need to be made, and it plays a key role in project governance. The project board ensures that there is a clear business case for the project, and that the capital funding for the project is adequate and well spent. The project board may cancel the project at any stage during project

---

[9]The project board in the Prince 2 methodology includes roles such as the project executive, senior supplier, senior user, project assurance, and the project manager. These roles have distinct responsibilities.

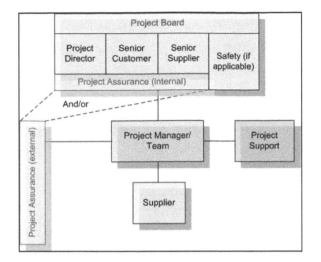

Fig. 2.4 Prince 2 project board

Table 2.6 Project board roles and responsibilities

Role	Responsibility
Project director	Ultimately responsible for the project. Provides overall guidance to the project
Senior customer	Represents the interests of users
Senior supplier	Represents the resources responsible for implementation of project (e.g. IS manager)
Project manager	Link between project board and project team
Project assurance	Internal role (optional) that provides an independent (of project manager) objective view of the project
Safety (optional)	Ensure adherence to health and safety standards

execution should there cease to be a business case, or should project spending exceed tolerance and go out of control.[10]

The project manager reports to the project board and sends regular status reports to highlight progress made as well as key project risks and issues. The project board meets at an appropriate frequency during the project (with extra sessions held should serious project issues arise) (Fig. 2.4).

There are several roles on the project board (an individual could perform more than one role) and their responsibilities include (Table 2.6) the following:

---

[10]The project plan will usually specify a *tolerance level* for schedule and spending, where the project may spend (perhaps less than 10%) in excess of the allocated capital for the project before seeking authorization for further capital funding for the project.

2.10   Project Reporting

The frequency of project reporting is defined in the project plan (or the communications plan). The project report advises management and the key stakeholders of the current status of the project and includes key project information such as:

- Completed deliverables (during period),
- New risks and issues,
- Schedule, effort and budget status (e.g. RAG metrics[11]),
- Quality and test status,
- Key risks and issues,
- Milestone status,
- Deliverables planned (next period).

The project manager discusses the project report with management and the project board and presents the current status of the project as well as the key risks and issues. The project manager will present a recovery plan (exception report) to deal with the situation where the project has fallen significantly outside the defined project tolerance (i.e. it is significantly behind schedule or over budget).

The key risks and issues will be discussed, and the project manager will explain how the key issues are being dealt with, and how the key risks will be managed. The new risks and issues will also be discussed, and the project board will carefully consider how the project manager plans to deal with these and will provide appropriate support.

The project board will carefully consider the status of the project as well as the input from the project manager before deciding on the appropriate course of action (which could include the immediate termination of the project if there is no longer a business case for it).

2.11   Project Closure

A project is a temporary activity, and once the project goals have been achieved and the product handed over to the customer and support group, it is ready to be closed. The project manager will prepare an end of project report detailing the extent to which the project achieved its targeted objectives. The report will include a summary of key project metrics including key quality metrics and the budget and timeliness metrics.

---

[11]Often, a colour coding mechanism is employed with a red flag indicating a serious issue; amber highlighting a potentially serious issue; and green indicating that everything is ok.

Fig. 2.5 Project
management triangle

The success of the project is judged on the extent to which the defined objectives
have been achieved, and on the extent to which the project has delivered the agreed
functionality on schedule, on budget and with the right quality. This is often
referred to as the project management triangle (Fig. 2.5).

The project manager presents the end project report to the project board,
including any factors (e.g. change requests) that may have affected the timely
delivery of the project or the allocated budget. The project is then officially closed.

The project manager then schedules a meeting with the team review the lessons
learned from the project. The team records the lessons learned during the project
(typically in a lessons learned log), and the key lessons learned are summarized in
the lessons learned report. Any actions identified are assigned to individuals and
followed through to closure, and the lessons learned report is made available to
other projects (with the goal of learning from experience). The project team is
disbanded, and the project team members are assigned to other duties.

2.12 Prince 2 Methodology

Prince 2 (*Projects in controlled environments*) is a popular project management
methodology that is widely used in the UK and Europe. It is a structured,
process-driven approach to project management, with processes for project start-up,
initiating a project, controlling a stage, managing stage boundaries, closing a project, managing product delivery, planning and directing a project (Fig. 2.6). It has
procedures to coordinate people and activities in a project, as well as procedures to
monitor and control project activities.

These key processes are summarized in Table 2.7, and more detailed information on Prince 2 is in [1].

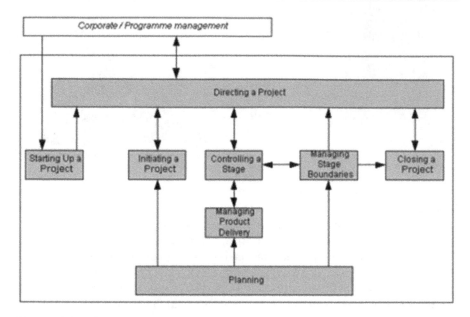

Fig. 2.6 Prince 2 processes

Table 2.7 Key processes in Prince 2

Process	Description
Start-up	Project manager and project board appointed, project approach and project brief defined
Initiating	Project and quality plan completed, business case and risks refined, project files set up and project authorized
Controlling a stage	Stage plan prepared, quality and risks/issues managed, progress reviewed and reported
Managing stage boundary	Stage status reviewed and next stage planned, actual products produced versus original stage plan compared, stage or exception report produced
Closing a project	Orderly closure of project with project board, end project report and lessons learned report
Managing product delivery	Covers product creation by the team or a third party supplier. Ensure that the planned deliverables meet quality criteria
Planning	Prince 2 employs product-based planning which involves identifying the products required, and the activities and resources to provide them
Directing a project	The project board consists of senior management, and it controls the project. It has the authority to authorize and define what is required from the project, commitment of resources and funds and management direction

2.13   Review Questions

1. What is a project? What is project management?
2. Describe various approaches to estimation.
3. What activities take place at project start-up and initiation?
4. What skills are required to be a good project manager?
5. What is the purpose of the project board? Explain project governance.
6. What is the purpose of risk management? How are risks managed?
7. Describe the main activities in project management.
8. What is the difference between a risk and an issue?
9. What is the purpose of project reporting?
10. How is quality managed in a project?

2.14   Summary

Project management is concerned with the effective management of projects, and the goal is to deliver a high-quality product, on time and on budget, to the customer. It involves good project planning and estimation; managing resources; managing changes and issues that arise; managing quality; managing risks; managing the budget; monitoring progress and taking corrective action; communicating progress; and delivering a high-quality product to the customer.

The scope of the project needs to be determined and estimates established. The project plan is developed and approved by the stakeholders, and it will contain or reference several other plans. It needs to be maintained during the project. Project estimation and scheduling are difficult as often software projects are quite different from previous projects. Gantt charts are often employed for project scheduling, and these show the work breakdown for the project, as well as task dependencies and the assignment of staff to the various tasks.

The effective management of risk during a project is essential to project success. Risks arise due to uncertainty, and the risk management cycle involves risk identification; risk analysis and evaluation; identifying responses to risks; selecting and planning a response to the risk; and risk monitoring.

Once the planning is complete, the project execution commences, and the focus moves to monitoring progress, replanning as appropriate, managing risks and issues, providing regular progress reports to the project board and so on. Finally, there is an orderly close of the project.

Reference

1. Office of Government Commerce, Managing Successful Projects with PRINCE2, 2004

Requirements Engineering

3

Abstract

This chapter discusses requirements engineering and discusses activities such as requirements gathering, requirements elicitation, requirements analysis, requirements management, and requirements verification and validation.

Keywords

User requirements · System requirements · Functional and non-functional requirements · Requirements elicitation · Requirements analysis · Requirements verification and validation · Requirements management · Requirements traceability

3.1 Introduction

The user requirements specify what the customer wants and define *what* the software system is required to do, as distinct from *how* this is to be done. The requirements are the foundation for the system, and if they are incorrect then irrespective of the best software development processes in the world, the implemented system will be incorrect. The process of determining the requirements, analysing and validating them and managing them throughout the project lifecycle is termed *requirements engineering*.

Often, the initial requirements for a project arise due to a particular problem that the business or customer needs to solve. This leads to a project to implement an appropriate solution, and the first step is to determine the scope of work and the actual requirements for the project, and whether the project is feasible from the cost, time and technical considerations.

© Springer International Publishing AG 2017

G. O'Regan, *Concise Guide to Software Engineering*, Undergraduate Topics in Computer Science, DOI 10.1007/978-3-319-57750-0_3

The *user requirements* are determined from discussions with the customer to determine their actual needs, and they are then refined into the *system requirements*, which state the *functional* and *non-functional* requirements of the system.

The requirements must be precise and unambiguous to ensure that all stakeholders are clear on what is (and what is not) to be delivered, and prototyping may be employed to clarify the requirements and to assist in their definition.

Requirements verification is concerned with ensuring that the requirements are properly implemented (i.e. *building it right*). In other words, it is concerned with ensuring that the requirements are properly addressed in the design and implementation, and a traceability matrix and testing are often employed as part of the verification activities.

Requirements validation (i.e. *building the right system*) is concerned with ensuring that the right requirements are defined and that they are precise, complete, consistent, realizable and reflect the actual needs of the customer. The validation of the requirements is done by the stakeholders, and it involves several reviews of the requirements (and prototype), reviews of the design and user acceptance testing.

The Agile software development methodology (discussed in more detail in Chap. 18) has become very popular in recent years, and its lightweight approach is to be contrasted with the traditional waterfall model. It argues that requirements change so quickly that a requirements document is unnecessary, since such a document would be out of date as soon as it was written.

However, this chapter will focus on requirements engineering as it is in traditional software engineering, and the reader may consult Chap. 18 and the various texts on Agile to understand its approach.

3.2   Requirements Process

The process of determining the requirements for a proposed system involves discussions with the relevant stakeholders to determine their needs and to explicitly define what functionality the system should provide, as well as any hardware and performance constraints.

The specification of the requirements needs to be precise and unambiguous to ensure that all parties involved share a common understanding of the system and fully agree on what is to be developed and tested. A feasibility study may be needed to demonstrate that the requirements are feasible and may be implemented within the defined schedule and cost constraints.

The requirements are the foundation for the system, and project planning is based on the defined requirements. It is therefore essential that the requirements are *complete* (all services required by the user are defined), *consistent* (requirements should not contradict one another) and *unambiguous* (the requirements are clear and definite in meaning). Table 3.1 presents characteristics of good requirements.

Table 3.1 Characteristics of good requirements

No.	Characteristics of good requirements
1.	Each requirement is clear and unambiguous
2.	Each requirement has a priority to indicate its importance
3.	Each requirement may be implemented
4.	Each requirement is testable
5.	Each requirement is necessary
6.	Any conflicts between the requirements are resolved
7.	Each requirement is broken down as fully as possible
8.	Each requirement is consistent with the project's objectives
9.	Each requirement is stated as a stakeholder need (i.e. premature design/solution or implementation information is not included)
10.	The user (business) requirements are traceable (in both directions) throughout the development cycle
11.	The requirements are complete and consistent

Prototyping may be employed to assist in the definition and validation of the requirements, and a suitable prototype will include key parts of the system. It will allow users to give early feedback on the proposed system and on the extent to which it meets their needs. Prototyping is useful in clarifying the requirements and helps to reduce the risk of implementing the incorrect solution.

The implications of the proposed set of requirements need to be understood, as the choice of a particular requirement may affect the choice of another requirement. For example, in the telecommunication domain, two features may work correctly in isolation, but when present together, they interact in an undesirable way. Therefore, feature interactions need to be identified and investigated at the requirements phase to determine how interactions should be resolved.

In situations where an inadequate requirements process is employed, then there may be serious problems in the project. This may be manifested by requirements that are poorly defined or controlled, or requirements that are incomplete, inadequately documented or untestable. In other cases, there may be major scope creep with requirements accepted from any source.

Changes to the requirements may lead to a high level of rework, or cause major delays to the project schedule, or major increases in project cost. In other cases, where poor configuration management practices are employed, the changes to the requirements may not be reflected in the project plan, and the deliverables may be inconsistent with the requirements. Table 3.2 presents symptoms of a poor requirements process:

The following activities are involved in the requirements process, and they are discussed in more detail in the following sections:

- Requirements elicitation and specification
- Requirements analysis
- Requirements verification and validation

Table 3.2 Symptoms of poor requirements process

No.	Symptom
1.	High level of requirements creep during the project
2.	Requirements changing regularly during the project
3.	Missing requirements
4.	Changes to the requirements are not controlled
5.	Requirements accepted from any source
6.	High level of rework during the project
7.	Design, implementation and test products inconsistently interpret the requirements
8.	Deliverables are inconsistent with the requirements
9.	Untestable requirements
10.	Inability to demonstrate that the implementation satisfies the requirements

- Requirements traceability
- Requirements management.

We distinguish between the user (or business) requirements and the system requirements. The *user requirements* are the high-level requirements for the system (they tend to be high-level statements in a natural language with diagrams and tables), whereas the *system requirements* are a more detailed description of what the system is to do. The user requirements are more abstract than the system requirements, and a user requirement is typically expanded into several system requirements. The system requirements provide more detailed information on the system to be implemented, and it details the functionality to be provided and any operational constraints.

The system requirements include the functional and non-functional requirements. A *functional requirement* is a statement about the functionality of the system, i.e. a description of the behaviour of the system and how it should respond to particular inputs. A *non-functional requirement* is a constraint on the functionality of the system (e.g. a timing, performance, reliability, availability, portability, usability, safety, security, dependability or a hardware constraint).

It is essential that the functional and non-functional requirements are stated precisely, and the *non-functional requirements are often quantitatively specified* so that it may be objectively determined (by testing) whether they are satisfied or not. Further, it is essential that the non-functional requirements are satisfied, as otherwise the delivered system may be unusable or unacceptable to the client. The non-functional requirements often affect the overall architecture of the system, rather than the individual components of the system.

Next, we discuss the process of determining the requirements for the system and specifying them in a requirements document.

3.2.1 Requirements Elicitation and Specification

Requirements elicitation is the process of determining the requirements for the proposed system, and it involves discussions with the relevant stakeholders to determine their needs and to explicitly define what functionality the system should provide, as well as any operational and performance constraints. The process of eliciting the requirements from the stakeholders is difficult as

- Stakeholders often do not know what they want from the system.
- Stakeholders often do not know what is or what is not technically feasible and may have unrealistic expectations.
- Stakeholders express the requirements in the language of their domain, which may differ from the language of the business analysts.
- Different stakeholders may want different things from the system resulting in conflicts that need to be resolved.

The project manager/business analyst and the relevant stakeholders will conduct a brainstorming session to define the high-level requirements for the proposed system (or modification to an existing system). The requirements gathering may involve interviews with the stakeholders to allow them to talk about how they currently perform their work and to determine their requirements from the proposed system. It may also include observation session where the business analyst observes the users to see how the work is currently performed.

Further requirements workshops will review and analyse the draft user and system requirements documents and identify all other relevant information for the proposed system. There will typically be two requirements documents produced, and these are the *user* (sometimes called business) *requirements specification* (URS or BRS) and the *system requirements specification* (SRS). These two documents could potentially be combined into one document (Fig. 3.1).

The user requirements document is usually written in a natural language such as English (it may include diagrams and tables), and it describes the external behaviour of the system and specifies the functional and non-functional requirements in non-technical language. The systems requirements document will be an expanded version of the user requirements, and it provides the detail as to how the user requirements are provided in the system. It is a detailed specification of the entire system, with the aim of describing the external behaviour of the system and excluding (as far as possible) design information.[1] The SRS may be written in:

---

[1] It is desirable that the user or system requirements describe what is to be provided rather than how it is to be provided. That is, in theory, design or implementation information should be excluded in the specification. However, in practice, it is sometimes difficult to exclude all design information (e.g. consider the case where a system needs to work with an existing system).

Fig. 3.1 Requirements process

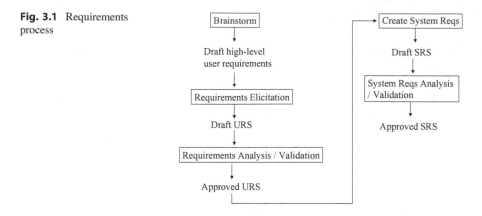

- A natural language
- A graphical language
- Formal specification language.

The system specification is generally written in a natural language such as "*English*" (with diagrams and tables included). Natural language is inherently ambiguous, and therefore, care is required to ensure that the definition is precise and unambiguous, and the specification needs to be carefully reviewed to ensure that any ambiguities are identified and removed.

The specification may be written in a graphical specification language such as UML, which is often employed in defining the functional requirements of a system using use case diagrams, state diagrams and sequence diagrams. Finally, extra precision is needed for the specification of the requirements in the safety critical and security critical fields, and a formal mathematical specification language (such as VDM or Z) is often used in these domains.

Prototyping may be employed, and it helps in identifying gaps and misunderstandings in the definition of the requirements. The prototype is an early working version of the system, it is used to give the users a flavour of what the working system will look like, and its evaluation by the stakeholders helps in clarifying the requirements. The prototype may be thrown away at the end of prototyping, or it may be reused in the development of the system. Prototyping involves:

- Define prototype objectives
- Decide which functional requirements will be prototyped
- Develop the prototype
- Evaluate the prototype.

The project manager (or a business analyst) will facilitate the requirements workshops, and the initial workshop is an interview and brainstorming session[2]

---

[2]It may involve getting end-users to talk about how they currently do a certain task and brainstorming on better ways in which the proposed system can do the same task.

focused on *requirements discovery*. This involves identifying and gathering the requirements from the various stakeholders, analysing and prioritising them, resolving conflicts between them and consolidating them into a coherent set of user requirements.

This leads to the first draft of the user requirements, which is prepared by the project manager/business analyst, and the draft document is circulated to the stakeholders for review and comments. Further requirements workshops are then held to discuss and analyse the current draft of the user requirements, to ensure that they meet the needs of the stakeholders, as well as identifying new requirements and resolving any conflicts.[3] This process continues until all stakeholders are in agreement with the user requirements and are prepared to approve them. In some cases, the user requirements may already be defined and documented by the customer.

The project manager/business analyst may employ a checklist as an aid to determine that the requirements process has been followed and to verify that the user requirements have been fully specified and that every requirement specified is actually necessary. The final version of the user requirements document is circulated to all participants for their final review and approval.

Once the user requirements have been approved by all stakeholders, the work on the *system requirements* commences, and the business analyst expands the user requirements into more specific and detailed system requirements. Several workshops/reviews of the system requirement specification take place with the stakeholders, with the goal of ensuring that the system requirements are valid with respect to the business requirements and that they meet stakeholders' needs and are fit for purpose. Finally, the stakeholders approve the SRS.

Scenarios are useful in adding detail to the requirements, with each scenario covering a small number of possible interactions with the system. Use cases are often used to identify the actors involved in the interactions, and they provide a useful way to elicit the requirements from the stakeholders who interact directly with the system.

The ambiguity of natural language has led to interest in more precise notations to express requirements unambiguously. We mentioned the graphical unified modelling language (UML) [1], which has become popular in recent years. Its use case diagram is often used for requirements elicitation, with the use cases (Fig. 14.2) describing the functional requirements of the system graphically. The use cases describe the scenarios (or sequences of actions) in the system from the user's viewpoint (actor). It shows how the actor interacts with the system, where an actor represents the set of roles that a user can play, and the actor may be human or an automated system. Use case diagrams and various UML diagrams are discussed in Chap. 14.

---

[3]Conflicts are inevitable as stakeholders will have different needs, and so discussion and negotiation are required to resolve these conflicts and achieve consensus.

Formal specification notations such as Z or VDM are often employed in the safety critical or security critical fields. The advantage of these mathematical languages is that they are precise and amenable to proof, and mathematical analysis may be employed in a sense to debug[4] the requirements. This provides increased confidence in the correctness and validity of the requirements. However, these notations are perceived as being difficult to use by industrialists, and they are not widely employed in mainstream software engineering. Formal methods are discussed in more detail in Chap. 12.

3.2.2 Requirements Analysis

The requirements analysis activities are conducted as part of requirements elicitation, and the requirements are analysed to ensure that they are those that are actually required; that they are precisely and unambiguously stated; that they are complete and consistent; that they are categorized and prioritised; and that any conflicts between them are identified and resolved. There may be an initial feasibility study prior to the commencement of the project to ensure that the proposed system is technically feasible and achievable within the defined budget and time constraints.

The resolution of any conflicts is through discussion and negotiations with the stakeholders. The requirements are generally prioritised to define the importance of each requirement, and a number of development models (e.g. the Rational Unified Process) implement the most important requirements first. Requirements analysis is an iterative process with feedback going back to the stakeholders in the requirements elicitation process.

The requirements workshops will verify that the system requirements are valid with respect to the user requirements, and technical workshops will need to be conducted to determine the appropriate approach to their implementation.

3.2.3 Requirements Verification and Validation

The difference between requirements validation and verification is illustrated by the phrase *"Building the right thing"* versus *"building it right"*. In other words, *validation* is concerned with ensuring that the correct requirements are being implemented, whereas *verification* is concerned with ensuring that the defined requirements are being implemented correctly.

The stakeholders *validate* the requirements to ensure that they are the right set of requirements and that their implementation will result in a system that is fit for purpose. It is essential to validate the requirements, as the cost of correction of a requirements defect increases the later that the defect is discovered. Therefore, it is essential to identify a requirements defect as early as possible, as otherwise there

---

[4]Essentially, the mathematical language provides the facility to prove that certain properties are true of the specification, and that certain undesirable properties are false in the specification.

may be major cost and time involved in its correction, especially if the defect is discovered late in the software development lifecycle.

The validation activities may involve checks that the requirements are complete, consistent, feasible, testable and are fit for purpose. The validation may involve prototyping and several reviews (and updates) of the requirements (and prototype) by the stakeholders, until all stakeholders are ready to approve the requirements of the system.

The validation of the requirements will ensure that the requirements are complete and consistent, as well as reflecting the needs of the customer. The final validation step is the user acceptance testing, and this is performed by the customer to confirm that the completed system is fit for purpose and satisfies customer expectations. The lifecycle model employed determines the verification and validation activities to be conducted during the project, with models such as joint application development (JAD) and Agile involving a high level of customer involvement throughout the lifecycle.

Requirements verification is concerned with ensuring that the system as built (from design, to implementation, to testing and deployment) properly implements the defined requirements. A traceability matrix (Table 3.4) shows how the requirements are implemented and tested, and it may be employed as part of requirements verification.

It shows how the user requirements have been addressed in the system requirements, and how they have been implemented in the design of the system, as well as showing how the test cases have verified that the implementation has implemented the requirements correctly.

3.2.4 Requirements Managements

Requirements management is concerned with managing changes to the requirements, and in ensuring that the project maintains an up-to-date approved set of requirements throughout the project lifecycle. It is essential that the project deliverables are kept consistent with the latest version of the requirements, and that when the requirements document changes then all other project deliverables such as the design document, software modules and test specifications are kept consistent with the new version of the requirements.

It is an important area to get right as all project activities are planned from the approved set of requirements. Requirements management is concerned with managing changes to the requirements of the project, and in identifying inconsistencies between the requirements and the project plans and work products. Its focus is on the *activities for managing changes to the requirements*, as distinct from the activities in gathering and defining the requirements.

It is important that changes to the requirements are controlled, and that the impacts of the changes are fully understood prior to authorization. Once the system requirements have been approved, any proposed changes to the requirements are subject to formal change control. The project will set up a group that is responsible for authorizing changes to the requirements [usually called the *change control board* (CCB)]. The CCB is responsible for analysing requests to change the requirements, and it makes an informed decision on whether to accept or reject the change request based on its impacts and risks.

The need to change the requirements may be due to business or regulatory changes, or to a customer need becoming apparent at a late stage of the project when the project is nearing completion. A request to change the requirements is termed a *change request* (CR), and this is a stakeholder request for a change to the scope of the project, and it may arise at any time during the project. The impacts of the CR (e.g. technical, risks, cost, budget, and schedule) need to be carefully considered, as a change introduces new risks to the project, and may adversely affect cost, schedule and quality.

Therefore, it is essential that the impacts of the CR be fully considered prior to its authorization. The CR is considered by the CCB, and an informed decision is made to authorize or reject the request. The activities involved in managing change requests are summarized in Table 3.3.

Following the approval of a CR, the affected documents such as the system requirements, the design and software modules are modified accordingly. This is done to ensure that all of the project deliverables are kept consistent with the latest version of the requirements. Testing is carried out to verify that the changes have been implemented correctly.

3.2.5   Requirements Traceability

The objective of requirements traceability is to verify that all of the defined requirements for the project have been implemented and tested. One way to do this is to consider each requirement number and to go through every part of the design document to find where the requirement is being implemented in the design and similarly to go through the test documents and find any reference to the requirement number to show where it is being tested. This would demonstrate that the particular requirement number has been implemented and tested.

A more effective mechanism to do this is to employ a traceability matrix, which may be employed to map the user requirements to the system requirements; the system requirements to the design; the design to the unit test cases; the system test cases; and the UAT test cases. That is, traceability is defined through the project lifecycle, and the matrix provides a crisp summary of how the requirements have been implemented and tested.

The traceability of the requirements is *bidirectional*, and the traceability matrix may be maintained as a separate document, or as part of the requirements document. The basic idea is that a mapping between the requirement numbers and sections of the design or test plan is defined, and this provides confidence that all of the requirements have been implemented and tested.

Requirements will usually be numbered, and a single requirement number may map on to several sections of the design or to several test cases, i.e. the mapping is

Table 3.3 Managing change requests

Activity	Change request
Log change request	The change request is logged and a unique reference number and priority assigned
Assess impact	The cost, schedule, technical and quality impacts are determined and the risks identified
Decision	The CCB authorizes or rejects the change request
Implement solution	The affected project documents and software modules are identified and modified accordingly
Verify solution	Testing (unit, system and UAT) is employed to verify the correctness of the solution
Close CR	The change request is closed

often *one to many*. The traceability matrix (Table 3.4) provides the mapping between individual requirement numbers, and the sections in the design or test plan corresponding to the particular requirement number.

It is essential to keep the traceability matrix up to date during the project and especially after changes to the requirements. The traceability matrix is useful as a tool whenever there are changes to the requirements as it allows the impacts of the change on the other requirements (and other project deliverables) to be easily determined.

3.3 System Modelling

A model is an abstraction (simplification) of the physical world, and it acts as a representation of reality. The aim of the model is to capture the essential details of the real world, and as it is a simplification of the reality, it does not include all aspects of the physical world. However, it is important that all of the key aspects to be studied are included in the model and to determine the adequacy of the model as a representation of the real world.

A model is considered suitable if its properties closely match those of the system being modelled. It is common to employ models in engineering: for example, in civil engineering, it is normal to develop models of bridges and traffic flow prior to constructing a bridge. These models help in understanding the anticipated stresses on the bridge and play an important role in the design of a bridge that is safe to use. It is important that the models are an adequate representation of the reality, as otherwise there is the potential for serious consequences. For example, the model of the Tacoma Narrows Bridge did not include aerodynamic forces, and this proved to be a major factor in its subsequent collapse [2].

A good model will allow predictions of future behaviour to be made, and the adequacy of the model is determined from model exploration. This involves asking questions and determining the extent to which the model provides accurate answers

Table 3.4 Sample trace
matrix

Requirement no.	Sections in design	Test cases in test plan
R1.1	D1.4, D1.5, D3.2	T1.2, T1.7
R1.2	D1.8, D8.3	T1.4
R1.3	D2.2	T1.3
R1.50	D20.1, D30.4	T20.1, T24.2

to the questions. Inadequate models are replaced over time with better models that provide a better explanation of the reality. For example, the Ptolemaic cosmological model was replaced by the Copernican model, and Newtonian mechanics was replaced the theory of relativity when dealing with velocities that are close to the speed of light [3].

The adequacy of the model will determine its acceptability as a representation of the physical world. Models that are ineffective will be replaced with models that offer a better explanation of the manifested physical behaviour.

Occam's Razor[5] ('*principle of parsimony*') is a key principle employed in modelling [4]. It states that the number of entities employed to explain the reality should be kept to a minimum, with every entity used actually required for the explanation. In other words, the simplest model should be chosen with the least number of assumptions, and all superfluous concepts that are not required to explain the phenomena should be removed. This results in a crisp and simpler model.

System modelling is an abstraction of the existing and proposed system, and it helps in clarifying what the existing system does and in communicating and clarifying requirements of the proposed system. The model is a simplification of the system, and it may be explored to identify strengths and weaknesses in the existing system. This leads to requirements for the new system.

Models of the new system may be used to communicate the proposed requirements to the other stakeholders, and more than one model (e.g. using several UML diagrams) may be employed to represent the system from a number of different viewpoints (e.g. environment, behaviour, structural or behaviour). The use of the graphical UML diagrams to represent the software system is a useful type of system modelling.

Another important approach (used mainly in the safety and security critical field) is the use of mathematical models that provide abstract mathematical models of the proposed software system.

Model-driven engineering is concerned with the generation of the programs from the models, and the Rational/IBM tools allow programs to be generated from the UML diagrams.

---

[5]This principle is named after the medieval philosopher, William of Ockham.

3.4   Review Questions

1. What is the difference between a functional and non-functional requirement?
2. What is the difference between requirements verification and validation?
3. What is requirements engineering? How are requirements elicited from the customer?
4. Explain the difference between a user requirement and a system requirement?
5. How are changes to the requirements managed? Why is it important to keep project deliverables consistent with the requirements?
6. What is the purpose of requirements traceability?
7. Explain the advantages and disadvantages of specifying the system requirements in a natural language. Describe other approaches.
8. Explain the purpose of a model and how models may be used in requirements engineering.

3.5   Summary

The user requirements specify what the customer wants and define what the software system is required to do, as distinct from how this is to be done. The requirements are the foundation for the system, and so if they are incorrect, then the implemented system will be incorrect. The process of determining the requirements, analysing and validating them and managing them throughout the project lifecycle is termed requirements engineering.

The user requirements are determined from discussions with the customer to determine their actual needs, and they are then refined into the system requirements, which state the functional and non-functional requirements of the system. The requirements must be precise and unambiguous to ensure that all stakeholders are clear on what is (and what is not) to be delivered.

Prototyping may be employed to assist in the definition of the requirements. Requirements verification is concerned with ensuring that the requirements are properly implemented, and it is concerned with ensuring that the requirements are properly addressed in the design and implementation. A traceability matrix and testing are often employed as part of the verification activities.

Requirements validation is concerned with ensuring that the right requirements are defined and that they are complete, consistent and reflect the actual needs of the customer. The validation of the requirements is done by the stakeholders, and it involves several reviews of the requirements (and prototype), reviews of the design and user acceptance testing.

Requirements management is concerned with managing changes to the requirements, and in ensuring that the project maintains an up-to-date approved set of requirements throughout the project lifecycle. It ensures that the project deliverables are kept consistent with the latest version of the requirements, and when the requirements document changes, then all other project deliverables need to be kept consistent with the new version of the requirements.

The objective of requirements traceability is to verify that all of the defined requirements for the project have been implemented and tested. The traceability matrix provides a crisp summary of how the requirements have been implemented and tested, and it provides a bidirectional mapping of the requirements to the design and test case.

References

1. I. Jacobson, G. Booch, J. Rumbaugh, *The Unified Software Modelling Language User Guide* (Addison-Wesley, Reading, 1999)
2. G. O'Regan, *A Practical Approach to Software Quality* (Springer, New York, 2002)
3. T. Kuhn, *The Structure of Scientific Revolutions* (University of Chicago Press, Chicago, 1970)
4. M.M.A. Airchinnigh, Conceptual models and computing. PhD Thesis. Department of Computer Science, University of Dublin. Trinity College, Dublin, 1990

Software Design and Development

4

Abstract

This chapter discusses design and development, and software design is the blueprint of the solution to be developed. It is concerned with the high-level architecture of the system, as well as the detailed design that describes the algorithms and functionality of the individual programs. The detailed design is then implemented in a programming language such as C++ or Java. We discuss software development topics such as software reuse, customized-off-the-shelf software (COTS) and open-source software development.

Keywords

Architectural design · Detailed design · Function-oriented design · Object-oriented design · Object-oriented development · User interface design · Open-source development · Customized off-the-shelf software (COTS) · Software reuse · Software maintenance and evolution

4.1 Introduction

The user requirements specify what the customer wants and define *what* the software system is required to do, as distinct from *how* this is to be done. The user requirements are determined from discussions with the stakeholders to determine their actual needs, and they are then refined into the system requirements, which state the functional and non-functional requirements of the system.

The software design of the system is a blueprint of the solution of the system to be developed. It is concerned with the high-level architecture of the system, as well as the detailed design that describes the algorithms and functionality of the individual programs. The detailed design is then implemented in a programming language such as C++ or Java.

Software design is a creative process that is concerned with how the system will be organized and implemented. It consists of the high-level system architecture and the low-level detailed design. The system architecture may include hardware such as personal computers and servers, as well as the definition of the subsystems with the various software modules and their interfaces. The choice of the architecture of the system is a key design decision, as it affects the performance and maintainability of the system.

The architecture is often modelled with block diagrams that give a high-level picture of the system structure, where each diagram represents a subsystem (or component) with arrows indicating the flow of data or control. The architecture facilitates discussion of the system design, as well as recording the design decisions. Architecture in the small is concerned with the architecture of individual programs, whereas architecture in the large is concerned with the architecture of large complex systems that may include other systems.

The system architecture is analogous to the architecture of a building, and it describes how the system is organized as a set of communicating structures (or subsystems). It presents the high-level design of the system, and there may be several views of the architecture (e.g. Kruchten's 4+1 model), which describe the system from different viewpoints (e.g. end-users and managers). The views (e.g. logical, development, process and physical) may be presented using various UML diagrams (e.g. class, activity and state diagrams).

The choice of the architectural design will determine the extent to which key non-functional requirements such as performance, reliability and availability are satisfied. Further, the architecture of the system is costly and difficult to modify, and so it is essential that the right architecture be chosen first time (issues such as scalability may also need to be considered). Detailed (Low-level) design is concerned with the specification of the design of the modules or individual programs.

The software development is concerned with the actual implementation of the design, and it is implemented in some programming language such as C++ or Java. The software may be developed internally or it may be outsourced to another company; existing open-source software may be employed or modified accordingly or a solution may be purchased off-the-shelf. It is essential that the design is valid with respect to the requirements and that the implemented system is valid with respect to the design.

4.2 Architecture Design

The design of the system consists of engineering activities to describe the *architecture model or structure of the system* that will satisfy the functional and non-functional requirements, as well as the *design of the individual programs* to describe the algorithms and functionality required to implement the system requirements.

The design is concerned with how the system will be organized, and the architecture design is often presented as a set of interacting components. The design activities include architecture design, interface design, component design, algorithm design, and data structure design. There are often several possible design solutions for a particular system, and the designer will need to choose the most appropriate design of the system.

The architectural model of the system is an abstract visual representation of the structure of the system, and it is often presented as a set of boxes or block diagrams. It shows the major components of the system (i.e., the subsystems) and their interactions, and each box represents a component with the architecture showing all of the components and their connections. A box within a box represents a sub component, and arrows are used to represent the flow of data between the components. This abstract description of the system provides a high-level view of the system and is an effective way to facilitate discussion about the system design with the relevant stakeholders.

There is a need to present multiple views of the system architecture such as how the system is decomposed into modules, how the run-time processes interact and how the hardware is distributed across the processors in the system. These views may include Krutchen's 4+1 model (Table 4.1) [1].

The process view may be described by data flow diagrams (part of the SSADM method), which show the flow of data through a system. UML is a popular design method that gives several views of the architecture of the system.

The interface design defines the interfaces between the system components, and this allows a component to be used without knowing how it is implemented. Once the interface designs have been specified, the components may be designed and developed concurrently. The component design defines how each component will operate, and the database design defines the data structures that are required. It is essential to validate the design with respect to the system requirements and to ensure that the architecture will satisfy the functional and non-functional requirements.

Table 4.1 Views of system architecture

View	Description
Logical	This view shows the key abstractions in the system as objects or object classes
Process view	This view shows how the system is composed of interacting processes at run-time
Development view	This view shows how the software is decomposed into modules/components for development
Physical view	This view shows the system hardware and how the software components are distributed across the processors in the system

Fig. 4.1 C.A.R Hoare
(public domain)

Architectural design patterns are popular and date back to the mid-1990s. A design pattern is an abstract description of best practice that has worked successfully in different systems and environments, and it acts as a reusable solution that may be used in many situations. It is more a description or template on how to solve the problem within a particular context, rather than a finished solution. There are many examples of design patterns (e.g. the client server pattern includes servers and clients with services delivered from the servers).

The views of C.A.R. Hoare (Fig. 4.1) on software design are interesting. He states that there are two ways of constructing a software design.

One way is to make it so simple that there are obviously no deficiencies.

The other way is to make it so complex that there are no obvious deficiencies.

He argues that the first method is far more difficult to achieve and that it requires skill and insight. The starting point in design is always the problem domain, and it is essential that the problem to be solved be understood from a number of different viewpoints. A number of potential solutions may then be identified, and each potential solution is evaluated. This leads to the chosen solution that may, for example, be the simplest and least costly.

Design is an iterative process and the goal is to describe the system architecture that will satisfy the functional and non-functional requirements. It involves describing the system at a number of different levels of abstraction, with the designer starting off with an informal picture of the design that is then refined by adding more information.

Parnas's ideas on architecture and design have been quite influential, and he recognized that the structure of a software system matters, and getting the structure right is important. His 1972 paper "*On the criteria to be used in decomposing systems into modules*" [2] is a classic in software engineering. He introduced the

Fig. 4.2 David Parnas

revolutionary *information hiding* principle, which allows software to be *designed in a way to deal with change* (Fig. 4.2).

A module is characterized by its knowledge of a design decision (*secret*) that it hides from all other modules. Every information-hiding module has an *interface* that provides the only means to access the services provided by the modules. *The interface hides the module's implementation.* Information hiding is a fundamental principle that is used in object-oriented programming, and Parnas argues in his 1972 paper that:

> It is almost always incorrect to begin the decomposition of a system into modules on the basis of a flowchart. We propose instead that one begins with a list of difficult design decisions or design decisions which are likely to change. Each module is then designed to hide such a decision from the others

The design may be specified in various ways such as graphical notations that display the relationships between the various components making up the design. The notation may include block diagrams, flow charts or various UML diagrams such as sequence diagrams and state charts.

The design of programs may employ pseudocode to specify the algorithms, as well as the data structures that are the basis for implementation. Natural language is often used to express information that cannot be expressed formally, but it is essential that the natural language description is precise and unambiguous. The design activities include:

– Architecture Design of system (with all subsystems)
– Abstract specification of each subsystem

- Interface Design (for each subsystem)
- Component Design
- Data Structure Design
- Algorithm Design.

The quality of the software architecture directly impacts the robustness, performance and maintainability of the system. The software architecture needs to manage the inherent complexity of the system, and it must ensure a solid performance of the implemented system, with safety, security, availability and maintainability requirements properly addressed.

4.3 Detailed Design and Development

The design of the system consists of engineering activities to describe the components of the system, as well as the algorithms and functions required to implement the system requirements. Design and development are concerned with developing an executable software system.

Function-oriented design involves starting with a high-level view of the system and refining it into a more detailed design. The system state is centralized and shared between the functions operating on that state. Functional design has been overtaken by object-oriented design, and so it is mainly of historic interest today.

Object-oriented design (OOD) is popular, and it is based on the concept of information hiding developed by Parnas. The system is viewed as a collection of *objects* rather than functions, with each object managing its own state information. The system state is decentralized and an object is a member of an object class. The definition of a *class* includes *attributes* and *operations* on class members, and these may be inherited from superclasses. Objects communicate by exchanging *messages*, and messages are the only way to access an object. The internal details of the object are kept private.

Software design and development are closely linked, and often proceed in parallel. Software design is the creative process that identifies the software components and their relationships, whereas software development is concerned with the implementation of the design in some programming language. The choice of language reflects the problem domain, and it may be an object-oriented language such as C++ or Java, or a procedural language such as C or FORTRAN. It is important that the software code is subject to a peer review to ensure that it is of high quality and that it is a valid implementation of the requirements and design. The coding standards for the language need to be followed, as this helps with the maintainability of the code.

Software reuse has become important and organizations recognize the importance of reuse during software development. Its advantages are that it improves software productivity and potentially provides higher quality software. Customized off-the-shelf software (COTS) provides specific functionality that may be purchased and tailored for use in the software development. It may be possible to buy the entire system off-the-shelf, and so one of the earliest design decisions is whether *to buy* or *build* the application.

Open-source software development has become popular, and the idea is that the source code is not proprietary, but is freely available (under an open-source licence) for software developers to use and modify as they wish. It offers a way to speed up software development, as well as potentially providing a high-quality cost-effective solution.

4.3.1 Function-Oriented Design

Function-oriented design is one of the older design methodologies, and it involves starting with a high-level view of the system and refining it into a more detailed design. The system is considered to be a set of modules with clearly defined behaviour, which interact with each other in a defined manner to produce some system behaviour.

Function-oriented design views the software design as a set of functions that share state, and the functions transform the inputs to the desired outputs. The system state is centralized and shared between the functions operating on the state, and at the end of the phase, all of the major modules (as well as their interactions) and all of the main data structures of the system have been defined.

The system design (top level design) first determines which modules are needed for the system, and the detailed design expands on the system design and is focused on the internal design and specification of the modules. The detailed design is concerned with how the modules are interconnected and implemented.

The functional design is a refinement of the architectural design in that the architectural design has identified the key components, and the functional design then in a sense then determines the module structure for each component (the modules created need to be consistent with the architecture). Functional design is mainly of historic interest, as it has been overtaken by OOD.

4.3.2 Object-Oriented Design

OOD is a design method that models the system as a set of cooperating objects (rather than as a set of functions), and where the individual objects are viewed as instances of a class. OOD is concerned with the object-oriented decomposition of the system, and it involves defining the required objects and their interactions to solve the particular problem. The system state is decentralized with each object managing its own state information. The objects have a collection of attributes that define their state and operations that act on the state. The data in the object is hidden, and the only access to the data is with the operations.

The difference between a class and an object may be seen from the example that walls and windows are classes, whereas individual doors and windows are objects.

A class is a set of objects (rather than an individual object), and all members of the class share the same attributes, operations and relationships. A class may represent a software thing or a hardware thing.

A class may inherit its behaviour from one or more superclasses, with the class definition setting out the differences between the class and its superclasses. The communication between objects is done by exchanging messages (in practice, an object calls a procedure associated with another object).

An object is a "black box" that sends and receives *messages*. A black box consists of *code* (computer instructions) and *data* (information which these instructions operate on). The traditional way of programming kept code and data separate. For example, functions and data structures in the C programming language are not connected. However, in the object-oriented world, code and data are merged into a single indivisible thing called an *object*.

The reason that an object is called a black box is that the user of an object never needs to look inside the box, since all communication to it is done via messages. Messages define the *interface* to the object. Everything an object can do is represented by its message interface. Therefore, there is no need to know anything about what is in the black box (or object) in order to use it. The access to an object is only through its messages, while keeping the internal details private. This is called *information hiding* and is due to work by Parnas in the early 1970s.

The main features of the object-oriented paradigm are described in Table 4.2.

There is a need to understand the relationship between the software to be designed and its external environment. This may involve using UML to develop models such as a system context model that shows the other systems in its environment, and an interaction model that shows the interaction between the system and its environment.

This leads to the architectural design where the major components of the system and their interactions are identified. The UML diagrams help in identifying the objects and operations in the system, and the various UML models (e.g. sequence diagrams and state diagrams) show the relationships between the objects. Design patterns (best practice of solutions to common problems that may be reused) are often employed in OOD. The various UML diagrams are described in more detail in Chap. 14.

4.3.3 User Interface Design

User interface design is concerned with the design of the user interface for machines and software. The user interface is the boundary between the user and the system, and the usability of the system (as well as the user experience) will be determined by the quality of the user interface design. The user interface needs to take into account the knowledge and experience of the user, and the user interactions with the system should be as simple and efficient as possible.

Table 4.2 Object-oriented paradigm

Feature	Description
Class	A class defines the abstract characteristics of a thing, including its attributes (or properties) and its behaviours (or methods). The members of a class are termed objects
Object	An object is a particular instance of a class with its own set of attributes. The set of values of the attributes of a particular object is called its state
Method	The methods associated with a class represent the behaviours of the objects in the class
Message passing	Message passing is the process by which an object sends data to another object or asks the other object to invoke a method
Inheritance	A class may have subclasses (or children classes) that are more specialized versions of the class. A subclass inherits the attributes and methods of the parent class. This allows the programmer to create new classes from existing classes. The derived classes inherit the methods and data structures of the parent class
Encapsulation (information hiding)	One fundamental principle of the object-oriented world is encapsulation (or information hiding). The internals of an object are kept private to the object and may not be accessed from outside the object. That is, encapsulation hides the details of how a particular class works, and it requires a clearly specified interface around the services provided
Abstraction	Abstraction simplifies complexity by modelling classes and removing all unnecessary detail. All essential detail is represented, and non-essential information is ignored
Polymorphism	Polymorphism is a behaviour that varies depending on the class in which the behaviour is invoked. Two or more classes may react differently to the same message. The same name is given to methods in different subclasses: i.e. one interface and multiple methods

User interface design requires a good understanding of user needs, as well as how the user will interact with the system. It may involve prototyping of the interface and usability testing of the prototypes to judge its fitness for use. There are usability standards (e.g. ISO 9241 and ISO 16982) that provide guidance on usability.

Today's graphical user interfaces (GUI) have become ubiquitous for applications on personal computers, and a GUI is characterized by:

- Multiple windows on the screen
- Use of icon to represent information
- Command selection via menus
- Use of a mouse.

The advantages of GUIs are that they are easy to learn and use, with users with limited computing experience able to learn the user interface quite quickly.

4.3.4 Open-Source Development

Open-source development is a modern approach to software development in which the source code is published, and thousands of volunteer software developers from around the world participate in developing and improving the software. The idea is that the source code is not proprietary, and that it is freely available for software developers to use and modify as they wish. One useful benefit is that it may potentially speed up development time thereby shortening time to market.

The roots of open-source development are in the Free Software Foundation (FSF). This is a non-profit organization founded by Richard Stallman [3] to promote the free software movement, and it has developed a legal framework for the free software movement.

The Linux operating system is a well-known open-source product, and other products include mySQL, Firefox and Apache HTTP server. The quality of software produced by the open-source movement is good, and defects are generally identified and fixed faster than with proprietary software development.

A company needs to decide whether the product to be developed should use an open-source approach, as well as determining the risks and benefits associated with this approach. The type of open-source licence required needs to be identified and obtained.

4.3.5 Customized Off-the-Shelf Software

Customized off-the-shelf software (COTS) is a software (or a system) that is ready made and may be purchased off-the-shelf and adapted to the user's requirements. A COTS product typically needs to be configured for the specific use required, and the tailoring is within the parameters of the commercial software, and so custom development is usually not required.

The use of COTS components may shorten the time to market and help to reduce software development costs, as the components may be purchased from a third-party vendor rather than developed internally. Further, there is greater confidence in the quality and reliability of the COTS software (compared to custom built software), as its reliability has already been shown through its use with other organizations.

The disadvantages of COTS are that it could lead to dependency on a particular vendor, or the risk that the COTS product could become obsolete with the vendor no longer supporting it. Further, there may also be security risks if the COTS software contains security vulnerabilities (this is even more serious if the COTS software is integrated with other software products to create larger systems). For this reason, the product development strategy needs to be clearly thought through, with all risks carefully considered.

4.3.6 Software Reuse

Software reuse is the systematic reuse of existing software technology to build software. It involves the reuse of software deliverables produced during the software development lifecycle (e.g. designs, code and test suites), and its successful implementation may shorten the time to market, as well as reducing software costs and improving software quality and productivity.

The successful introduction of reuse in an organization requires an infrastructure to support reuse. It is a lot more than creating a repository of software assets, where software engineers add software items to the depository, with the hope that other software engineers will use the contents of the repository.[1]

The reuse process involves activities to manage the reuse infrastructure, and establishing the reuse goals and the roles involved. It includes activities to create reusable assets which involve understanding the domain in which the software will be used, and designing the software for use in multiple products, as well as identifying, collecting and representing the required software assets.

Finally, it involves activities to classify and retrieve the assets in the reuse library, and activities to search and retrieve the required software assets from the library.

4.3.7 Object-Oriented Programming

Object-oriented programming has become popular in large-scale software development, and it became the dominant paradigm in programming from the early 1990s. Its proponents argue that it is easier to learn, and simpler to develop and maintain such programs, and its growth in popularity was helped by the rise in popularity of GUI, which are well suited to object-oriented programming. The C++ programming language has become popular, and it is an object-oriented extension of the C programming language.

The traditional view of programming is that a program is a collection of functions, or a list of instructions to be performed on the computer. *Object-oriented programming* is a paradigm shift in programming, where a computer program is considered to be a collection of objects that act on each other. Each object is capable of sending and receiving messages and processing data. That is, each object may be viewed as an independent entity or actor with a distinct role or responsibility.

---

[1] I recall Parnas making a joke many years ago that we have developed all of this reusable software that nobody reuses.

The origins of object-oriented programming go back to the invention of Simula 67 at the Norwegian Computing Research Centre[2] in the late 1960s. It introduced the notion of a class and instances of a class.[3] Simula 67 influenced later languages such as the Smalltalk object-oriented language developed at Xerox PARC in the mid-1970s.

Xerox introduced the term *"Object-oriented programming"* for the use of objects and messages as the basis for computation. Most modern programming languages support object-oriented programming, and object-oriented features have been added to many existing languages such as BASIC, FORTRAN and Ada.

C++ and Java Bjarne Stroustrup developed the C++ programming language in 1983 as an object-oriented extension of the C programming language. It was designed to use the power of object-oriented programming and to maintain the speed and portability of C. It provides a significant extension of C's capabilities, but it does not force the programmer to use the object-oriented features of the language.

A key difference between C++ and C is the concept of a class. A *class* is an extension to the C concept of a structure. The main difference is that while a C data structure can hold only data, a C++ class may hold both data and functions. An *object* is an instantiation of a class: i.e. the class is essentially the type, whereas the object is essentially a variable of that type. Classes are defined in C++ by using the keyword class.

Java is an object-oriented programming language developed by James Gosling and others at Sun Microsystems in the early 1990s. C and C++ influenced the syntax of the language, and the language was designed with portability in mind. The objective is for a program to be written once and executed anywhere. Platform independence is achieved by compiling the Java code into Java bytecode, which are simplified machine instructions specific to the Java platform.

This code is then run on a Java virtual machine (JVM) that interprets and executes the Java bytecode. The JVM is specific to the native code on the host hardware. The problem with interpreting bytecode is that it is slow compared to traditional compilation. However, Java has a number of techniques to address this including just in time compilation and dynamic recompilation. Java also provides automatic garbage collection. This is a very useful feature as it protects programmers who forget to deallocate memory (thereby causing memory leaks).

The reader is referred to [4] for a more detailed explanation of the design and development activities.

---

[2]The inventors of Simula-67 were Ole-Johan Dahl and Kristen Nygaard.

[3]Dahl and Nygaard were working on ship simulations and were attempting to address the huge number of combinations of different attributes from different types of ships. Their insight was to group the different types of ships into different classes of objects, with each class of objects being responsible for defining its own data and behaviour.

4.4 Software Maintenance and Evolution

Software maintenance is the process of changing a system after it has been delivered to the customer, and it involves correcting any defects that are present in the software and enhancing the system to meet the evolving needs of the customer. The defects may be due to coding, design or requirements errors, with coding defects the cheapest to fix and requirements defects the most expensive to correct. The resolution to the defects involves identifying the affected software components and modifying them, and verifying that the solution is correct and that no new problems have been introduced.

Software systems often have a long lifetime (e.g. some systems have a lifetime of 20–30 years), and so the software needs to be continuously enhanced over its lifetime to meet the evolving needs of the customer. Software evolution is concerned with the continued development and maintenance of the software after its initial release, with new releases of the software prepared each year. Each new release includes new functionality and corrections to the known defects.

4.5 Review Questions

1. What is the difference between requirements and design?
2. Explain the difference between architectural design and detailed design.
3. Explain the difference between functional-oriented design and OOD.
4. What are the advantages and disadvantages of COTS software.
5. What is object-oriented programming?
6. What is software reuse and how is it accomplished?
7. Explain the differences between COTS, software reuse and open-source software.
8. Explain the difference between software maintenance and evolution.

4.6 Summary

The success of business is highly influenced by software, and companies may develop their own software internally, or they may acquire software solutions off-the-shelf or from bespoke software development.

The user requirements specify what the customer wants and define *what* the software system is required to do, as distinct from *how* this is to be done. The requirements are the foundation for the system, and it is essential that they are correct and reflect the needs of the customer.

The software design of the system is a blueprint of the system to be developed. It is concerned with the high-level architecture of the system, as well as the detailed design that describes the algorithms and functionality of the individual programs. Software design is a creative process that is concerned with how the system will be organized and implemented.

The system architecture may include hardware such as computers and servers, as well as the definition of the subsystems with the various software modules and their interfaces. The choice of the architecture of the system is a key design decision, as it affects the performance and maintainability of the system.

The detailed software design of the system is concerned with activities to describe the algorithms and functions required to implement the system requirements. It may include hardware as well as the various software modules and their interfaces. Design and development are concerned with developing an executable software system.

The software development is concerned with the actual implementation of the design in some programming language such as C++ or Java. The software may be developed internally or it may be outsourced to another company or a solution may be purchased off-the-shelf. It is essential that the design is valid with respect to the requirements and that the implemented system is valid with respect to the design.

References

1. P. Kruchten, Architectural blueprints—the "4+1" view model of software architecture. IEEE Softw. **12**(6), 42–50 (1995)
2. D. Parnas, On the criteria to be used in decomposing systems into modules. Commun. ACM **15** (12) (1972)
3. G. O'Regan, *Giants of Computing* (Springer, London, 2013)
4. I. Sommerville, *Software Engineering*, 9th edn. (Pearson, Boston, 2011)

Configuration Management

5

Abstract

This chapter discusses configuration management and discusses the fundamental concept of a baseline. Configuration management is concerned with identifying those deliverables that must be subject to change control and controlling changes to them.

Keywords

Configuration management system · Configuration items · Baseline · File naming conventions · Version control · Change control · Change control board · Configuration management audits

5.1 Introduction

Software configuration management (SCM) is concerned with tracking and controlling changes to the software and project deliverables, and it provides full traceability of the changes made during the project. It provides a record of what has been changed, as well as who changed it. SCM involves identifying the configuration items of the system; controlling changes to them; and maintaining integrity and traceability.

The origins of software configuration management go back to the early days of computing when the principles of configuration management used in the hardware design field were applied to software development in the 1950s. It has evolved over time to a set of procedures and tools to manage changes to the software.

© Springer International Publishing AG 2017
G. O'Regan, *Concise Guide to Software Engineering*, Undergraduate Topics in Computer Science, DOI 10.1007/978-3-319-57750-0_5

The configuration items are generally documents in the early part of the software development lifecycle, whereas the focus is on source code control management and software release management in the later parts of development. Software configuration management involves:

- Identifying what needs to be controlled
- Ensuring those items are accurately defined and documented
- Ensuring that changes are made in a controlled manner
- Ensuring that the correct version of a work product is being used
- Knowing the version and status of a configuration item at any time
- Ensuring adherence to standards
- Planning builds and releases.

Software configuration management allows the orderly development of software, and it ensures that only authorized changes to the software are made. It ensures that releases are planned and that the impacts of proposed changes are considered prior to their authorization. The integrity of the system is maintained at all times, and the constituents of the software (including their version numbers) are known at any time.

Effective configuration management allows questions such as the following (Table 5.1) to be easily answered:

The symptoms of poor configuration management include corrected defects that suddenly begin to reappear, difficulty in or failure to locate the latest version of source code or failure to determine the source code that corresponds to a software release.

Therefore, it is important to employ sound configuration management practices to enable high-quality software to be consistently produced. Poor configuration management practices lead to quality problems resulting in a loss of the credibility and reputation of a company. Several symptoms of poor configuration management practices are listed in Table 5.2.

Table 5.1 Features of good configuration management	Features of good configuration management
	What is the correct version of the software module to be updated?
	Where can I get a copy of R4.7 of software system X?
	What versions of the software system X are installed at the various customer sites?
	What changes have been introduced in the new release of software (version R4.8 from the previous release of R4.7)?
	What version of the design document corresponds to software system version R3.5?
	What customers use R3.5 of the software system?
	Are there undocumented or unapproved changes included in the released version of the software?

Table 5.2 Symptoms of poor configuration management

Symptoms of poor configuration management
Defects corrected suddenly begin to reappear
Cannot find the latest version of the source code
Unable to match the source code and object code
Wrong version of software sent to the customer
Wrong code tested
Cannot replicate previously released code
Simultaneous changes to same source component by multiple developers with some changes lost

Configuration management involves identifying the configuration items to be controlled and systematically controlling change to them, in order to maintain the integrity and traceability of the configuration throughout the software development lifecycle. There is a need to manage and control changes to documents and source code, including the project plan, the requirements document, design documents, code and test plans.

A key concept in configuration management is that of a "*baseline*," which is *a set of work products that have been formally reviewed and agreed upon and serves as the foundation for future development work.*

A baseline can only be changed through formal change control procedures, which leads to a new baseline. It provides a stable basis for the continuing evolution of the configuration items, and all approved changes move forward from the current baseline leading to the creation of a new baseline. The change control board (CCB) or a similar mechanism authorizes the release of baselines, and the content of each baseline is documented. All configuration items must be approved before they are entered into the released baselines.

Therefore, it is necessary to identify the configuration items that need to be placed under formal change control and to maintain a history of the changes made to the baseline. There are four key parts to software configuration management (Table 5.3).

A typical set of software releases (e.g., in the telecommunications domain) consists of incremental development, where the software to be released consists of a number of releases builds with the early builds consisting of new functionality, and the later builds consisting of fix releases.

Software configuration management is planned for the project, and each project will typically have a configuration management plan which will detail the planned delivery of functionality and fix release for the project (Table 5.4).

Each of the R.1.0.O.k baselines are termed release builds, and they consist of new functionality and fixes to the identified problems. The content of each release build is known; i.e., the project team and manager will target specific functionality and fixes for each build, and the actual content of the particular release baseline is documented. Each release build can be replicated, as the version of source code to create the build is known, and the source code is under control management.

Table 5.3 Software configuration management activities

Area	Description
Configuration identification	This requires identifying the configuration items to be controlled and implementing a sound configuration management system, including a repository where documents and source code are placed under controlled access. It includes a mechanism for releasing documents or code, a file naming convention and a version numbering system for documents and code and baseline/release planning. The version and status of each configuration item should be known
Configuration control	This involves tracking and controlling change requests and controlling changes to the configuration items. Any changes to the work products are controlled and authorized by a change control board or similar mechanism. Problems or defects reported by the test groups or customer are analyzed, and any changes made are subject to change control. The version of the work product is known, and the constituents of a particular release are known and controlled. The previous versions of releases can be recreated, as the source code constituents are fully known and available
Configuration auditing	This includes audits to verify the integrity of the baseline, and audits of the configuration management system verify that the standards and procedures are followed. The results of the audits are communicated to the affected groups, and corrective action is taken to address the findings
Status accounting	This involves data collection and report generation. These reports include the software baseline status, the summary of changes to the software baseline, problem report summaries and change request summaries

Table 5.4 Build plan for project

Release baseline	Contents	Date
R. 1.0.0.0	F_4, F_5, F_7	31.01.17
R. 1.0.0.1	F_1, F_2, F_6 + fixes	15.02.17
R. 1.0.0.2	F_3 + fixes	28.02.17
R. 1.0.0.3	F_8 + fixes (functionality freeze)	07.03.17
R. 1.0.0.4	Fixes	14.03.17
R. 1.0.0.5	Fixes	21.03.17
R. 1.0.0.6	Official release	31.03.17

There are various tools employed for software configuration management activities, and these include well-known tools such as Clearcase, PVCS and Visual Source Safe (VSS) for source code control management. The PV tracker tool and Clearquest may be used for tracking defects and change requests. A defect-tracking tool will list all of the open defects against the software, and a defect may require several change requests to correct the software (as a problem may affect different parts of the software product as well as different versions of the product, and a change request may be necessary for each part). The tool will generally link the

Table 5.5 CMMI requirements for configuration management

Specific goal	Specific practice	Description of specific practice/goal
SG 1		*Establish baselines*
	SP 1.1	Identify configuration items
	SP 1.2	Establish a configuration management system
	SP 1.3	Create or release baselines
SG 2		*Track and control changes*
	SP 2.1	Track change requests
	SP 2.2	Control configuration items
SG 3		*Establish integrity*
	SP 3.1	Establish configuration management records
	SP 3.2	Perform configuration audits

change requests to the problem report. The current status of the problem report can be determined, and the targeted release build for the problem identified.

The CMMI provides guidance on practices to be implemented for sound configuration management (Table 5.5).

The CMMI requirements are concerned with establishing a configuration management system; identifying the work products that need to be subject to change control; controlling changes to these work products over time; controlling releases of work products; creating baselines; maintaining the integrity of baselines; providing accurate configuration data to stakeholders; recording and reporting the status of configuration items and change requests; and verifying the correctness and completeness of configuration items with configuration audits. We shall discuss the key parts of configuration management in the following sections.

5.2   Configuration Management System

The configuration management system enables the controlled evolution of the documents and the software modules produced during the project. It includes

- Configuration management planning
- A document repository with check in/check out features
- A source code repository with check in/check out features
- A configuration manager (may be a part-time role)
- File naming convention for documents and source code
- Project directory structure
- Version Numbering System for documents
- Standard templates for documents
- Facility to create a baseline
- A release procedure
- A group (change control board) to approve changes to baseline

 – A change control procedure
 – Configuration management audits to verify the integrity of baseline.

5.2.1   Identify Configuration Items

The configuration items are the work products to be placed under configuration management control, and they include project documents, source code and data files. They may also include compilers as well as any supporting tools employed in the project.

The project documentation will typically include project plans, the user requirements specification, the system requirements specification, the architecture and technical design documents and the test plans.

The items to be placed under configuration management control are identified and documented early in the project lifecycle. Each configuration item needs to be uniquely identified and controlled. This may be done with a naming convention for the project deliverables and source code and applying it consistently. For example, a simple approach is to employ mnemonics labels and version numbers to uniquely identify project deliverables. A user requirements specification for project 005 in the finance business area may be represented simply by:

FIN_005_URS

5.2.2   Document Control Management

The project documents are stored in a document repository using a configuration management tool such as PVCS or VSS. For consistency, a standard directory structure is often employed for projects, as this makes it easier to locate particular configuration items. A single repository may be employed for both documents and software code (or a separate repository for each).

Clearly, it is undesirable for two individuals to modify the same document at the same time, and the document repository will include *check in/check out* procedures. The document must be checked out prior to its modification, and once it is checked out, another user may not modify it until it has been checked back in. An audit trail of all modifications made to a particular document is maintained, including details of the person who made the change, the date that the change was made and the rationale for the change.

Version Numbering of Documents
A simple version numbering system may be employed to record the versions of documents: e.g., v0.1, v0.2 and v0.3 is often used for draft documents, with version v1.0 being the first approved version of the document. Each time a document is modified its version number is incremented, and the document history records the reasons for the modification.

- V0.1 Initial draft of document
- V0.x Revised draft ($x > 0$)
- V1.0 Approved baseline version
- V1.x Approved minor revision ($x > 0$)
- Vn.0 Approved major revision ($n > 1$)
- Vn.x Approved minor revision ($x > 0$, $n > 1$).

The document will provide information on whether it is a draft or approved, as well as the date of last modification, the person who made the modification, and the rationale for the modification. The configuration management system will provide records of the configuration management activities, as well as the status of the configuration items and the status of the change requests. The revision history of the configuration items will be maintained.

5.2.3   Source Code Control Management

The source code and data files are stored in a source code repository using a tool such as PVCS, VSS or Clearcase, and the repository provides an audit trail of all the changes made to the source code. An item must first be checked out for modification, the changes are made, and it is then checked back into the repository. The source code management system provides security and control of the configuration items, and the procedures include:

- Access controls
- Checking in/out configuration items
- Merging and Branching
- Labels (labelling releases)
- Reporting.

The source code configuration management tool ensures the integrity of the source code and prevents more than one person from altering the software code at the same time.

5.2.4   Configuration Management Plan

A software *configuration management plan* (it may be part of the project plan or a separate plan) is prepared early in the project, and it defines the configuration management activities for the project. It will detail the items to be placed under configuration management control, the standards for naming configuration items, the version numbering system, as well as version control and release management.[1] The CM plan is placed under configuration management control.

The content of each software release is documented as well as installation and rollback instructions. The content includes the requirements and change requests implemented, as well as the defects corrected and the version of the new release. A list is maintained of the customer sites of where the release has been installed. All software releases are tested prior to their approval. The CM plan will include:

– Roles and responsibilities
– Configuration Items
– Naming Conventions
– Version Control
– Filing Structure for the project.

The stakeholders and roles involved are identified and documented in the CM plan. Often, the role of a *software configuration manager* is employed, and this may be a full time or part-time role.[2] The CM manager ensures that the configuration management activities are carried out correctly and will conduct and report the results of the CM audits.

5.3   Change Control

A change request (CR) database[3] is set up to record change requests made during the project. The change requests are documented and considered by the change control board (CCB). The CCB may just consist of the project manager and the system owner for small projects, or a management and technical team for larger projects.

The impacts and risks of the proposed change need to be considered, and an informed decision made on whether to reject or approve the CR. The proposed change may have technical impacts, as well as introducing new project risks, and may adversely affect the schedule and budget. It is important to keep change to a minimum at the later stages of the project in order to reduce risks to quality.

Figure 5.1 describes a simple process for raising a change request, performing an impact assessment, deciding on whether to approve or reject the change request and proceeding with implementation (where applicable).

The results of the CCB review of each change request (including the rationale of the decision made) will be recorded. Change requests and problem reports for all configuration items are recorded and analyzed, reviewed, approved (or rejected) and tracked to closure.

---

[1]These may be defined in a Configuration Management procedure and referenced in the CM plan.
[2]This depends on the size of the organization and projects. The project manager may perform the CM manager role for small projects.
[3]This may just be a simple Excel spread sheet or a sophisticated tool.

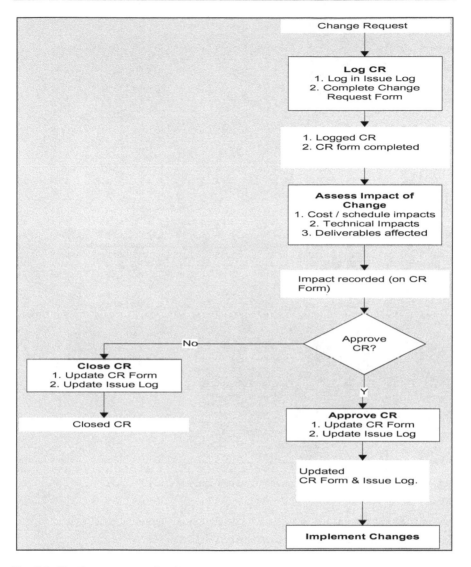

Fig. 5.1 Simple process map for change requests

A sample configuration management process map is detailed in Fig. 5.2, and it shows the process for updates to configuration information following an approved change request. The deliverable is checked out of the repository; modifications are made and the changes approved; configuration information is updated and the deliverable is checked back into the repository.

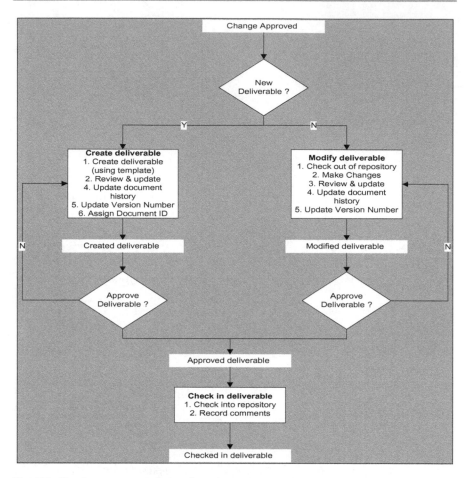

Fig. 5.2 Simple process map for configuration management

5.4   Configuration Management Audits

Configuration management audits are conducted during the project to verify that the configuration is consistent and complete. Every project should have at least one configuration audit, and the objective is to verify the completeness and correctness of the configuration system for the project. The audit will check that the records correctly identify the configuration and that the configuration management standards and procedures have been followed. Table 5.6 presents a sample configuration management checklist.

Table 5.6 Sample configuration management audit checklist

No.	Item to check
1.	Is the Directory Structure set up for the project?
2.	Are the configuration items identified and listed?
3.	Have the latest versions of the templates been used?
4.	Is a unique document Id employed for each document?
5.	Is the standard version numbering system followed for the project?
6.	Are all versions of documents and software modules in the document/source code repository?
7.	Is the Configuration Management plan up to date?
8.	Are the roles defined in the Configuration Management Plan performing their assigned responsibilities?
9.	Are changes to the approved documents formally controlled?
10.	Is the version number of a document incremented following an agreed change to an approved document?
11.	Is there a change control board set up to approve change requests?
12.	Is there a record of which releases are installed at the various customer sites?
13.	Are all documents/software modules produced by vendors under appropriate configuration management control?

There may also be a *librarian role* in setting up the filing structure for the project, or the configuration manager may perform this role. The project manager assigns responsibilities for performing configuration management activities. All involved in the process receive appropriate training on the process.

5.5   Review Questions

1. What is software configuration management?
2. What is change control?
3. What is a baseline?
4. Explain source code control management.
5. Explain document control management.
6. What is a configuration management audit and explain how it differs from a standard audit?
7. Describe the role of the configuration manager and librarian.
8. Describe the main elements in a software configuration management system.

5.6 Summary

Software configuration management is concerned with the orderly development and evolution of the software. It is concerned with tracking and controlling changes to the software and project deliverables, and it provides full traceability of the changes made during the project.

It involves identifying the configuration items that are subject to change control, controlling changes to them, and maintaining integrity and traceability throughout the software development lifecycle. The configuration items are generally documents in the early part of the development lifecycle, whereas the focus is on source code control management and software release management in the later parts of the development lifecycle.

The company standards need to be adhered to, and the correct version of a work product should be known at all time. There is a need for a document and source code repository, which has access controls, checking in and checking out procedures and labelling of releases.

A project will have a configuration management plan, and the configuration manager role is responsible for ensuring that the configuration management activities are carried out correctly.

Configuration management ensures that the impacts of proposed changes are considered prior to authorization. It ensures that releases are planned and that only authorized changes to the software are made. The integrity of the system is maintained, and the constituents of the software system and their version numbers are known at all times. Configuration audits will be conducted to verify that the CM activities have been carried out correctly.

Software Inspections

6

Abstract

This chapter discusses software inspections, which play an important role in building quality into a product. The well-known Fagan inspection process that was developed at IBM in the 1970s is discussed, as well as lighter review and walkthrough methodologies.

Keywords

Informal review · Structured walk-through · Fagan inspection · Gilb inspections · Economic benefits of inspections · Inspection guides · Entry and exit criteria · Automated software inspections

6.1 Introduction

The objective of software inspections is to build quality into the software product, rather than adding quality later. There is clear evidence that the cost of correction of a defect increases the later that it is detected, and it is therefore more cost effective to build quality in rather than adding it later in the development cycle. Software inspections are an effective way of doing this.

There are several approaches to software inspections, and these vary in the formality of the process. An informal review consists of a walk-through of the document or code by an individual other than the author. The meeting usually takes place at the author's desk (or in a meeting room), and the reviewer and author discuss the document or code informally.

There are formal software inspection methodologies such as the well-known *Fagan inspection* methodology [1] and the Gilb methodology [2]. These methodologies include pre-inspection activity, an inspection meeting and post-inspection

© Springer International Publishing AG 2017

G. O'Regan, *Concise Guide to Software Engineering*, Undergraduate Topics in Computer Science, DOI 10.1007/978-3-319-57750-0_6

Fig. 6.1 Michael Fagan

activity. Several inspection roles are typically employed, including an *author* role, an *inspector* role, a *tester* role and a *moderator* role.

The Fagan inspection methodology was developed by Michael Fagan (Fig. 6.1) at IBM in the mid-1970s, and Tom Gilb developed Gilb's approach in the early 1990s. The formality of the software inspection methodology employed is influenced by the impacts of software failure on the customer's business, as a failure may have a major negative impact on the customer. For example, an incorrect one-line change to telecommunications software could lead to failure resulting in a major telecommunications outage and significant disruption to customers.

Further, there may be financial impacts, as the service level agreement details the service level that will be provided, and the compensation given for service disruption. Consequently, a telecommunications company needs to ensure that its software is fit for purpose, and a formal software inspection process tends to be employed to ensure that quality is built in. This means that requirement documents, high-level and detailed design documents and software code are all inspected, and generally inspections are explicitly planned in the project schedule.

Another words, an organization needs to define an inspection process that is appropriate to its business, and it may adopt a rigorous approach such as the Fagan or Gilb methodology, or a less formal process where the impact of failure is less severe. It may not be possible to have all of the participants present in a room, and participation by conference call or video link may need to be employed. A formal process may not suit some organizations, and a structured walk-through may be the adopted approach.

Software inspections play an important role in building quality into the software, and in ensuring that the quality of the delivered product is good. The quality of the delivered software product is only as good as the quality at the end each phase, and therefore a phase should be exited only when the desired quality has been achieved.

The effectiveness of an inspection is influenced by the expertise of the inspectors, adequate preparation, the speed of the inspection and compliance to the inspection process. The inspection methodology provides guidelines on the inspection and preparation rates for an inspection, and guidelines on the entry and exit criteria for an inspection.

There are typically at least two roles in the inspection methodology. These include the *author* role and the *inspector* role. The *moderator, tester* and the *reader* roles may also be present in the methodology.

The next section describes the benefits of software inspections, and this is followed by a discussion of a simple review methodology where the reviewers send comments directly to the author. Then, a structured walk-through and a semi-formal review process are described, and finally the Fagan inspection process is described in detail.

6.2   Economic Benefits of Software Inspections

There is clear evidence that a software inspection program provides a return on investment and has tangible benefits in terms of quality, productivity, time to market and customer satisfaction. For example, IBM Houston employed software inspections for the space shuttle missions: 85% of the defects were found by inspections and 15% were found by testing. There were no defects found on the space missions, and about 2 million lines of computer software were inspected. IBM, North Harbour in the UK quoted a 9% increase in productivity with 93% of defects found by software inspections.

Software inspections are useful for educating new employees on the product, and on the standards and procedures used in the organization. They ensure that knowledge is shared among the employees, rather than understood by just one individual. Inspections improve software productivity, as less time is spent in correcting defective software.

The cost of correction of a defect increases the later that it is identified in the lifecycle. Boehm [3] states that the *cost of correction of a requirements defect identified in the field is over 40 times more expensive than if it were detected at the requirements phase,* and so it is most economical to detect and fix the defect in phase. The cost of correction of a requirements defect identified at the customer site includes the cost of correcting the requirements, the cost of design, coding, unit testing, system testing and regression testing. It may be necessary to send an engineer on site to fix the problem, and there may be hidden costs in the negative perception of the company with a subsequent loss of sales.

There is a powerful argument to identify defects as early as possible, and software inspections are a cost-effective way of doing this. There are various estimates of the *cost of poor quality* (COPQ) in an organization (Fig. 10.29), and some estimates suggest that it could be as high as 20–40% of sales. The exact calculation may be determined by a time sheet accountancy system, which details the cost of internal and external failure, and the cost of appraisal and prevention.

The return on investment from the introduction of software inspections may be calculated, and the evidence is that it leads to reductions in the cost of poor quality. Inspections provide a cost-effective way of improving quality and productivity.

6.3 Informal Reviews

This type of review involves reviewers sending comments directly to the author (e.g. email or written), and there is no actual review meeting. It is not as effective as the Fagan inspection process, but it helps in identifying some defects in the work products.

The author is responsible for making sure that the review happens and advises the participants that comments are due by a certain date. The author analyses the comments received, makes the required changes and circulates the document for approval. The activities are described in Table 6.1:

Comment:

The informal review process may help to improve quality in an organization. It is dependent on the participants adequately reviewing the deliverable and sending comments to the author. The author can only request the reviewer to send comments. There is no independent monitoring of the author to ensure that the review actually happens and is effective, and that comments are requested, received and implemented.

Table 6.1 Informal review

Step	Description
1.	The author circulates the deliverable (either physically or electronically) to the review audience
2.	The author advises the review audience of the due date for comments
3.	The due date for comments is typically one week or longer
4.	The author checks that all comments have been received by the due date
5.	The author contacts any reviewers who have not provided feedback and requests comments
6.	The author analyses all comments received and implements the appropriate changes
7.	The deliverable is circulated to the review audience for sign off
8.	The reviewers sign off (with any final comments) indicating that the document has been correctly amended by the author
9.	The author/project leader stores the comments received

6.4   Structured Walk-through

A structured walk-through is a peer review in which the author of a deliverable (e.g. a project document or actual code) brings one or more reviewers through the deliverable. The objective is to get feedback from the reviewers on the quality of the document or code and to familiarize the review audience with the author's work. The walk-through includes several roles, namely, the *review leader* (usually the author), the *author*, the *scribe* (may be the author) and the *review audience* (Table 6.2).

6.5   Semi-formal Review Meeting

A semi-formal review (a simplified version of the Fagan inspection) is a moderated review meeting chaired by the review leader. The author selects the reviewers and appoints a review leader (who may be the author). The review leader chairs the meeting and verifies that the follow-up activity has been completed. The author distributes the deliverable to be reviewed and provides a brief overview as appropriate. The material in this section is adapted from [4].

The review leader schedules the review meeting with the reviewers (with possible participation via a conference call). The review leader chairs the meeting and is responsible for keeping the meeting focused and running smoothly, resolving any conflicts, recording actions and completing the review form.

The review leader checks that all participants including conference call participants are present, and that all have done adequate preparation. Each reviewer is invited to give general comments, as this will determine whether the deliverable is

Table 6.2 Structured walk-throughs

Step	Description
1.	The author circulates the deliverable (either physically or electronically) to the review audience
2.	The author schedules a meeting with the reviewers
3.	The reviewers familiarize themselves with the deliverable
4.	The review leader (usually the author) chairs the meeting
5.	The author brings the review audience through the deliverable, explaining what each section is aiming to achieve, and requesting comments from them as to its correctness
6.	The scribe (usually the author) records errors, decisions and any action items
7.	A meeting outcome is agreed, and the author addresses all agreed items. If the meeting outcome is that a second review should be held then go to Step 1
8.	The deliverable is circulated to reviewers for sign off, and the reviewers sign off (with any final comments) indicating that the deliverable has been correctly amended by the author
9.	The author/project leader stores the comments and sign offs

ready to be reviewed, and whether the review should take place. Participants who are unable to attend are required to send their comments to the review leader prior to the review, and the review leader will present these comments at the meeting.

The material is typically reviewed page by page for a document review, and each reviewer is invited to comment on the current page. Code reviews may focus on coding standards, or on both coding standards and on finding defects in the software code. The issues noted during the review are recorded, and these may include items requiring further investigation.

The review outcome is decided at the end of the review (i.e. whether the deliverable needs a second review). The author then carries out the necessary corrections and investigation, and the review leader verifies that the follow-up activities have been completed. The document is then circulated to the review audience for sign off.

Comment:

The semi-formal review process works well for an organization when the review leader is not the author. This ensures that the review is conducted effectively, and that the follow-up activity takes place. It may work with the author acting as review leader provided the author has received the right training on software inspections and follows the review process.

The process for semi-formal reviews is summarized in Table 6.3. Figure 6.2 presents a template to record the issues identified during the review.

6.6   Fagan Inspections

The Fagan methodology (Table 6.4) is a well-known software inspection methodology. It is a seven-step process that includes planning, overview, preparation, an inspection meeting, process improvement, rework and follow-up activities. Its objectives are to identify and remove errors in the work products, and to identify any systemic defects in the processes used to create the work products.

The Fagan inspection process stipulates that requirement documents, design documents, source code and test plans all be formally inspected by experts independent of the author, and the inspection is conducted from different viewpoints such as requirements, design and test.

There are various roles defined in the inspection process, including the *moderator*, who chairs the inspection; the *reader*, who paraphrases the particular deliverable; the *author*, who is the creator of the deliverable; and the *tester*, who is concerned with the testing viewpoint. The inspection process will also consider whether the design is correct with respect to the requirements, and whether the source code is correct with respect to the design.

The goal is to identify as many defects as possible and to confirm the correctness of a particular deliverable. Inspection data is recorded and may be used to determine the effectiveness of the organization in detecting and preventing defects.

Table 6.3 Activities for semi-formal review meeting

Phase	Review task	Roles
Planning	Ensure document/code is ready to be reviewed Appoint *review leader* (may be author) Select reviewers with appropriate knowledge/experience and assign roles	Author Leader
Distribution	Distribute document/code and other material to reviewers (at least 3 days before the meeting) Schedule the meeting	Author Leader
Optional meeting	Give overview of deliverable to be reviewed Allow reviewers to ask any questions	Author Reviewers
Preparation	Read through document/code, marking up issues/questions Mark minor issues on their copy of the document/code	Reviewers
Review meeting	Review leaders chairs the meeting Explains purpose of the review and how it will proceed Set time limit for meeting Keep review meeting focused and moving Review document page by page Code reviews may focus on standards/defects Resolve any conflicts or defer as investigates Note comments/shortcomings on review form **Raise issues—(Do not fix them)** Present comments/suggestions/questions Pass review documents/code with marked up minor issues directly to the author Respond to any questions or issues raised Propose outcome of review meeting Complete review summary form/return to author Keep a record of the review form	Leader Reviewers
Post-review	Investigate and resolve any issues/shortcomings identified at review Verify that the author has made the required corrections	Author Leader

The moderator records the defects identified during the inspection, and the defects are classified according to their type and severity. The defect data may be entered into an inspection database to enable analysis to be performed and metrics to be generated. The severity of the defect is recorded, and the major defects are classified [e.g. according to the Fagan defect classification or some other scheme such as the *orthogonal defect classification* (ODC)].

The next section describes the Fagan inspection guidelines, which include recommendations on the time to spend on the various inspection activities. An organization may need to tailor the Fagan inspection process to suit its needs, and the tailored guidelines need evidence to confirm that they are effective.

6.6.1 Fagan Inspection Guidelines

The Fagan inspection guidelines are based on studies by Michael Fagan, and they provide recommendations on the time to spend on the various inspection activities. It

Date _____ Deliverable _____ Version No. _____ #Reviews _____
Author _____Review Leader _____
Reviewers_____
Page/Line No.   Description   Action

Unresolved Issued / Investigates
Issue   **Reason unresolved**   **Verified.**

Review Outcome (Tick)
No changes required □   Verification by Review Leader only □   Full review required □
Review incomplete □

Review Summary (Optional)
#Major Defects_____ # Minor Defects _____ Estimated Rework time _____
Hours Preparation _____ #Hours Review _____ Amount Reviewed _____

Fig. 6.2 Template for semi-formal review

Table 6.4 Overview Fagan inspection process

Activity	Role/Responsibility	Objective
Planning	Moderator	Identify inspectors and roles Verify material is ready for inspection Distribute inspection material Book a room for the inspection
Overview (Optional)	Author	Brief participants on material Give background information
Preparation	Inspectors	Prepare for the meeting and role Checklist may be employed Read through the deliverable and mark up issues/questions
Inspection meeting	Moderator/Inspectors	The moderator will cancel the inspection if inadequate preparation is done Time limit set for inspection Moderator keeps meeting focused The inspectors perform their roles Emphasis on finding defects not solutions Defects are recorded and classified Author responds to any questions The duration of the meeting is recorded An inspection outcome is agreed
Process improvement	Inspectors	Continuous improvement of development and inspection process The causes of major defects are recorded Root cause analysis to identify any systemic defect with development or inspection process Recommendations are made to the process improvement team
Rework	Author	The author corrects the defects and carries out any necessary investigations
Follow-up	Moderator/Author	The moderator verifies that the author has resolved the defects and investigations

is important that sufficient time is spent on the various inspection activities, and that the speed of the inspection is appropriate. We present the strict Fagan guidelines as defined by the Fagan methodology (Table 6.5), and more relaxed guidelines that have been shown to be effective in the telecommunications field (Table 6.6).

The effort involved in adherence to the strict Fagan guidelines is substantial, and this led to the development of tailored guidelines. The tailoring of any methodology requires care, and the effectiveness of the tailored process needs to be demonstrated by empirical evidence. (e.g. as a pilot prior to its deployment as well as quantitative data to show that the inspection is effective and results in a low number of escaped customer defects).

It is important to comply with the guidelines once they are deployed in the organization, and trained moderators and inspectors will ensure awareness and compliance. Audits may be employed to verify compliance.

The tailored guidelines are presented in Table 6.6.

Table 6.5 Strict Fagan
inspection guidelines

Activity	Area	Amount/Hr	Max/Hr
Preparation time	Requirements	4 pages	6 pages
	Design	4 pages	6 pages
	Code	100 LOC	125 LOC
	Test plans	4 pages	6 pages
Inspection time	Requirements	4 pages	6 pages
	Design	4 pages	6 pages
	Code	100 LOC	125 LOC
	Test plans	4 pages	6 pages

Table 6.6 Tailored
(Relaxed) Fagan inspection
guidelines

Activity	Area	Amount/Hr	Max/Hr
Preparation time	Requirements	10–15 pages	30 pages
	Design	10–15 pages	30 pages
	Code	300 LOC	500 LOC
	Test plans	10–15 pages	30 pages
Inspection time	Requirements	10–15 pages	30 pages
	Design	10–15 pages	30 pages
	Code	300 LOC	500 LOC
	Test plans	10–15 pages	30 pages

6.6.2 Inspectors and Roles

There are four inspector roles identified in a Fagan Inspection and these include
(Table 6.7):

6.6.3 Inspection Entry Criteria

There are explicit entry and exit criteria defined for the various types of inspections.
These criteria need to be satisfied to ensure that the inspection is effective. The entry
criteria (Table 6.8) for the various inspections are as follows:

6.6.4 Preparation

Preparation is a key part of the inspection process, as the inspection will be ineffective if the inspectors are insufficiently prepared. The moderator is required to
cancel the inspection if any of the inspectors has been unable to do appropriate
preparation.

Table 6.7 Inspector roles

Role	Responsibilities
Moderator	Manages the inspection process and ensures compliance to the process
	Plans the inspection and chairs the meeting
	Keeps the meeting focused and resolves any conflicts
	Keeps to the inspection guidelines
	Verifies that the deliverables are ready to be inspected
	Verifies that the inspectors have done adequate preparation
	Records the defects on the inspection sheet
	Verifies that the agreed follow-up work has been completed
	Skilled in the inspection process and appropriately trained
	Skilful, diplomatic and occasionally forceful
Reader	Paraphrases the deliverable and gives an independent view of it
	Actively participates in the inspection
Author	Creator of the work product being inspected
	Has an interest in finding all defects present in the deliverable
	Ensures that the work product is ready to be inspected
	Gives an overview to inspectors (if required)
	Participates actively during inspection and answers all questions
	Resolves all identified defects and carries out any required investigation
Tester	Role is focused on how the product would be tested
	Role often employed in requirements inspection/test plan inspection
	The tester participates actively in the inspection

Table 6.8 Fagan entry criteria

Inspection type	Entry criteria	Roles
Requirements	Inspector(s) with sufficient expertise available	Moderator/Inspectors
	Preparation done by inspectors	
	Correct requirements template used	
Design inspection	Requirements inspected and signed off	Moderator/Inspectors
	Correct design template used to produce design	
	Inspector(s) have sufficient domain knowledge	
	Preparation done by inspectors	
Code inspection	Requirements/Design inspected and signed off	Moderator/Inspectors
	Overview provided	
	Preparation done by inspectors	
	Code listing available	
	Clean compile of source code	
	Coding standards satisfied	
	Inspector(s) have sufficient domain knowledge	
Test plan inspection	Requirements/Design inspected and signed off	Moderator/Inspectors
	Preparation done by inspectors	
	Inspector(s) have sufficient domain knowledge	
	Correct test plan template employed	

6.6.5   The Inspection Meeting

The inspection meeting (Table 6.9) consists of a formal meeting between the author and at least one inspector. It is concerned with finding defects in the particular deliverable and verifying the correctness of the inspected material. The effectiveness of the inspection is influenced by

- The expertise and experience of the inspector(s)
- Preparation done by inspector(s)
- The speed of the inspection

These factors are quite clear since an inexperienced inspector will lack the appropriate domain knowledge to understand the material in depth. Second, an inspector who has inadequately prepared will be unable to make a substantial contribution during the inspection. Third, the inspection is ineffective if it tries to cover too much material in a short space of time. The moderator will complete the inspection form (Fig. 6.4) to record the results from the inspection.

The final part of the inspection is concerned with process improvement. The inspector(s) and author examine the major defects, identify the root causes of the defect and determine corrective action to address any systemic defects in the software process. The moderator is responsible for completing the inspection summary form and the defect log form, and for entering the inspection data into the inspection database. The moderator will give any process improvement suggestions directly to the process improvement team.

Table 6.9 Inspection meeting

Inspection type	Purpose	Procedure
Requirements	Find requirements defects Confirm requirements correct	Inspectors review each page of requirements and raise questions or concerns. Defects recorded by moderator
Design	Find defects in design Confirm correct (with respect to requirements)	Inspectors review each page of design (compare to requirements) and raise questions or concerns. Defects recorded by moderator
Code	Find defects in the code Confirm correct (with respect to design/reqs)	Inspectors review the code and compare to requirements/design and raise questions or concerns. Defects recorded by moderator
Test	Find defects in test cases/test plan Confirm test cases can verify design/requirements	Inspectors review each page of test plan/specification, compare to requirements/design and raise questions or concerns. Defects recorded by moderator

6.6.6   Inspection Exit Criteria

The exit criteria (Table 6.10) for the various inspections are as follows:

6.6.7   Issue Severity

The severity of an issue identified in the Fagan inspection may be classified as major, minor, a process improvement item or an item requiring further investigation. It is classified as *major* if its non-detection would lead to a defect report being raised later in the development cycle, whereas a defect report would generally not be raised for a *minor* issue. An issue classified as an investigate item requires further study, and an issue classified as process improvement is used to improve the software development process (Table 6.11).

Table 6.10 Fagan exit criteria

Inspection type	Exit criteria
Requirements	Requirements satisfy the customer's needs All requirements defects are corrected
Design	Design satisfies the requirements All identified defects are corrected Design satisfies the design standards
Code	Code satisfies the design and requirements Code satisfies coding standards and compiles cleanly All identified defects are corrected
Test	Test plan sufficient to test the requirements/design Test plan follows test standards All identified defects corrected

Table 6.11 Issue severity

Issue severity	Definition
Major (M)	A defect in the work product that would lead to a customer-reported problem if undetected
Minor (m)	A minor issue in the work product
Process improvement (PI)	A process improvement suggestion based on analysis of major defects
Investigate (INV)	An item to be investigated

6.6.8   Defect Type

There are several defect-type classification schemes employed in software inspections. These include the Fagan inspection defect classification (Table 6.12) and the orthogonal defect classification scheme (Table 6.13).

The orthogonal defect classification (ODC) scheme was developed at IBM [5], and a defect is classified according to three (orthogonal) viewpoints. The *defect trigger* is the catalyst that led the defect to manifest itself; the *defect type* indicates the change required for correction; and the *defect impact* indicates the impact of the defect at the phase in which it was identified. The ODC classification yields a rich pool of information about the defect, but effort is required to record this information. The defect-type classification is described in Table 6.13.

The defect impact provides a mechanism to relate the impact of the software defect to customer satisfaction. The impact of a defect identified pre-release is

Table 6.12 Classification of defects in Fagan inspections

Code inspection	Type	Design inspections	Type	Requirements inspections	Type
Logic (code)	LO	Usability	UY	Product objectives	PO
Design	DE	Requirements	RQ	Documentation	DS
Requirements	RQ	Logic	LO	Hardware interface	HI
Maintainable	MN	Systems inter-	IS	Competition	CO
Interface	IF	face		Analysis	
Data usage	DA	Portability	PY	Function	FU
Performance	PE	Reliability	RY	Software interface	SI
Standards	ST	Maintainability	MN	Performance	PE
Code	CC	Error handling	EH	Reliability	RL
Comments		Other	OT	Spelling	GS

Table 6.13 Classification of ODC defect types

Defect type	Code	Definition
Checking	CHK	Omission or incorrect validation of parameters or data in conditional statements
Assignment	ASN	Value incorrectly assigned or not assigned at all
Algorithm	ALG	Efficiency or correctness issue in algorithm
Timing	TIM	Timing/serialization error between modules, shared resources
Interface	INT	Interface error (error in communications between modules, operating system, etc.)
Function	FUN	Omission of significant functionality
Documentation	DOC	Error in user guides, installation guides or code comments
Build/Merge	BLD	Error in build process/library system or version control
Miscellaneous	MIS	None of the above

Fig. 6.3 Sample defect types
in a project (ODC)

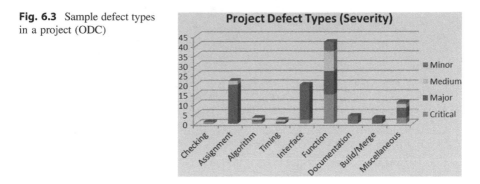

viewed as the impact of it being detected by an end-user, and for a
customer-reported defect its impact is the actual information reported by the
customer.

The inspection data is typically recorded in an inspection database, which allows
analysis to be performed on the most common types of defects, and the preparation
of action plans to minimize reoccurrence (Fig. 6.3). The frequency of defects per
category is identified, and causal analysis is employed to identify preventive
actions. Often, the most problematic areas are targeted first (as identified in a Pareto
chart), and an investigation into the particular category is conducted. The action
plans will identify actions to be carried out to improve the existing processes.

The ODC classification scheme may be used to give early warning on the quality
and reliability of the software, as its use leads to an expected profile of defects for
the various lifecycle phases. The actual profile may then be compared to the
expected profile, and the presence of significant differences between these may
indicate risks to quality.

For example, if the actual defect profile at the system test phase resembles the
defect profile of the unit-testing phase, then it is likely that there are quality
problems. This is clear since the unit-testing phase is expected to yield a certain
pool of defects, with system testing receiving higher quality software with the
defects found during unit testing corrected. Consequently, ODC may be applied to
make a judgment of product quality and performance.

The inspection data will enable the *phase containment effectiveness* (PCE) metric to be determined (Fig. 10.19), and to determine if the software is ready for
release to the customer.

6.7   Automated Software Inspections

Static code analysis is the analysis of software code without executing the code. It is
usually performed with automated tools, and the sophistication of the tool determines the actual analysis done. Some tools may analyse individual statements or

Inspection Type _____ Deliverable _____ Project _____
Date _____ Amount Inspected _____ Version No. ____
Author_____ Moderator_____ No. of Reviews _____
Inspectors _____
#Hours Preparation _____ # Hours Inspection _____#Hours Rework _____
Summary of Findings: # Majors _____ # Minors ____ # PIs _____ # INVs ____
  ODC Summary (Majors): #CHK__#ASS__#ALG__#TIM__# INT_#FUN___# DOC__# BLD__

_____

No. Page/Line No. Severity   Type Description

Top 3 Root Causes of Major Defects / Process Improvement Actions
1.
2.
3.

Review Outcome
No changes □   Verification by Moderator □   Full Review □ Review Incomplete □
Defects per KLOC _____ Defects per page _____ Verification of Rework _____
Date Verified _____ Inspection Data in Database ____

Fig. 6.4 Template for Fagan inspection

declarations, whereas others may analyse the whole source code. The objective of the analysis is to highlight potential coding errors early in the software development lifecycle.

These automated software inspection tools provide quality assessment reports on the extent to which the coding standards are satisfied. Many integrated development environments (IDEs) provide basic functionality for automated code reviews. These include Microsoft Visual Studio and Eclipse.

The LDRA Testbed tool automatically determines the complexity of the source code, and it provides metrics that give an indication of the maintainability of the code. A useful feature of the LDRA tool is that it gives a visual picture of system complexity, and it has a re-factoring tool to assist with reducing complexity. It automatically generates code assessment reports listing all of the files examined and provides metrics on the clarity, maintainability and testability of the code.

Compliance to coding standards is important in producing readable code and in preventing error-prone coding styles. There are several tools available to check conformance to coding standards including the LDRA TBvision tool, which has reporting capabilities to show code quality as well as fault detection and avoidance measures. It includes functionality to allow users to view the results presented intuitively in various graphs and reports. A selection of LDRA tools are presented in Chap. 17.

6.8 Review Questions

1. What are software inspections?
2. Explain the difference between informal reviews, structured walk-throughs, semi-formal reviews and formal inspections.
3. What are the benefits of software inspections?
4. Describe the seven steps in the Fagan inspection process.
5. What is the purpose of entry and exit criteria in software inspections?
6. What factors influence the effectiveness of a software inspection?
7. Describe the roles involved in a Fagan inspection.
8. Describe the benefits of automated inspections.

6.9 Summary

The objective of software inspections is to build quality into the software product, and there is clear evidence that the cost of correction of a defect increases the later in the software development cycle in which it is detected. Consequently, there is an economic argument to employing software inspections, as it is more cost effective to build quality in rather than adding it later in the development cycle.

There are several approaches to software inspections, and these vary in the level of formality employed. A simple approach consists of a walk-through of the document or code by an individual other than the author. The meeting is informal and usually takes place at the author's desk or in a meeting room, and the reviewer and author discuss the document or code informally.

There are formal software inspection methodologies such as the well-known *Fagan inspection* methodology. This approach includes pre-inspection activity, an inspection meeting and post-inspection activity. Several inspection roles are typically employed, including an *author* role, an *inspector* role, a *tester* role and a *moderator* role.

An organization will need to devise an inspection process that is suitable for its particular needs. The level of formality is influenced by its business, its culture and the potential impact of a software defect on its customers. It may not be possible to have all of the participants present in a room, and participation by conference call may be employed.

Software inspections play an important role in building quality into each phase, and in ensuring that the quality of the delivered product is good. The quality of the delivered software product is only as good as the quality at the end each phase, and therefore a phase should be exited only when the desired quality has been achieved.

The effectiveness of an inspection is influenced by the expertise of the inspectors, adequate preparation and speed of the inspection, and compliance to the inspection process. The inspection methodology provides guidelines on the inspection and preparation rates for an inspection, and guidelines on the entry and exit criteria for an inspection.

References

1. M. Fagan, Design and code inspections to reduce errors in software development. IBM Syst. J. **15**(3) (1976)
2. T. Gilb, D. Graham, *Software Inspections* (Addison Wesley, Boston, 1994)
3. B. Boehm, *Software Engineering Economics* (Prentice Hall, New Jersey, 1981)
4. F. O'Hara, *Peer Reviews—The Key to Cost Effective Quality*. (European SEPG, Amsterdam, 1998)
5. I. Bhandari, A case study of software process improvement during development. IEEE Trans. Softw. Eng. **19**(12), 1157–1170 (1993)

Software Testing

7

Abstract

This chapter is concerned with software testing and discusses the various types of testing that may be carried out during the project. We discuss test planning, test case definition, test environment set-up, test execution, test tracking, test metrics, test reporting and testing in an e-commerce environment.

Keywords

Test planning · Test case design · Unit testing · System testing · Performance testing · e-commerce testing · Acceptance testing · White box testing · Black box testing · Test tools · Test environment · Test reporting

7.1 Introduction

Testing plays a key role in verifying the correctness of software and confirming that the requirements have been correctly implemented. It is a constructive and destructive activity in that while on the one hand it aims to verify the correctness of the software, on the other hand it aims to find as many defects as possible in the software. The vast majority of defects (e.g. 80%) will be detected by software inspections in a mature software organization, with the remainder detected by the various types of testing carried out during the project.

Software testing provides confidence that the product is ready for release to potential customers, and the recommendation of the testing department is crucial in the decision as to whether the software product should be released or not. The test manager highlights any risks associated with the product, and these are considered prior to its release. The test manager and test department can be influential in an organization by providing strategic advice on product quality, and in encouraging

© Springer International Publishing AG 2017
G. O'Regan, *Concise Guide to Software Engineering*, Undergraduate Topics in Computer Science, DOI 10.1007/978-3-319-57750-0_7

organization change to improve the quality of the software product through the use of best practice in software engineering.

The testers need a detailed understanding of the software requirements to enable them to develop appropriate test cases to verify the correctness of the software. Test planning commences at the early stages of the project, and testers play a role in building quality into the software product and verifying its correctness. The testers generally participate in the review of the requirements, and the testing viewpoint is important during the review to ensure that the requirements are correct and are testable.

The test plan for the project is documented (this could be part of the project plan or a separate document), and it includes the personnel involved, the resources and effort required, the definition of the testing environment to enable effective testing to take place, any special hardware and test tools required, and the planned schedule. There is a separate test specification plan for the various types of testing, and it records the test cases, including the purpose of the test case, the inputs and expected outputs and the test procedure for the particular test case.

Various types of testing are performed during the project, including unit, integration, system, regression, performance and user acceptance testing. The software developers perform the unit testing, and the objective is to verify the correctness of a module. This type of testing is termed "*white box*" testing and is based on knowledge of the internals of the software module. White box testing typically involves checking that every path in a module has been tested, and it involves defining and executing test cases to ensure code and branch coverage. The objective of "*black box*" testing is to verify the functionality of a module (or feature or the complete system itself), and knowledge of the internals of the software module is not required.

Test reporting is an important part of the project, and it ensures that all project participants understand the current quality of the software, as well as understanding what needs to be done to ensure that the product achieves the required quality criteria. The test status is reported regularly during the project, and once the tester discovers a defect, a problem report is opened, and the problem is analysed and corrected by the software developers. The problem may indicate a genuine defect, a misunderstanding by the tester or a request for an enhancement.

An *independent test group* is generally more effective than a test group that is directly reporting to the development manager. The independence of the test group helps to ensure that quality is not compromised when the project is under pressure to make its committed delivery dates. A good test group will play a proactive role in quality improvement, and this may involve participation in the analysis of the defects identified during testing phase at the end of the project, with the goal of prevention or minimization of the reoccurrence of the defects.

Real-world issues such as the late delivery of the software from the developers often complicate the software testing. Software development is challenging and deadline-driven, and missed developer deadlines may lead to compression of the testing schedule, as the project manager may wish to stay with the original schedule. There are risks associated with shortening the test cycle, as the testers may be unable to complete the planned test activities. This means that insufficient data are available to make an informed judgment as to whether the software is ready for release, leading to risks that a defect-laden product may be shipped to the customer.

Test departments may be understaffed, as management may consider additional testers to be expensive and may wish to minimize costs. The test manager needs to be assertive in presenting the test status of the project, stating the known quality and risks, and the recommendation of the test manager needs to be carefully considered by the project manager and other stakeholders.

7.2 Test Process

The quality of the testing is dependent on the maturity of the test process, and a good test process will include test planning, test case analysis and design, test execution and test reporting. A simplified test process is sketched in Fig. 7.1, and the test process will include as follows:

- Test planning and risk management.
- Dedicated test environment and test tools.
- Test case definition.
- Test automation.
- Test execution.
- Formality in handover to test department.
- Test result analysis.
- Test reporting.
- Measurements of test effectiveness.
- Lessons learned and test process improvement.

Test planning consists of a documented plan defining the scope of testing and the various types of testing to be performed, the definition of the test environment, the required hardware or software for the test environment, the estimation of effort and resources for the various activities, risk management, the deliverables to be produced, the key test milestones and the test schedule.

The test plan is reviewed to ensure its fitness for purpose and to obtain commitment to the plan, as well as ensuring that all involved understand and agree to their responsibilities. The test plan may be revised in a controlled manner during the project. It is described in more detail in Sect. 7.3.

The test environment varies according to the type of business and project requirements. Large organizations may employ dedicated test laboratories, whereas a single workstation may be sufficient in a small organization. A dedicated test environment may require significant capital investment, but it will pay for itself in reducing the cost of poor quality, by identifying defects, and verifying that the software is fit for purpose.

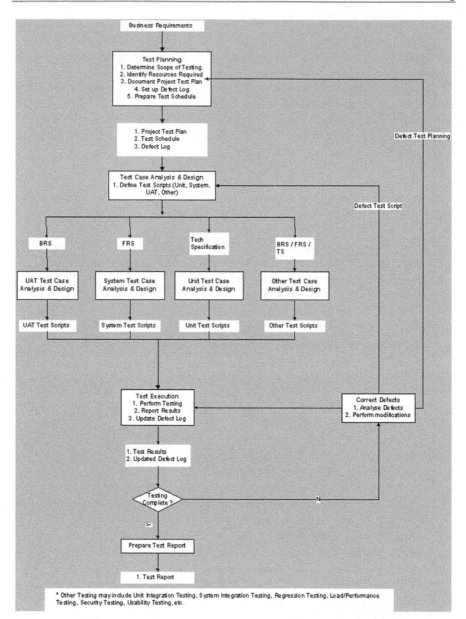

Fig. 7.1 Simplified test process

The test environment includes the hardware and software needed to verify the correctness of the software. It is defined early in the project so that any required hardware or software may be ordered in time. It may include simulation tools, automated regression and performance test tools, as well as tools for defect reporting and tracking.

The software developers produce a software build under configuration management control, and the build is verified for integrity to ensure that testing may commence. There is generally a formal or informal handover of the software to the test department, and a formal handover includes criteria that must be satisfied for the handover to take place. The test department must be ready for testing with the test cases and test environment prepared.

The various types of testing employed to verify the correctness of the software are described in Table 7.1. They may include:

The effectiveness of the testing is dependent on the definition of good test cases, which need to be complete in the sense that their successful execution will provide confidence in the correctness of the software. Hence, the test cases must relate or cover the software requirements, and we discussed the concept of a traceability matrix (that maps the requirements to the design and test cases) in Chap. 3 (Table 3.4). The traceability matrix provides confidence that each requirement has a corresponding test case for verification. The test cases will consist of a format similar to the following:

Table 7.1 Types of testing

Test type	Description
Unit testing	This testing is performed by the software developers, and it verifies the correctness of the software modules
Component testing	This testing is used to verify the correctness of software components to ensure that the component is correct and may be reused
System testing	This testing is (usually) carried out by an independent test group to verify the correctness of the complete system
Performance testing	This testing is (usually) carried out by an independent test group to ensure that the performance of the system is within the defined parameters. It may require tools to simulate clients and heavy loads, and precise measurements of performance are made
Load/stress testing	This testing is used to verify that the system performance is within the defined limits for heavy system loads over long or short periods of time
Browser compatibility	This testing is specific to web-based applications and verifies that the website functions correctly with the supported browsers
Usability testing	This testing verifies that the software is easy to use, and that the look and feel of the application is good
Security testing	This testing verifies that the confidentiality, integrity and availability requirements are satisfied
Regression testing	This testing verifies that the core functionality is preserved following changes or corrections to the software. Test automation may be employed to increase its productivity and efficiency
Test simulation	This testing simulates part of the system where the real system currently does not exist, or where the real live situation is hard to replicate
Acceptance testing	This testing carried out by the customer to verify that the software matches the customer's expectations prior to acceptance

- Purpose of the test case.
- Set-up required to execute the test case.
- Inputs to the test case.
- The test procedure.
- Expected outputs or results.

The test execution will follow the procedure defined in the test cases, and the tester will compare the actual results obtained with the expected results. The test completion status will be passed, failed or blocked (if unable to run at this time). The test results summary will indicate which test cases could be executed, which passed, which failed and which could not be executed.

The tester documents the test results including detailed information on the passed and failed tests. This will assist the software developers in identifying the precise causes of failure and the appropriate corrective actions. The developers and tester will agree to open a defect report in the defect-tracking system to track the successful correction of the defect.

The test status (Fig. 7.2) consists of the number of tests planned, the number of test cases run, the number that have passed and the number of failed and blocked tests. The test status is reported regularly to management during the testing cycle. The test status and test results are analysed and extra resources provided where necessary to ensure that the product is of high quality with all defects corrected prior to the acceptance of the product.

Test tools and test automation are used to support the test process and lead to improvements in quality, reduced cycle time and productivity. Tool selection (see Chap. 17) needs to be performed in a controlled manner, and it is best to identify the requirements for the tool first and then to examine a selection of tools to determine which best meets the requirements. Tools may be applied to test management and reporting, test results management, defect management and to the various types of testing.

Fig. 7.2 Sample test status

A good test process will maintain measurements to determine its effectiveness, and an end of testing review is conducted to identify any lessons that need to be learned for continual improvement. The test metrics employed will answer questions such as:

- What is the current quality of the software?
- How stable is the product at this time?
- Is the product ready to be released at this time?
- What are the key risks and are they all managed?
- How good was the quality of the software that was handed over?
- How does the product quality compare to other products?
- How effective was the testing performed on the software?
- How many open problems are there and how serious are they?
- How much testing remains to be done?

7.3   Test Planning

Testing is a sub-project of a project and needs to be managed as such, and so good project planning and monitoring and control are required. The IEEE 829 standard includes a template for test planning, and test planning involves defining the scope of the testing to be performed, defining the test environment, estimating the effort required to define the test cases and to perform the testing, identifying the resources needed (including people, hardware, software and tools), assigning the resources to the tasks, defining the schedule, and identifying any risks to the testing and managing them.

The monitoring and control of the testing involves tracking progress and taking corrective action, replanning as appropriate where the scope of the testing has changed, providing test reports to give visibility of the test status to the project team (including the number of tests planned, executed, passed, blocked and failed), retesting corrections to the failed or blocked test cases, taking corrective action to ensure quality and schedule are achieved, managing risks and providing a final test report with a recommendation to go to acceptance testing. Test management involves as follows:

- Identify the scope of testing to be done.
- Determine types of testing to be performed.
- Estimates of time, resources, people, hardware, software and tools.
- Determine how test progress and results will be communicated.
- Define how test defects will be logged and reported.
- Provide resources needed.
- Definition of test environment.
- Assignment of people to tasks.

Table 7.2 Simple test schedule

Activity	Resource name(s)	Start date	End/Re-plan date	Comments
Review requirements	Test team	15.02.2017	16.02.2017	Complete
Project test plan/review	J. DiNatale	15.02.2017	28.02.2017	Complete
System test plan/review	P. Cuitino	01.03.2017	22.03.2017	Complete
Performance test plan/review	L. Padilla	15.03.2017	31.03.2017	Complete
Regression plan/review	P. Cuitino	01.03.2017	15.03.2017	Complete
Set-up test environment	P. Cuitino	15.03.2017	31.03.2017	Complete
System testing	P. Cuitino	01.04.2017	31.05.2017	In progress
Performance testing	L. Padilla	15.04.2017	07.05.2017	In progress
Regression testing	L. Padilla	07.05.2017	31.05.2017	In progress
Test reporting	J. DiNatale	01.04.2017	31.05.2017	In progress

- Define the schedule.
- Identify and manage risks.
- Track progress and take corrective action.
- Provide regular test status of passed, blocked, failed tests.
- Re-plan if scope of the project changes.
- Conduct post-mortem to learn any lessons.

Table 7.2 presents a simple test schedule for a small project, and the test manager will often employ Microsoft Project (or a similar scheduling tool) for planning and tracking of larger projects (e.g. Fig. 2.2). The activities in the test schedule are tracked and updated accordingly to record the tasks that have been completed, and dates are rescheduled as appropriate. Testing is a key sub-project of the main project, and the project manager will track the key test milestones and will maintain close contact with the test manager.

It is prudent to consider risk management early in test planning, to identify risks that could potentially arise during the testing, to estimate the probability of occurrence of the risk and its impact should it occur, and to identify (as far as is practical) actions to mitigate the risk or a contingency plan to address the risk if it materializes.

7.4   Test Case Design and Definition

Several types of testing that may be performed during the project were described in Table 7.1, and there is often a separate test plan for unit, system and UAT testing. The unit tests are based on the software design, the system tests are based on the system requirements, and the UAT tests are based on the business (or user) requirements.

Each of these test plans contains test scripts (e.g. the unit test plan contains the unit test scripts), and the test scripts are traceable to the design (for the unit tests), and for the system requirements (for the system test scripts). The unit tests are more focused on white box testing, whereas the system test and UAT tests are focused on black box testing.

Each test script contains the objective of the test script and the procedure by which the test is carried out. Each test script includes as follows:

- Test case ID
- Test type (e.g. unit, system, UAT)
- Objective/description
- Test script steps
- Expected results
- Actual results
- Tested by

Regression testing involves carrying out a subset of the defined tests to verify that the core functionality of the software remains in place following changes to the system.

7.5   Test Execution

The software developers will carry out the unit and integration testing as part of the normal software development activities. The developers will correct any identified defects, and the development continues until all unit and integration tests pass, and the software is fit to be released to the test group.

The test group will usually be *independent* (i.e. it has an independent reporting channel), and it will usually perform the system testing, performance testing, usability testing and so on. There is usually a formal handover from development to the test group prior to the commencement of testing, and the handover criteria need to be satisfied in order for the software to be accepted for testing by the test group.

The handover criteria will generally require that all unit and integration tests have been run and passed, that all known risks have been identified, that the test environment is ready for independent testing, and that the system, performance and all other relevant test scripts are available, and that all required resources required for testing are available.

Test execution then commences and the testers run the system tests and other tests, log any defects in the defect-tracking tool and communicate progress to the test manager. The test status is communicated to the project team, and the developers correct the identified defects and produce new releases. The test group retests the failed and blocked tests and performs regression testing to ensure that the core functionality remains in place. This continues until the quality goals for the project have been achieved.

7.6   Test Reporting and Project Sign-Off

The test manager will report progress regularly during the project. The report provides the current status of testing for the project and includes as follows:

- Quality status (including tests run, passed and blocked).
- Risks and issues.
- Status of test schedule.
- Deliverables planned (next period).

The test manager discusses the test status with management and highlights the key risks and issues to be dealt with. The test manager may require management support to deal with these.

The test status is important in judging whether the software is ready to be released to the customer. Various quality metrics may be employed to measure the quality of the software, and the key risks and issues are considered. The test manager will make a recommendation to release or not based on the actual test status. One useful metric (one of many) is the cumulative arrival rate (Fig. 7.3) that gives an indication of the stability of the product.

The slope of the curve is initially steep as testing commences and defects are detected. As testing continues and defects are corrected and retested, the slope of the curves levels off, and over time the indications are that the software has stabilized and is potentially ready to be released to the customer.

However, it is important not to rush to conclusions based on an individual measurement. For example, the above chart could possibly indicate that testing halted on May 13th with no testing since then, and that would explain why the defect arrival rate per week is zero. Careful investigation and analysis needs to be done before the interpretation of a measurement is made, and usually several measurements rather than one are employed to make a sound decision.

Fig. 7.3 Cumulative defects

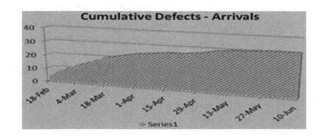

7.7 Testing and Quality Improvement

Testing is an essential part of the software development process, and the recommendation of the test manager is carefully considered in the decision to release the software product. Decision-making is based on objective facts, and measurements are employed to assess the quality of the software. The open-problem status (Figs. 10.16 and 10.17), the problem arrival rate (Fig. 10.18) and the cumulative problem arrival rate (Fig. 7.3) give an indication of the quality and stability of the software product and may be used in conjunction with other measures to decide on whether it is appropriate to release the software, or whether further testing should be performed.

Test defects are valuable in the sense that they provide the organization the opportunity to improve its software development process to prevent the defects from reoccurring in the future. A mature development organization will perform internal reviews of requirements, design and code prior to testing. The effectiveness of the internal review process and the test process may be seen in the phase containment metric (PCE), which is discussed in Chap. 10.

Figure 10.19 indicates that the project had a phase containment effectiveness of approximately 54%. That is, the developers identified 54% of the defects, the system-testing phase identified approximately 23% of the defects, acceptance testing identified approximately 14% of the defects, and the customer identified approximately 9% of the defects. Many organizations set goals with respect to the phase containment effectiveness of their software. For example, a mature organization might aim for their software development department to have a phase containment effectiveness goal of 80%. This means that 80% of the defects should be found by software inspections.

The improvement trends in phase containment effectiveness may be tracked over time. There is no point in setting a goal for a particular group or area unless there is a clear mechanism to achieve the goal. Thus to achieve a goal of 80% phase containment effectiveness, the organization will need to implement a formal software inspection methodology as described in Chap. 6. Training on inspections will be required, and the effectiveness of software inspections was monitored and improved.

A mature organization will aim to have 0% of defects reported by the customer, and this goal requires improvements in its software inspection methodology and its software testing methodology. Measurements provide a way to verify that the improvements have been successful. Each defect is potentially valuable as it, in effect, enables the organization to identify weaknesses in the software process and to target improvements.

Escaped customer defects offer an opportunity to improve the testing process, as it indicates a weakness in the test process. The defects are categorized, causal analysis is performed, and corrective actions are identified to improve the testing process. This helps to prevent a reoccurrence of the defects. Thus, software testing plays an important role in quality improvement.

7.8   Traceability of Requirements

The objective of requirements traceability (as discussed in Chap. 3) is to verify that all of the requirements have been implemented and tested. One way to do this would be to examine each requirement number and to go through every part of the design document to find any reference to the particular requirement number, and similarly to go through the test plan and find any reference to the requirement number. This would demonstrate that the particular requirement number has been implemented and tested.

A more effective mechanism to do this is with a traceability matrix (Table 3.4). This may be a separate document or part of the test documents. The idea is that a mapping between the requirement numbers and the associated test cases is defined, and this provides confidence that all of the requirements have been implemented and tested.

A requirement number may map on to several test cases, i.e., the mapping may be one to many with several test cases employed to verify the correctness of a particular requirement. Traceability provides confidence that each requirement number has been implemented in the software design and tested via the test plan.

7.9   Test Tools

Test tools are employed to support the test process and are used to enhance quality, reduce cycle time and increase productivity. Tool selection needs to be planned, and the evaluation and selection of a particular tool involves defining the requirements for the proposed tool and identifying candidate tools to evaluate against the requirements. Each tool is then evaluated to yield an evaluation profile, and the results are analysed to enable an informed decision to be made. Tools to support the various software engineering activities (including testing) are described in Chap. 17.

There are various tools to support testing such as test planning and management tools, defect-tracking tools, regression test automation tools, performance tools. There are tools available from various vendors such as Compuware, Software Research, Inc., HP, LDRA, McCabe and Associates, and IBM Rational.

7.9.1   Test Management Tools

There are various test management tools available (e.g. the Quality Center tool from HP), and the main features of such a tool are as follows:

- Management of entire testing process.
- Test planning.
- Support for building and recording test scripts.

- Test status and reporting.
- Graphs for presentation.
- Defect control system.
- Support for many testers.
- Support for large volume of test data.
- Audit trail proof that testing has been done.
- Test automation.
- Support for various types of testing.

The Quality Center™ tool standardizes and manages the entire test and quality process, and it is a web-based system for automated software quality management and testing. It employs dashboard technology to give visibility into the process.

It provides a consistent repeatable process for gathering requirements, planning and scheduling tests, analysing results and managing defects. It supports a high level of collaboration and communication between the stakeholders. It allows the business analysts to define the application requirements and testing objectives. The test managers and testers may then design test plans, test cases and automated scripts. The testers then run the manual and automated tests, report results and log the defects.

The developers review and correct the logged defects. Project and test managers can create status reports and manage test resources. Test and product managers decide objectively whether the application is ready to be released.

7.9.2   Miscellaneous Testing Tools

There is a wide collection of test tools to support activities such as static testing, unit testing, system testing, performance testing and regression testing.

Code coverage tools are useful for unit testing, and, for example, the LDRA Testbed is able to analyse source files to report on areas of code that were not executed at run-time, thereby facilitating the identification of missing test data. Code coverage tools are useful in identifying the sources of errors, as they will typically show the code areas that were executed through textual or graphic reports.

Regression testing involves rerunning existing test cases to verify that the software remains correct following the changes made. It is often automated with capture and playback tools, and the Winrunner tool[1] that was developed by Mercury (now part of HP) captures, verifies and replays user interactions, and allows regression testing to be automated. Effort is required to set-up the tests for automation, but the payback is improvements in quality and productivity.

The purpose of performance testing is to verify that system performance is within the defined limits, and it requires measures on the server side, network side and client side (e.g. processor speed, disk space used, memory used,). It includes load testing and stress testing. Mercury's LoadRunner (now called HP Loadrunner)

---

[1]The Winrunner tool has been replaced by HP Unified Functional Testing Software.

tool allows the software application to be tested with hundreds or thousands of concurrent users to determine its performance under heavy loads. It allows the scalability of the software system to be tested, to determine whether can support the predicted growth.

The decision on whether to automate and what to automate often involves a test process improvement team. It tends to be difficult for a small organization to make a major investment in test tools (especially if the projects are small). However, larger organizations will require a more sophisticated testing process to ensure that high-quality software is consistently produced.

7.10   e-commerce Testing

There has been an explosive growth in electronic commerce, and website quality and performance is a key concern. A website is a software application, and so standard software engineering principles are employed to verify the quality of a website. e-commerce applications are characterized by:

- Distributed system with millions of servers and billions of participants.
- High availability requirements (24 * 7 * 365).
- Look and feel of the website is highly important.
- Browsers may be unknown.
- Performance may be unpredictable.
- Users may be unknown.
- Security threats may be from anywhere.
- Often rapid application development is required.
- Design a little, implement a little and test a little.
- Rapidly changing technologies.

The standard waterfall life cycle model is rarely employed for the front end of a web application, and instead, RAD/JAD/Agile models are employed. The use of lightweight development methodologies does not mean that anything goes in software development, and similar project documentation should be produced (except that the chronological sequence of delivery of the documentation is more flexible). Joint application development allows early user feedback to be received on the look and feel and correctness of the application, and the method of design a little, implement a little and test a little is valid for web development. The various types of web testing include as follows:

- Static testing.
- Unit testing.
- Functional testing.
- Browser compatibility testing.
- Usability testing.

- Security testing.
- Load/performance/stress testing.
- Availability testing.
- Post-deployment testing.

Static testing generally involves inspections and reviews of documentation. The purpose of static testing of websites is to check the content of the web pages for accuracy, consistency, correctness and usability, and also to identify any syntax errors or anomalies in the HTML. There are tools available (e.g. NetMechanic) for statically checking the HTML for syntax correctness.

The purpose of unit testing is to verify that the content of the web pages corresponds to the design, that the content is correct, that all the links are valid and that the web navigation operates correctly.

The purpose of functional testing is to verify that the functional requirements are satisfied. It may be quite complex as e-commerce applications may involve product catalogue searches, order processing, credit checking and payment processing, and the application may liaise with legacy systems. Also, testing of cookies, whether enabled or disabled, needs to be considered.

The purpose of browser compatibility testing is to verify that the web browsers that are to be supported are actually supported. The purpose of usability testing is to verify that the look and feel of the application is good and that web performance (loading web pages, graphics, etc.) is good. There are automated browsing tools which go through all of the links on a page, attempt to load each link and produce a report including the timing for loading an object or page. Usability needs to be considered early in design and is important in GUI applications.

The purpose of security testing is to ensure that the website is secure. The purpose of load, performance and stress testing is to ensure that the performance of the system is within the defined parameters.

The purpose of post-deployment testing is to ensure that website performance remains good, and this may be done as part of a service level agreement (SLA). A SLA typically includes a penalty clause if the availability of the system or its performance falls outside the defined parameters. Consequently, it is important to identify performance and availability issues early before they become a problem. Thus, post-deployment testing includes monitoring of website availability, performance and security and taking corrective action. e-commerce sites operate 24 h a day for 365 days a year, and major financial loss is incurred in the case of a major outage.

7.11 Test-Driven Development

Test-driven development (TDD) was developed by Kent Beck and others as part of extreme programming, and it ensures that test cases are written early with the software code written to pass the test cases. It is a paradigm shift from traditional software engineering, where unit tests are written and executed after the code has been written.

The set of test cases is derived from the requirements, and the software is then written to pass the test cases. Another words, the test-driven development of a new feature begins with writing a suite of test cases based on the requirements for the feature, and the code for the feature is then written to pass the test cases.

Initially, all tests fail as no code has been written, and so the first step is to write some code that enables the new test cases to pass. This new code may be imperfect (it will be improved later), but this is initially acceptable as the only purpose is to pass the new test cases. The next step is to ensure that the new feature works with the existing features, and this involves executing all new and existing test cases.

This may involve modification of the source code to enable all of the tests to pass and to ensure that all features work correctly together. The final step is refactoring the code, and this involves cleaning up and restructuring the code. The test cases are rerun during the refactoring to ensure that the functionality is not altered in any way. The process repeats with the addition of each new feature. TDD is described in more detail in Chap. 18.

7.12   Review Questions

1. Describe the main activities in test planning.
2. What does the test environment consist of? When should it be set-up?
3. Explain the traceability of the requirements to the test cases?
4. Describe the various types of testing that may be performed.
5. Investigate available test tools to support testing? What areas of testing do they support and what are their benefits?
6. Describe an effective way to evaluate and select a test tool.
7. What are the characteristics of e-commerce testing that make it unique from other domains.
8. Discuss test reporting and the influence of the test manager in project sign-off.
9. Explain test-driven development.

7.13   Summary

This chapter discussed software testing and how testing may be used to verify that the software is of a high quality and fit to be released to potential customers. Testing is both a constructive and destructive activity, in that while on the one hand it aims to verify the correctness of the software, on the other hand it aims to find as many defects as possible.

Various test activities were discussed including test planning, setting up the test environment, test case definition, test execution, defect reporting, and test management and reporting.

We discussed black box testing and white box testing, unit and integration testing, system testing, performance testing, security and usability testing. Testing in an e-commerce environment was considered.

Test reporting enables all project participants to understand the current quality of the software and to understand what needs to be done to ensure that the product meets the required quality criteria.

Various tools to support the testing process were discussed, and a methodology to assist in the selection and evaluation of tools is essential. Metrics are useful in providing visibility into test progress and into the quality of the software. The role of testing in promoting quality improvement was discussed.

Testing is often complicated by the late delivery of the software from the developers, and this may lead to the compression of the testing schedule. The recommendation of the test manager on whether to release the product needs to be carefully considered.

Supplier Selection and Management

8

Abstract

This chapter is concerned with the selection and management of a software supplier. It discusses how candidate suppliers may be identified, formally evaluated against defined selection criteria, and how the appropriate supplier is selected. We discuss how the selected supplier is managed during the project.

Keywords

Request for proposal · Supplier evaluation · Formal agreement · Statement of work · Managing supplier · Service level agreement · Escrow · Acceptance of software

8.1 Introduction

Supplier selection and management is concerned with the selection and management of a third-party software supplier. Many large projects involve total or partial outsourcing of the software development, and it is therefore essential to select a supplier that is capable of delivering high-quality and reliable software on time and on budget.

This means that the process for the selection of the supplier needs to be rigorous and that the capability of the supplier is clearly understood, and the associated risks are known prior to selection. The selection is based on objective criteria such as cost, the approach, the ability of the supplier to deliver the required solution, and the supplier capability, and while cost is an important criterion, it is just one among several other important factors.

Once the selection of the supplier is finalized, a legal agreement is drawn up between the contractor and supplier, which states the terms and condition of the contract, as well as the statement of work. The statement of work details the work to be carried out, the deliverables to be produced, when they will be produced, the personnel involved their roles and responsibilities, any training to be provided, and the standards to be followed.

The supplier then commences the defined work and is appropriately managed for the duration of the contract. This will involve regular progress reviews, and acceptance testing is carried out prior to accepting the software from the supplier. The following activities are generally employed for supplier selection and management (Table 8.1).

Table 8.1 Supplier selection and management

Activity	Description
Planning and requirements	This involves defining the approach to the procurement. It involves: – Defining the procurement requirements – Forming the evaluation team to rate each supplier against objective criteria
Identify suppliers	This involves identifying suppliers and may involve research, recommendations from colleagues or previous working relationships. Usually, three to five potential suppliers will be identified
Prepare and issue RFP	This involves the preparation and issuing of the Request for Proposal (RFP) to potential suppliers. The RFP may include the evaluation criteria and a preliminary legal agreement
Evaluate proposals	The received proposals are evaluated and a shortlist was produced. The shortlisted suppliers are invited to make a presentation of their proposed solution
Select supplier	Each supplier makes a presentation followed by a Q&A session. The evaluation criteria are completed for each supplier and reference sites were checked (as appropriate). The decision on the preferred supplier is made
Define supplier agreement	A formal agreement is made with the preferred supplier. This may include the following: – Negotiations with the supplier/involvement with Legal Department – Agreement may vary (statement of work, service level agreement, Escrow, etc.) – Formal agreement signed by both parties – Unsuccessful parties informed – Purchase order raised
Managing the supplier	This is concerned with monitoring progress, project risks, milestones and issues, and taking action when progress deviates from expectations
Acceptance	This is concerned with the acceptance of the software and involves acceptance testing to ensure that the supplied software is fit for purpose
Roll-out	This is concerned with the deployment of the software and support/maintenance activities

8.2 Planning and Requirements

The potential acquisition of software arises as part of a make-or-buy analysis at project initiation. The decision is whether the project team should (or has the competence to) develop a particular software system (or component of it), or whether there is a need to outsource (or purchase off-the-shelf) the required software. The supplied software may be the complete solution to the project's requirements, or it may need to be integrated with other software produced for the project. The following tasks are involved:

- The requirements are defined (these may be a subset of the overall business requirements).
- The solution may be available as an off-the-shelf software package (with configuration needed to meet the requirements).
- The solution may be to outsource all or part of the software development.
- The solution may be a combination of the above.

Once the decision has been made to outsource or purchase an off-the-shelf solution, an evaluation team is formed to identify potential suppliers and evaluation criteria is defined to enable each supplier's solution to be objectively rated.

A plan will be prepared by the project manager detailing the approach to the procurement, defining how the evaluation will be conducted, defining the members of the evaluation team and their roles and responsibilities, and preparing a schedule of the procurement activities to be carried out.

The remainder of this chapter is focused on the selection of a supplier for the outsourcing of all (or part) of the software development, but it could be easily adapted to deal with the selection of an off-the-shelf software package.

8.3 Identifying Suppliers

A list of potential suppliers may be determined in various ways including:

- Previous working relationship with suppliers.
- Research via the Internet/Gartner.
- Recommendations from colleagues or another company.
- Advertisements/other.

A previous working relationship with a supplier provides useful information on the capability of the supplier, and whether it would be a suitable candidate for the work to be done. Companies will often maintain a list of preferred suppliers, and these are the suppliers that have worked previously with the company and whose capability is known. The risks associated with a supplier on the preferred supplier list are known and are generally less than those of an unknown supplier. If the experience of working with the supplier is poor, then the supplier may be removed from the preferred supplier list.

There may be additional requirements for public procurement to ensure fairness in the procurement process, and often-public contracts need to be more widely advertised to allow all interested parties the opportunity to make a proposal to provide the product or service.

The list of candidate suppliers may potentially be quite large, and so short listing may be employed to reduce the list to a more manageable size of around five candidate suppliers.

8.4   Prepare and Issue RFP

The Request for Proposal (RFP) is prepared and issued to potential suppliers, and the suppliers are required to complete a proposal detailing the solution that they will provide, as well as the associated costs, by the closing date. The proposal will need to detail the specifics of the supplier's solution, and it needs to show how the supplier plans to implement the requirements.

The RFP details the requirements for the software and must contain sufficient information to allow the candidate supplier to provide a complete and accurate response. The completed proposal will include technical and financial information, which allows a rigorous evaluation of each received proposal to be carried out.

The RFP may include the criteria defined to evaluate the supplier, and often weightings are employed to reflect the importance of individual criteria. The evaluation criteria may include several categories such as the following:

- Functional (related to business requirements).
- Technology (related to the technologies/non-functional requirements).
- Supplier capability and maturity.
- Delivery approach.
- Overall cost.

Once the proposals have been received further short listing may take place to limit the formal evaluation to around three suppliers.

8.5   Evaluate Proposals and Select Supplier

The evaluation team will evaluate all received proposals using an evaluation spreadsheet (or similar mechanism), and the results of the evaluation yield a short list of around three suppliers. The shortlisted suppliers are then invited to make a presentation to the evaluation team, and this allows the team to question each supplier in detail to gain a better understanding of the solution that they are offering, and any risks associated with the supplier and their proposed solution.

Following the presentations and Q&A sessions, the evaluation team will follow up with checks on reference sites for each supplier. The evaluation spread sheet is updated with all the information gained from the presentations, the reference site checks, and the risks associated with individual suppliers.

Finally, an evaluation report is prepared to give a summary of the evaluation, and this includes the recommendation of the preferred supplier. The project board then makes a decision to accept the recommendation; select an alternate supplier; or restart the procurement process.

8.6   Formal Agreement

The preferred supplier is informed on the outcome of the evaluation, and negotiations on a formal legal agreement commences. The agreement will need to be signed by both parties and may (depending on the type of agreement) include the following:

- Legal contract.
- Statement of work.
- Implementation plan.
- Training plan.
- User guides and manuals.
- Customer support to be provided.
- Service level agreement.
- Escrow agreement.
- Warranty period.

The *statement of work* (SOW) is employed in bespoke software development, and it details the work to be carried out, the activities involved, the deliverables to be produced, the personnel involved, and their roles and responsibilities.

A *service level agreement* (SLA) is an agreement between the customer and service provider which specifies the service that the customer will receive as well as the response time to customer issues and problems. It will also detail the penalties should the service performance fall below the defined levels.

An *Escrow agreement* is an agreement made between two parties where an independent trusted third party acts as an intermediary between both parties. The intermediary receives money from one party and sends it to the other party when contractual obligations are satisfied. Under an Escrow agreement, the trusted third party may also hold documents and source code.

8.7 Managing the Supplier

The activities involved in the management of the supplier are similar to the standard project management activities discussed in Chap. 2. The supplier may be based in a different physical location (possibly in another country), and so regular communication is essential for the duration of the contract. The project manager is responsible for managing the supplier and will typically communicate with the supplier on a daily basis. The supplier will send regular status reports detailing progress made as well as any risks and issues. The activities involved include the following:

- Monitoring progress.
- Managing schedule, effort and budget.
- Managing risks and issues.
- Managing changes to the scope of the project.
- Obtaining weekly progress reports from the supplier.
- Managing project milestones.
- Managing quality.
- Reviewing the supplier's work.
- Performing audits of the project.
- Monitoring test results and correction of defects.
- Acceptance testing of the delivered software.

The project manager will maintain daily/weekly contact with the supplier and will monitor progress, milestones, risks, and issues. The risks associated with the supplier include the supplier delivering late or delivering poor quality, and all risks need to be managed.

8.8 Acceptance of Software

Acceptance testing is carried out to ensure that the software developed by the supplier is fit for purpose. The supplied software may just be a part of the overall system, and it may need to be integrated with other software. The acceptance testing involves the following:

- Preparation of acceptance test cases (this is the acceptance criteria).
- Planning and scheduling of acceptance testing.
- Setting up the test environment.
- Execution of test cases (UAT testing) to verify acceptance criteria is satisfied.
- Test reporting.
- Communication of defects to supplier.
- Correction of the defects by supplier.
- Re-testing and Acceptance of software.

The project manager will communicate the identified defects with the software to the supplier, and the supplier makes the required corrections and modifications to the software. Re-testing then takes place, and once all acceptance tests have successfully passed, the software is accepted.

8.9 Roll-out and Customer Support

This activity is concerned with the roll-out of the software at the customer site, and the handover to the support and maintenance team. It involves:

- Deployment of the software at customer site.
- Provision of training to staff.
- Handover to the Support and Maintenance Team.

8.10 Review Questions

1. What are the main activities in supplier selection and management?
2. What factors would lead an organization to seek a supplier rather than developing a software solution in-house?
3. What are the benefits of outsourcing?
4. Describe how a supplier should be selected.
5. Describe how a supplier should be managed.
6. What is a service level agreement?
7. Describe the purpose of a statement of work?
8. What is an Escrow agreement?

8.11 Summary

Supplier selection and management is concerned with the selection and management of a third-party software supplier. Many large projects often involve total or partial outsourcing of the software development, and it is therefore essential to select a supplier who is capable of delivering high-quality and reliable software on time and on budget.

This means that the process for the selection of the supplier needs to be rigorous, and that the capability of the supplier is clearly understood, as well as knowing any risks associated with the supplier. The selection is based on objective criteria, and the evaluation team will rate each supplier against the criteria and recommend their preferred supplier.

Once the selection is finalized, a legal agreement is drawn up (which usually includes the terms and condition of the contract as well as a statement of work). The supplier then commences the defined work and is appropriately managed for the duration of the contract.

The project manager is responsible for managing the supplier, and this involves communicating with the supplier on a daily basis and managing issues and risks. The software is subject to acceptance testing before it is accepted from the supplier.

Software Quality Assurance

9

Abstract

This chapter discusses software quality assurance and the importance of process quality. It is a premise in the quality field that good processes and conformance to them are essential for the delivery of high-quality product, and this chapter discusses audits and describes how they are carried out.

Keywords

Auditor · Independence of auditor · SQA team · Audit planning · Audit meeting · Audit reporting · Audit actions · Tracking actions · Audit escalation · Training

9.1 Introduction

The purpose of software quality assurance is to provide visibility to management on the processes being followed and the work products being produced in the organization. It is a systematic enquiry into the way that things are done in the organization, and involves conducting audits of projects, suppliers and departments. It provides:

- Visibility into the extent of compliance to the defined processes and standards.
- Visibility into the processes and standards in use in the organization.
- Visibility into the effectiveness of the defined processes.
- Visibility into the fitness for use of the work products produced.

Software quality assurance involves planning and conducting audits; reporting the results to the affected groups; tracking the assigned audit actions to completion;

© Springer International Publishing AG 2017   131
G. O'Regan, *Concise Guide to Software Engineering*, Undergraduate Topics
in Computer Science, DOI 10.1007/978-3-319-57750-0_9

Table 9.1 Auditing activities

Activity	Description
Audit planning	– Select projects/areas to be audited during period – Agree audit dates with affected groups – Agree scope of audit and advise attendees what needs to be brought to the meeting – Book room and send invitation to the attendees – Prepare/update the audit schedule
Audit meeting	– Ask attendees as to their specific role (in the project), the activities performed and determine the extent to which the process is followed – Employ an audit checklist as an aid – Review agreed documentation – Determine if processes are followed and effective
Audit reporting	– Revise notes from the audit meeting and review any appropriate additional documentation – Prepare audit report and record audit actions (consider getting feedback on report prior to publication) – Agree closure dates of the audit actions – Circulate approved report to attendees/management
Track actions	– Track audit actions to closure – Record the audit action status – Escalation (where appropriate) to resolve open actions
Audit closure	– Once all actions are resolved, the audit is closed

and conducting follow-up audits, as appropriate. It is generally conducted by the SQA group,[1] and this group is independent of the groups being audited. The activities involved include (Table 9.1):

All involved in the audit process need to receive appropriate training. This includes the participants in the audit who receive appropriate orientation on the purpose of audits and their role in it. The auditor needs to be trained in interview techniques, including asking open and closed questions, as well as possessing effective documentation skills in report writing, in order to record the results of the audit. The auditor needs to be able to deal with any conflicts that might arise during an audit.[2]

The flow of activities in a typical audit process is sketched in Fig. 9.1, and they are described in more detail in the following sections.

---

[1]This group may vary from a team of auditors in a large organization to a part-time role in a small organization.

[2]The auditor may face a situation where one or more individuals become defensive and will need to reassure individuals that the objective of the audit is not to find fault with individuals, rather the objective is to determine whether the process is fit for purpose and to promote continuous improvement, as well as identifying any quality risks with the project. The culture of an organization has an influence on how open individuals will be during an audit (e.g. individuals may be defensive if there is a blame culture in the organization rather than an emphasis on fixing the process).

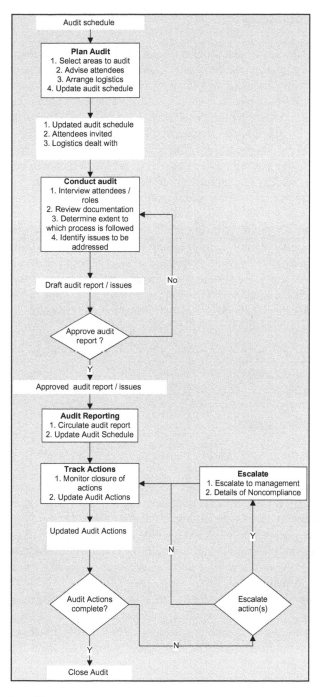

Fig. 9.1 Sample audit process

9.2 Audit Planning

Organizations vary in size and complexity and so the planning required for audits will vary. In a large organization, the quality manager or auditor is responsible for planning and scheduling the audits. In a small organization, the quality assurance activities may be performed by a part-time auditor who plans and schedules the audits.

A representative sample of projects/areas in the organization will be audited, and the number and types of audits conducted will depend on the current maturity of the organization. Mature organizations with a strong process culture will require fewer audits, whereas immature organizations may need a larger number of audits to ensure that the process is ingrained in the way that work is done.

It is essential that the *auditor is independent of the area being audited*. That is, the auditor should not be reporting to the manager whose area is being audited, as otherwise important findings in the audit could be omitted from the report. The independence of the auditor helps to ensure that the findings are fair and objective, as the auditor may state the facts as they are without fear of negative consequences.

The auditor needs to be familiar with the process and in a position to judge the extent to which the standards have been followed. The audit report needs to be accurate, as incorrect statements made will damage the credibility of the auditor. The planning and scheduling activities will include:

- Project/area to be audited.
- Planned date of audit.
- Scope of audit.
- Checklist to be used.
- Documentation required.
- Auditor.
- Attendees.

The auditor may receive orientation on the project/area to be audited prior to the meeting and may review relevant documentation in advance. A checklist may be employed by the auditor as an aid to structure the interview.

The role requires good verbal and documentation skills, as well as the ability to deal with any conflicts that may arise during the audit. The auditor needs to be fair and objective, and audit criteria will be employed to establish the facts in a non-judgmental manner.

Software quality assurance requires that an independent group (e.g. the SQA group) be set up. This may be a part-time group of one person in a small organization or a team of auditors in a large organization. The auditors must be appropriately trained to carry out their roles. The individuals being audited need to receive orientation on the purpose of audits and their role in the audit.

9.3 Audit Meeting

An audit consists of interviews and document reviews and involves a structured interview of the various team members. The goal is to give the auditor an understanding of the work done, the processes employed and the extent to which they are followed and effective. A checklist tailored to the particular type of audit being conducted is often employed. This will assist in determining relevant facts to judge whether the process is followed and effective. Table 9.2 gives a small selection of questions that may be part of an audit checklist.

The audit is an enquiry into the particular role of each attendee, the activities performed, the output produced, the standards followed and so on. The auditor needs to be familiar with the process and in a position to judge the extent to which it has been followed.

Table 9.2 Sample auditing checklist

Item to check
Project management
Has the project planning process been consistently followed?
Is the project plan complete and approved?
Are the risk log, issue log and lessons learned log set up?
Is the Microsoft Schedule (or equivalent) available and up to date?
Are the weekly status reports available and do they follow the template?
Configuration management
Are the appropriate people involved in defining, assessing the impact and approving the change request?
Are the affected deliverables (with the CR) identified and updated?
Are all documents and source code in the repository?
Are checking in/checking out procedures followed?
Supplier management
Is the statement of work complete?
Have the PM skills of the supplier been considered in the evaluation?
Does the formal agreement include strict change control?
Requirements, design and testing
Are the user requirements complete and approved?
Are the system requirements complete and approved?
Is the design complete and approved?
Are the requirements traceable to the design and test deliverables?
Are the unit test scripts available with the results recorded?
Are the system test cases available with results recorded?
Are UAT test cases available with results recorded?
Deployment and support
Are the user manuals complete and available?
Are all open problems documented?

Table 9.3 Sample audit report

Area	Description
Overview of audit	This gives an overview of the audit including the area audited, the date of the audit, its scope, the auditor and attendees, and the number of audit actions raised
Audit findings	These will vary depending on the type of audit, but it may include findings from project management, requirements, design, coding, configuration management, testing and peer reviews, customer support, etc.
Action plan	This will include an action plan to address the findings

The auditor opens the meeting with an explanation of the purpose and scope of the audit and usually starts with one or more open questions to get the participants to describe their particular role. Each attendee is asked to describe their specific role, the activities performed, the deliverables produced and the standards followed. Closed questions are employed to obtain specific information when required.

The auditor will take notes during the meeting, and these are reviewed and revised after the audit. There may be a need to review additional documentation after the meeting or to schedule follow-up meetings.

9.4 Audit Reporting

Once the audit meeting and follow-up activities have been completed, the auditor will need to prepare an audit report to communicate the findings from the audit. A draft audit report is prepared and circulated to the attendees, and the auditor reviews any comments received and makes final changes to address any valid feedback.[3] The approved audit report is then circulated to the attendees and management.

The audit report will include audit actions that need to be addressed by groups and individuals, and the auditor will track these actions to completion. In rare cases, the auditor may need to escalate the audit actions to management to ensure resolution.

The audit report generally includes three parts, namely the overview, the detailed findings and an action plan. This is described in Table 9.3.

9.5 Follow-Up Activity

Once the auditor has circulated the audit report to the affected groups, the focus then moves to closure of the assigned audit actions. The auditor will follow up with the affected individuals to monitor closure of the actions by the agreed date, and where

---

[3]It is essential that the audit report is accurate, as otherwise the auditor will lose credibility and become ineffective. Therefore, it is useful to get feedback from the attendees prior to publication of the report, in order to validate the findings. However, in some implementations of software quality assurance, the audit report is issued directly to the attendees without the performance of this step.

appropriate, a time extension may be granted. The auditor will update the status of an audit action to closed once it has been completed correctly. In rare cases, the auditor may need to escalate the audit action to management for resolution. This may happen when an assigned action has not been dealt with despite one or more time extensions. Once all audit actions have been closed, the audit is closed.

9.6   Audit Escalation

In rare cases, the auditor may encounter resistance from one or more individuals in completing the agreed audit actions. The auditor will remind the individual(s) of the audit process and their responsibilities in the process. In rare cases, where the individual (s) fail to address their assigned action(s) in a reasonable time frame, the auditor will escalate the non-compliance to management. The escalation may involve:

- Escalation of actions to middle management.
- Escalation to senior management.

Escalation is generally a rare occurrence, especially if good software engineering practices are embedded in the organization.

9.7   Review of Audit Activities

The results of the audit activities will be reviewed with management on a periodic basis. Audits provide important information to management on the processes being used in the organization; the extent to which they are followed; and the extent to which they are effective.

An independent audit (usually a third party or separate internal audit function) of SQA activities may be conducted to ensure that the SQA function is effective. Any non-compliance issues are identified and assigned to the auditor and quality manager for resolution.

9.8   Other Audits

The audit process that we discussed has been focused on process audits conducted during a project. Other audits that may be conducted include supplier audits, where the auditor visits the supplier to determine the extent to which they are following the agreed processes and standards for the outsourced work.

The SQA team is often the point of contact to facilitate customer audits, where an audit team from the customer visits the organization to determine the extent to which they are following processes and standards.

9.9   Review Questions

1. What is the purpose of an audit?
2. What planning is done prior to the audit?
3. Explain why the auditor needs to be independent?
4. Describe the activities in the audit process.
5. What happens at an audit meeting?
6. What happens after an audit meeting?
7. How will the auditor deal with a situation where the audit actions are still open after the due date?

9.10   Summary

The purpose of software quality assurance is to provide visibility to management on the processes being followed and the work products being produced in the organization. It is a systematic enquiry into the way that things are done in the organization, and it involves conducting audits of projects, suppliers and departments.

It provides visibility into the processes and standards in use, their effectiveness and the extent of compliance to them. It involves planning and conducting audits; reporting the results to the affected groups; tracking the assigned audit actions to completion; and conducting follow-up audits, as appropriate. It is generally conducted by the SQA group, and this group is independent of the groups being audited.

The audit planning is concerned with selecting projects/areas to be audited, determining who needs to be involved and dealing with the logistics. The audit meeting is a formal meeting with the audit participants to discuss their specific responsibilities in the project, the processes followed and so on.

The audit report details the findings from the audit and includes audit actions that need to be resolved. Once the audit report has been published, the auditor will track the assigned audit actions to completion, and once all actions have been addressed, the audit may then be closed.

Software Metrics and Problem-Solving

10

Abstract

This chapter is concerned with metrics and problem-solving, and this includes a discussion of the Balanced Scorecard which assists in identifying appropriate metrics for the organization. The Goal, Question, Metrics (GQM) approach is discussed, and this allows metrics related to the organization goals to be defined. A selection of sample metrics for an organization is presented, and problem-solving tools such as fishbone diagrams, Pareto charts, trend charts are discussed.

Keywords

Measurement · Goal, Question, Metric · Balanced scorecard · Problem-solving · Data gathering · Fishbone diagram · Histogram · Pareto chart · Trend graph · Scatter graph · Statistical process control

10.1 Introduction

Measurement is an essential part of mathematics and the physical sciences, and it has been successfully applied to the software engineering field. The purpose of a measurement programme is to establish and use quantitative measurements to manage the software development processes and software quality in an organization; to assist the organization in understanding its current software engineering capability; and to provide an objective indication that software process improvements have been successful.

Measurements provide visibility into the various functional areas in the organization, and the quantitative data allows trends to be seen over time. The analysis of the measurements allows action plans to be produced for continuous

© Springer International Publishing AG 2017   139
G. O'Regan, *Concise Guide to Software Engineering*, Undergraduate Topics in Computer Science, DOI 10.1007/978-3-319-57750-0_10

improvement. Measurements may be employed to track the quality, timeliness, cost, schedule and effort of software projects. The terms *"metric"* and *"measurement"* are used interchangeably in this book. The formal definition of measurement given by Fenton [1] is:

> Measurement is the process by which numbers or symbols are assigned to attributes or entities in the real world in such a way as to describe them according to clearly defined rules.

Measurement plays a key role in the physical sciences and everyday life, for example, calculating the distance to the planets and stars; determining the mass of objects; computing the speed of mechanical vehicles; calculating the electric current flowing through a wire; computing the rate of inflation; estimating the unemployment rate. Measurement provides a more precise understanding of the entity under study.

Often several measurements are used to provide a detailed understanding of the entity under study. For example, the cockpit of an airplane contains measurements of altitude, speed, temperature, fuel, latitude, longitude, and various devices essential to modern navigation and flight, and clearly an airline offering to fly passengers using just the altitude measurement would not be taken seriously.

Metrics play a key role in problem-solving, and various problem-solving techniques will be discussed later in this chapter. Measurement data is essential in quantifying how serious a particular problem is, and they provide a precise quantitative measure of the extent of the problem. For example, a telecommunications outage is measured as the elapsed time between the downtime and the subsequent uptime, and the longer the outage lasts the more serious it is. It is essential to minimize outages and their impact, and measurement data is invaluable in proving an objective account of the extent of the problem. Measurement data may be used to perform analysis on the root cause of a particular problem, e.g. of a telecommunications outage, and to verify that the actions taken to correct the problem have been effective.

Metrics provide an internal view of the quality of the software product, but care is needed before deducing the behaviour that a product will exhibit externally from the various internal measurements of the product. A *leading measure* is a software measure that usually precedes the attribute that is under examination; for example, the arrival rate of software problems is a leading indicator of the maintenance effort. Leading measures provide an indication of the likely behaviour of the product in the field and need to be examined closely. A *lagging indicator* is a software measure that is likely to follow the attribute being studied; for example, escaped customer defects are an indicator of the quality and reliability of the software. It is important to learn from lagging indicators even if the data can have little impact on the current project.

10.2 The Goal, Question, Metric Paradigm

Many software metrics programmes have failed because they had poorly defined, or non-existent goals and objectives, with the metrics defined unrelated to the achievement of the business goals. The *Goal, Question, Metric* (GQM) paradigm was developed by Victor Basili and others of the University of Maryland [2]. It is a rigorous goal-oriented approach to measurement, in which goals, questions and measurements are closely integrated.

The business goals are first defined, and then questions that relate to the achievement of the goal are identified. For each question, a metric that gives an objective answer to the particular question is defined. The statement of the business goal is precise, and it is related to individuals or groups. The GQM approach is a simple one, and managers and engineers proceed according to the following three stages:

- Set goals specific to needs in terms of purpose, perspective and environment.
- Refine the goals into quantifiable questions.
- Deduce the metrics and data to be collected (and the means for collecting them) to answer the questions.

GQM has been applied to several domains, and so we consider an example from the software field. Consider the goal of determining the effectiveness of a new programming language L. There are several valid questions that may be asked at this stage, including who are the programmers that use L?; and what is their level of experience?; What is the quality of software code produced with language L?; and What is the productivity of language L? This leads naturally to the quality and productivity metrics as detailed in Fig. 10.1.

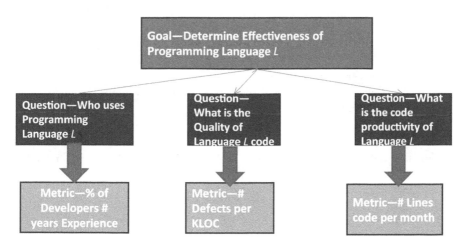

Fig. 10.1 GQM example

Goal

The focus on improvements should be closely related to the business goals, and the first step is to identify the key goals that are essential for business success (or to the success of an improvement programme). The business goals are related to the strategic direction of the organization and the problems that it is currently facing. There is little sense in directing improvement activities to areas that do not require improvement, or for which there is no business need to improve, or from which there will be a minimal return to the organization.

Question

These are the key questions that determine the extent to which the goal is being satisfied, and for each business goal the set of pertinent questions need to be identified. The information that is required to determine the current status of the goal is determined, and this naturally leads to the set of questions that must be answered to provide this information. Each question is analysed to determine the best approach to obtain an objective answer, and to define the metrics that are needed, and the data that needs to be gathered to answer the question objectively.

Metrics

These are measurements that give a quantitative answer to the particular question, and they are closely related to the achievement of the goals. They provide an objective picture of the extent to which the goal is currently satisfied. Measurement improves the understanding of a specific process or product, and the GQM approach leads to measurements that are closely related to the goal, *rather than measurement for the sake of measurement.*

GQM helps to ensure that the defined measurements will be relevant and used by the organizations to understand its current performance, and to improve and satisfy the business goals more effectively. Successful improvement is impossible without clear improvement goals that are related to the business goals. GQM is a rigorous approach to software measurement, and the measures may be from various viewpoints, e.g. manager viewpoint, project team viewpoint. The idea is always first to identify the goals, and once the goals have been decided, common-sense questions and measurement are employed.

There are two key approaches to software process improvement, i.e. *top-down* or *bottom-up* improvement. Top-down approaches are based on process improvement models and appraisals, e.g. models such as the CMMI, ISO 15504 and ISO 9000, whereas GQM is a bottom-up approach to software process improvement and is focused on improvements related to certain specific goals. The top-down and bottom-up approaches are often combined in practice.

10.3   The Balanced Scorecard

The Balanced Scorecard (BSC) (Fig. 10.2) is a management tool that is used to clarify and translate the organization vision and strategy into action. It was developed by Kaplan and Norton [3] and has been applied to many organizations. The European Software Institute (ESI) developed a tailored version of the BSC for the IT sector (the IT Balanced Scorecard).

The BSC assists in selecting appropriate measurements to indicate the success or failure of the organization's strategy. There are four perspectives in the scorecard: *customer, financial, internal process*, and *learning and growth*. Each perspective includes objectives to be accomplished for the strategy to succeed, measures to indicate the extent to which the objectives are being met, targets to be achieved in the perspective and initiatives to achieve the targets. The Balanced Scorecard includes financial and non-financial measures.

The BSC is useful in selecting the key processes that the organization should focus its process improvement efforts on in order to achieve its strategy (Fig. 10.3). Traditional improvement is based on improving quality; reducing costs; and

Fig. 10.2 The Balanced Scorecard

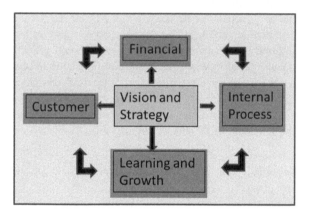

Fig. 10.3 Balanced Scorecard and implementing strategy

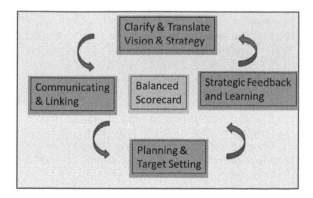

improving productivity, whereas the Balanced Scorecard takes the future needs of the organization into account and identifies the processes that the organization needs to excel at in the future to achieve its strategy. This results in focused process improvement, and the intention is to yield the greatest business benefit from the improvement programme.

The starting point is for the organization to define its *vision* and *strategy* for the future. This often involves strategy meetings with the senior management to clarify the vision and to achieve consensus on the strategic direction for the organization among the senior management team. The vision and strategy are then translated into *objectives* for the organization or business unit. The next step is communication, and the vision and strategy and objectives are communicated to all employees. These critical objectives must be achieved in order for the strategy to succeed, and so all employees (with management support) will need to determine their own local objectives to support the organization strategy. Goals are set and rewards are linked to performance measures.

The financial and customer objectives are first determined from the strategy, and the key business processes to be improved are then identified. These are the key processes that will lead to a breakthrough in performance for customers and share-holders of the company. It may require new processes with retraining of employees on the new processes necessary, and the Balanced Scorecard is very effective in driving organization change. The financial objectives require targets to be set for customer, internal business process and the learning and growth perspective. The learning and growth perspective will examine competencies and capabilities of employees and the level of employee satisfaction. Figure 10.3 describes how the Balanced Scorecard may be used for implementing the organization vision and strategy.

Table 10.1 presents sample objectives and measures for the four perspectives in the BSC for an IT service organization.

Table 10.1 BSC objectives and measures for IT service organization

Financial	Customer
Cost of provision of services	Quality service
Cost of hardware/software	Reliability of solution
Increase revenue	Rapid response time
Reduce costs	Accurate information
Timeliness of solution	Timeliness of solution
99.999% network availability	99.999% network availability
24 × 7 customer support	24 × 7 customer support
Internal business process	*Learning and growth*
Requirements definition	Expertise of staff
Software design	Software development capability
Implementation	Project management
Testing	Customer support
Maintenance	Staff development career structure
Customer support	Objectives for staff
Security/proprietary information	Employee satisfaction
Disaster prevention and recovery	Leadership

10.4 Metrics for an Organization

The objective of this section is to present a set of metrics to provide visibility into various areas in the organization and to show how metrics can facilitate improvement. The metrics presented may be applied or tailored to individual organizations, and the objective is to show how metrics may be employed for effective management. Many organizations have monthly quality or operation reviews, in which the presentation of metrics is an important part.

We present sample metrics for the various functional areas in a software development organization, including human resources, customer satisfaction, supplier quality, internal audit, project management, requirements and development, testing and process improvement. These metrics are typically presented at a monthly management review, and performance trends are observed. The main output from a management review is a series of improvement actions.

10.4.1 Customer Satisfaction Metrics

Figure 10.4 shows the customer survey arrival rate per customer per month, and it indicates that there is a customer satisfaction process in place in the organization and that the customers are surveyed and the extent to which they are surveyed. It does not provide any information as to whether the customers are satisfied, whether any follow-up activity from the survey is required, or whether the frequency of surveys is sufficient (or excessive) for the organization.

Figure 10.5 gives the customer satisfaction measurements in several categories including quality, the ability of the company to meet the committed dates and to deliver the agreed content, the ease of use of the software, the expertise of the staff and the value for money. Figure 10.5 is interpreted as follows:

Fig. 10.4 Customer survey arrivals

Fig. 10.5 Customer satisfaction measurements

8–10   Exceeds expectations,
7   Meets expectations,
5–6   Fair and
0–4   Below expectations.

Another words, a score of 8 for quality indicates that the customers considers the software to be of high quality, and a score of 9 for value for money indicates that the customers considers the solution to be excellent value. It is fundamental that the customer feedback is analysed (with follow-up meetings held with the customer where appropriate). There may be a need to produce an action plan to deal with customer issues, to communicate the plan to the customer and to execute the action plan in a timely manner.

10.4.2   Process Improvement Metrics

The objective of process improvement metrics is to provide visibility into the process improvement programme in the organization. Figure 10.6 shows the arrival rate of improvement suggestions from the software community. The chart indicates

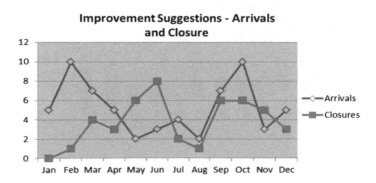

Fig. 10.6 Process improvement measurements

that initially the arrival rate is high and the closure rate is low, which is consistent with the commencement of a process improvement programme. The closure rate then improves which indicates that the improvement team is active and acting upon the improvement suggestions. The closure rate is low during July and August, which may be explained by the traditional holiday period.

The chart does not indicate the effectiveness of the process improvement suggestions, and the overall impact the particular suggestion has on quality, cycle time or productivity. There are no measurements of the cost of performing improvements, and this is important for a cost–benefit analysis of the benefits of the improvements obtained versus the cost of the improvements.

Figure 10.7 provides visibility into the status of the improvement suggestions, and the number of raised, open and closed suggestions per month. The chart indicates that gradual progress has been made in the improvement programme with a gradual increase in the number of suggestions that are closed.

Figure 10.8 provides visibility into the age of the improvement suggestions, and this is a measure of the productivity of the improvement team and its ability to do its assigned work.

Fig. 10.7 Status of process improvement suggestions

Fig. 10.8 Age of open process improvement suggestions

Fig. 10.9 Process improvement productivity

Figure 10.9 gives an indication of the productivity of the improvement pro-gramme, and it shows how often the team meets to discuss the improvement suggestions and to act upon them. This chart is slightly naive as it just tracks the number of improvement meetings that have taken place during the year, and it has no information on the actual productivity of the meeting. The chart could be considered with Figs. 10.6, 10.7 and 10.8, to get more accurate information on the productivity of the team.

There will usually be other charts associated with an improvement programme, for example, a metric to indicate the status of the CMMI programme is provided in Fig. 10.26. Similarly, a measure of the current status of an ISO 9000 implemen-tation could be derived from the number of actions which are required to implement ISO 9000, the number implemented and the number outstanding.

10.4.3 Human Resources and Training Metrics

These metrics give visibility into the human resources and training areas of a company. They provide visibility into the current headcount (Fig. 10.10) of the organization per calendar month and the turnover of staff in the organization (Fig. 10.11). The human resources department will typically maintain

Fig. 10.10 Employee headcount in current year

Fig. 10.11   Employee turnover in current year

measurements of the number of job openings to be filled per month, the arrival rate of resumes per month, the average number of interviews to fill one position, the percentage of employees that have received their annual appraisal, etc.

The key goals of the HR department are defined and the questions and metrics are associated with the key goals. For example, one of the key goals of the HR department is to attract and retain the best employees, and this breaks down into the two obvious subgoals of attracting the best employees and retaining them. The next chart gives visibility into the turnover of staff during the calendar year. It indicates the effectiveness of staff retention in the organization.

10.4.4   Project Management Metrics

The goal of project management is to deliver a high-quality product that is fit for purpose on time and on budget. The project management metrics provide visibility into the effectiveness of the project manager in delivering the project on time, on budget and with the right quality.

The timeliness metric provides visibility into the extent to which the project has been delivered on time (Fig. 10.12), and the number of months over or under

Fig. 10.12   Schedule timeliness metric

Fig. 10.13 Effort timeliness metric

schedule per project in the organization is shown. The schedule timeliness metric is a lagging measure, as it indicates that the project has been delivered within schedule or not after the event.

The on-time delivery of a project requires that the various milestones in the project be carefully tracked and corrective actions are taken to address slippage in milestones during the project.

The second metric provides visibility into the effort estimation accuracy of a project (Fig. 10.13). Effort estimation is a key component in calculating the cost of a project and in preparing the schedule, and its accuracy is essential. We mentioned the Standish research data on projects in an earlier chapter, and this report showed that accurate effort and schedule estimation is difficult.

The effort estimation chart is similar to the schedule estimation chart, except that the schedule metric is referring to time as recorded in elapsed calendar months, whereas the effort estimation chart refers to the planned number of person months required to carry out the work, and the actual number of person months that it actually took. Projects need an effective estimation methodology to enable them to be successful in project management, and the project manager will use metrics to determine how accurate the estimation has actually been.

The next metric is related to the commitments that are made to the customer with respect to the content of a particular release, and it indicates the effectiveness of the projects in delivering the agreed requirements to the customer (Fig. 10.14). This chart could be adapted to include enhancements or fixes promised to a customer for a particular release of a software product.

Fig. 10.14 Requirements delivered

10.4.5 Development Quality Metrics

These metrics give visibility into the development and testing of the software product, and we presented a sample of testing metrics in Chap. 7. Figure 10.15 gives an indication of the quality of the software produced and the quality of the definition of the initial requirements. It shows the total number of defects and the total number of change requests raised during the project, as well as details on their severities. The presence of a large number of change requests suggests that the initial definition of the requirement was incomplete and that there is considerable room for improvement in the requirements elicitation process.

Figure 10.16 gives the status of open issues with the project, which gives an indication of the current quality of the project, and the effort required to achieve the desired quality in the software. This chart is not used in isolation, as the project manager will need to know the arrival rate of problems to determine the stability of the software product.

The organization may decide to release a software product with open problems, provided that the associated risks with the known problems can be managed. It is

Fig. 10.15 Total number of issues in project

Fig. 10.16 Open issues in project

important to perform a risk assessment to ensure that these may be managed, and the known problems (and workarounds) should be documented in the release notes for the product.

The project manager will need to know the age of the open problems to determine the effectiveness of the project team in resolving problems in a timely manner. Figure 10.17 presents the age of the open defects, and it highlights the fact that there is one major problem that has been open for over one year. The project manager needs to prevent this situation from arising, as critical and major problems need to be swiftly resolved.

The problem arrival rate enables the project manager to judge the stability of the software, and this (with other metrics) helps in judging whether the software is fit for purpose and ready for release to potential customers. Figure 10.18 presents a sample problem arrival chart, and the chart indicates positive trends with the arrival rate of problems falling to very low levels.

The project manager will need to do analysis to determine whether there are other causes that could contribute to the fall in the arrival rate; for example, it may be the case that testing was completed in September, which would mean, in effect, that no testing has been performed since then, with an inevitable fall in the number of problems reported. The important point is not to jump to a conclusion based on a particular chart, as the circumstances behind the chart must be fully known and taken into account in order to draw valid conclusions.

Fig. 10.17 Age of open defects in project

Fig. 10.18 Problem arrivals per month

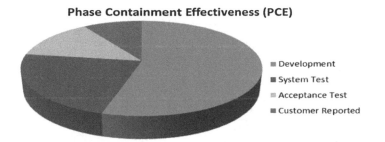

Fig. 10.19 Phase containment effectiveness

Figure 10.19 measures the effectiveness of the project in identifying defects in the development phase and the effectiveness of the test groups in detecting defects that are present in the software. The development portion typically includes defects reported on inspection forms and in unit testing.

The various types of testing (e.g. unit, system, performance, usability, acceptance) were discussed in Chap. 7. Figure 10.19 indicates that the project had a phase containment effectiveness of approximately 54%. That is, the developers identified 54% of the defects, the system-testing phase identified approximately 23% of the defects, acceptance testing identified approximately 14% of the defects and the customer identified approximately 9% of the defects. The objective is that the number of defects reported at acceptance test and after the product is officially released to customer should be minimal.

10.4.6 Quality Audit Metrics

These metrics provide visibility into the audit programme and include metrics for the number of audits planned and performed (Fig. 10.20), and the status of the audit actions (Fig. 10.21). Figure 10.20 presents visibility into the number of audits carried out in the organization and the number of audits that remain to be done.

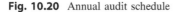

Fig. 10.20 Annual audit schedule

Fig. 10.21 Status of audit actions

It shows that the organization has an audit programme and gives information on the number of audits performed during a particular time period. The chart does not give a breakdown into the type of audits performed, e.g. supplier audits, project audits and audits of particular departments in the organization, but it could be adapted to provide this information.

Figure 10.21 chart gives an indication of the status of the various audits performed. An auditor performs an audit and the results are documented in an audit report, and the associated audit actions need to be completed by the affected individuals and groups. Figure 10.21 presents the status of the audit actions assigned to the affected groups.

Figure 10.22 gives visibility into the type of actions raised during the audit of a particular area. They could potentially include entry and exit criteria, planning issues, configuration management issues, issues with compliance to the lifecycle or templates, traceability to the requirements, issues with the review of various deliverables, issues with testing or process improvement suggestions.

Fig. 10.22 Audit action types

10.4.7 Customer Care Metrics

The goals of the customer care group in an organization are to respond efficiently and effectively to customer problems, to ensure that their customers receive the highest standards of service from the company and to ensure that its products function reliably at the customer's site. The organization will need to know its efficiency in resolving customer queries, the number of customer queries, the availability of its software systems at the customer site and the age of open queries. A customer query may result in a defect report in the case of a problem with the software.

Figure 10.23 presents the arrival and closure rate of customer queries (it could be developed further to include a severity attribute for the query). Quantitative goals are generally set for the resolution of queries (especially in the case of service level agreements). A chart for the age of open queries (similar to Fig. 10.17) is generally maintained. The organization will need to know the status of the backlog of open queries per month, and a simple trend graph would provide this. Figure 10.23 shows that the arrival rate of queries: in the early part of the year exceeds the closure rate of queries per month. This indicates an increasing backlog that needs to be addressed.

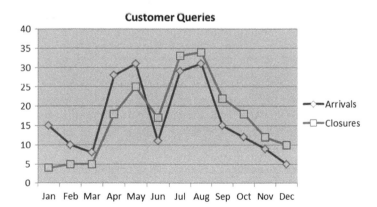

Fig. 10.23 Customer queries (arrivals/closures)

The customer care department responds to any outages and ensures that the outage time is kept to a minimum. Many companies set ambitious goals for network availability: for example, the *"five nines initiative"* has the objective of developing systems which are available 99.999% of the time, i.e. approximately five minutes of downtime per year. The calculation of availability is from the formula:

$$\text{Availability} = \frac{\text{MTBF}}{\text{MTBF} + \text{MTTR}}$$

where the mean time between failures (MTBF) is the average length of time between outages.

$$\text{MTBF} = \frac{\text{Sample interval time}}{\#\text{Outages}}$$

The formula for MTBF above is for a single system only, and the formula is adjusted when there are multiple systems.

$$\text{MTBF} = \frac{\text{Sample interval time}}{\#\text{Outages}} * \#\text{Systems}$$

The mean time to repair (MTTR) is the average length of time that it takes to correct the outage, i.e. the average duration of the outages that have occurred, and it is calculated from the following formula:

$$\text{MTTR} = \frac{\text{Total outage time}}{\#\text{Outages}}$$

Figure 10.24 presents outage information on the customers impacted by the outage during the particular month, and the extent of the impact on the customer.

An effective customer care department will ensure that a post-mortem of an outage is performed to ensure that lessons are learned to prevent a reoccurrence. This causal analysis details the root causes of the outage, and corrective actions are

Fig. 10.24 Outage time per customer

Fig. 10.25   Availability of system per month

implemented to prevent a reoccurrence. Metrics to record the amount of system availability and outage time per month will typically be maintained by the customer care group in the form of a trend graph.

Figure 10.25 provides visibility on the availability of the system at the customer sites, and many organizations are designing systems to be available 99.999% of the time. System availability and software reliability are discussed in more detail in Chap. 11.

10.4.8   Miscellaneous Metrics

Metrics may be applied to many other areas in the organization. This section includes metrics on the CMMI maturity of an organization (where an organization is implementing the CMMI), configuration management and the cost of poor quality. Figure 10.26 gives visibility into the time to create a software release from the configuration management system.

The internal CMMI maturity of the organization is given by Fig. 10.27, and this chart is an indication of its readiness for a formal CMMI assessment. A numeric score of 1–10 is used to rate each process area, and a score of 7 or above indicates that the process area is satisfied.

Crosby argued that the most meaningful measurement of quality is the cost of poor quality [4] and that the emphasis on the improvement activities in the

Fig. 10.26   Configuration management

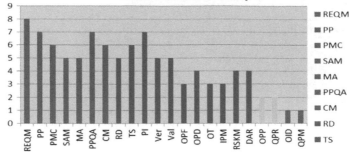

Fig. 10.27 CMMI maturity in current year

Table 10.2 Cost of quality categories

Type of cost	Description
Cost external	This includes the cost of external failure and includes engineering repair, warranties and a customer support function
Cost internal	This includes the internal failure cost and includes the cost of reworking and retesting of any defects found internally
Cost prevention	This includes the cost of maintaining a quality system to prevent the occurrence of problems and includes the cost of software quality assurance and the cost of training.
Cost appraisal	This includes the cost of verifying the conformance of a product to the requirements and includes the cost of provision of software inspections and testing processes

organization should therefore be to reduce the *cost of poor quality* (COPQ). The cost of quality includes the cost of external and internal failure, the cost of providing an infrastructure to prevent the occurrence of problems and the cost of the infrastructure to verify the correctness of the product.

The cost of quality was divided into four subcategories (Table 10.2) by Feigenbaum in the 1950s and evolved further by James Harrington of IBM.

The cost of quality graph (Fig. 10.28) will initially show high external and internal costs and low prevention costs, and the total quality costs will be high. However, as an effective quality system is put in place and becomes fully operational, there will be a noticeable decrease in the external and internal cost of quality and a gradual increase in the cost of prevention and appraisal.

The total cost of quality will substantially decrease, as the cost of provision of the quality system is substantially below the cost of internal and external failure. The COPQ curve will indicate where the organization is in relation to the cost of poor quality, and the organization will need to execute its improvement plan to put an effective quality management system in place to minimize the cost of poor quality.

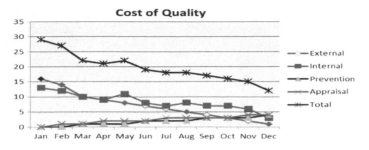

Fig. 10.28 Cost of poor quality (COPQ)

10.5 Implementing a Metrics Programme

The metrics discussed in this chapter may be adapted and tailored to meet the needs of organizations. The metrics are only as good as the underlying data, and good data gathering is essential. The following are typical steps in the implementation of a metrics programme (Table 10.3):

The business goals are the starting point in the implementation of a metrics programme, as there is no sense in measurement for the sake of measurement, and so metrics must be closely related to the business goals. The next step is to identify the relevant questions to determine the extent to which the business goal is being satisfied, and to define metrics that provide an objective answer to the questions.

The organization defines its business goals, and each department develops specific goals to meet the organization's goals. Measurement will indicate the extent to which specific goals are being achieved, and good data gathering and recording are essential. First, the organization will need to determine which data needs to be gathered and to determine methods by which the data may be recorded. The information that is needed to answer the questions related to the goals will determine the precise data to be recorded. A small organization may decide to record the data manually, but often automated or semi-automated tools will be employed. It is essential that the data collection and extraction is efficient, as otherwise the metrics programme is likely to fail.

Table 10.3 Implementing metrics	Implementing metrics in organization
	Define the business goals
	Determine the pertinent questions
	Define the metrics
	Identify tools to (semi-) automate metrics
	Determine data that needs to be gathered
	Identify and provide needed resources
	Gather data and prepare metrics
	Communicate the metrics and review monthly
	Provide training

The roles and responsibilities of staff with respect to the implementation and day-to-day operation of the metrics programme need to be defined. Training is needed to enable staff to perform their roles effectively. Finally, a regular management review is needed, where the metrics and trends are presented, and actions identified and carried out to ensure that the business goals are achieved.

10.5.1 Data Gathering for Metrics

Metrics are only as good as the underlying data, and so data gathering is a key activity in a metrics programme. The data to be recorded will be closely related to the questions, and the data is used to give an objective answer to the questions. The business goals are usually expressed quantitatively for extra precision, and Table 10.4 presents an example of how the questions related to a particular goal are identified.

Table 10.5 is designed to determine the effectiveness of the software development process and to enable the above questions to be answered. It includes a column for inspection data that records the number of *defects* recorded at the various inspections. The *defects* include the phase where the defect originated; for example, a defect identified in the coding phase may have originated in the requirements or design phase. This data is typically maintained in a spreadsheet, e.g. Excel (or a dedicated tool), and it needs to be kept up to date. It enables the phase containment effectiveness (PCE) to be calculated for the various phases.

Table 10.4 Goals and questions

Goal	Reduce escaped defects from each lifecycle phases by 10%
Questions	How many defects are identified within each lifecycle phase?
	How many defects are identified after each lifecycle phase is exited?
	What percentage of defects escaped from each lifecycle phase?

Table 10.5 Phase containment effectiveness

Phase of origin								
Phase	Inspect defects	Reqs	Design	Code	Accept test	In-phase defects	Other defects	% PCE
Reqs	4		1	1		4	6	40
Design	3					3	4	42
Code	20					20	15	57
Unit test		2	2	10				
System test		2	2	5				
Accept test								

We will distinguish between a defect that is detected *in-phase* and a defect that is detected *out-of-phase*. An in-phase defect is a problem that is detected in the phase in which it is created (e.g. usually by a software inspection). An out-of-phase defect is detected in a later phase (e.g. a problem with the requirements may be discovered in the design phase, which is a later phase from the phrase in which it was created).

The effectiveness of the requirements phase in Table 10.5 is judged by its success in identifying defects as early as possible, as the cost of correction of a requirements defect increases the later in the cycle that it is identified. The requirements PCE is calculated to be 40%, i.e. the total number of defects identified in phase divided by the total number of defects identified. There were four defects identified at the inspection of the requirements, and six defects were identified outside of the requirements phase: one in the design phase, one in the coding phase, two in the unit testing phase and two at the system-testing phase, i.e. 4/10 = 40%. Similarly, the code PCE is calculated to be 57%.

The overall PCE for the project is calculated to be the total number of defects detected in phase in the project divided by the total number of defects, i.e. 27/52 = 52%. Table 10.4 is a summary of the collected data and its construction consists of the following:

- Maintain inspection data of requirements, design and code inspections.
- Identify defects in each phase and determine their phase of origin.
- Record the number of defects in each phase per phase of origin.

The staff who perform inspections need to record the problems identified, whether it is a defect, and its phase of origin. Staff will need to be appropriately trained to do this consistently.

The above is just one example of data gathering, and in practice, the organization will need to collect various data to enable it to give an objective answer to the extent that the particular goal is being satisfied.

10.6   Problem-Solving Techniques

Problem-solving is a key part of quality improvement, and a *quality circle* (or problem-solving team) is a group of employees who do similar work and volunteer to come together on company time to identify and analyse work-related problems. Quality circles were first proposed by Ishikawa in Japan in the 1960s.

Various tools that assist problem-solving include *process mapping*, *trend charts*, *bar charts*, *scatter diagrams*, *fishbone diagrams*, *histograms*, *control charts* and *Pareto charts* [5]. These provide visibility into the problem and help to quantify the extent of the problem. The main features of a problem-solving team include:

- Group of employees who do similar work.
- Voluntarily meet regularly on company time.

- Supervisor as leader.
- Identify and analyse work-related problems.
- Recommend solutions to management.
- Implement solution where possible.

The facilitator of the quality circle coordinates the activities, ensures that the team leaders and team members receive sufficient training and obtains specialist help where required. The quality circle facilitator has the following responsibilities:

- Focal point of quality circle activities.
- Train circle leaders/members.
- Coordinate activities of all the circle groups.
- Assist in intercircle investigations.
- Obtain specialist help when required.

The circle leaders receive training in problem-solving techniques and are responsible for training the team members. The leader needs to keep the meeting focused and requires skills in team building. The steps in problem-solving include:

- Select the problem.
- State and restate the problem.
- Collect the facts.
- Brainstorm.
- Choose course of action.
- Present to management.
- Measurement of success.

The benefits of a successful problem-solving culture in the organization include:

- Savings of time and money.
- Increased productivity.
- Reduced defects.
- Fire prevention culture.

Various problem-solving tools are discussed in the following sections.

10.6.1 Fishbone Diagram

This well-known problem-solving tool consists of a cause-and-effect diagram that is in the shape of the backbone of a fish. The objective is to identify the various causes of some particular problem, and then, these causes are broken down into a number of subcauses. The various causes and subcauses are analysed to determine the root cause of the particular problem, and actions to address the root cause are then defined to prevent a reoccurrence of the manifested effect. There are various categories of causes, and these may include people, methods and tools, and training.

The great advantage of the fishbone diagram is that it offers a crisp mechanism to summarize the collective knowledge that a team has about a particular problem, as it focuses on the causes of the problem, and facilitates the detailed exploration of the causes.

The construction of a fishbone diagram involves a clear statement of the particular effect, and the effect is placed at the right-hand side of the diagram. The major categories of cause are drawn on the backbone of the fishbone diagram; brainstorming is used to identify causes; and these are then placed in the appropriate category. For each cause identified, the various subcauses may be identified by asking the question *"Why does this happen?"* This leads to a more detailed understanding of the causes and subcauses of a particular problem.

Example 10.1 An organization wishes to determine the causes of a high number of customer reported defects. There are various categories that may be employed such as people, training, methods, tools and environment. In practice, the fishbone diagram in Fig. 10.29 would be more detailed than that presented, as subcauses would also be identified by a detailed examination of the identified causes. The root cause(s) are determined from detailed analysis.

This example suggests that the organization has significant work to do in several areas and that an improvement programme is required. The improvements needed include the implementation of a software development process and a software test process; the provision of training to enable staff to do their jobs more effectively; and the implementation of better management practices to motivate staff and to provide a supportive environment for software development.

The causes identified may be symptoms rather than actual root causes: for example, high staff turnover may be the result of poor morale and a "blame culture", rather than a cause in itself of poor-quality software. The fishbone diagram

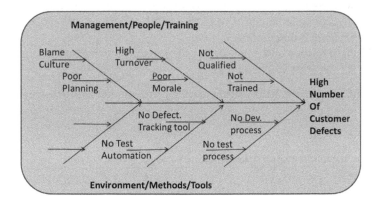

Fig. 10.29 Fishbone cause-and-effect diagram

gives a better understanding of the possible causes of the high number of customer defects. A small subset of these causes is then identified as the root cause(s) of the problem following further discussion and analysis.

The root causes are then addressed by appropriate corrective actions (e.g. an appropriate software development process and test process are defined and providing training to all development staff on the new processes). The management attitude and organization culture will need to be corrected to enable a supportive software development environment to be put in place.

10.6.2 Histograms

A histogram is a way of representing data in bar chart format, and it shows the relative frequency of various data values or ranges of data values. It is typically employed when there are a large number of data values, and it gives a very crisp picture of the spread of the data values and the centring and variance from the mean.

The histogram has an associated shape; for example, it may be a *normal distribution*, a *bimodal* or *multi-modal distribution*, or be positively or negatively skewed. The variation and centring refer to the spread of data and the relation of the centre of the histogram to the customer requirements. The spread of the data is important as it indicates whether the process is too variable, or whether it is performing within the requirements. The histogram is termed process centred if its centre coincides with the customer requirements; otherwise, the process is too high or too low. A histogram enables predictions of future performance to be made, assuming that the future will resemble the past.

The construction of a histogram first requires that a frequency table be constructed, and this requires that the range of data values be determined. The data is divided into a number of data buckets, where a bucket is a particular range of data values, and the relative frequency of each bucket is displayed in bar format. The number of class intervals or buckets is determined, and the class intervals are defined. The class intervals are mutually disjoint and span the range of the data values. Each data value belongs to exactly one class interval and the frequency of each class interval is determined.

The histogram is a well-known statistical tool and its construction is made more concrete with the following example.

Example 10.2 An organization wishes to characterize the behaviour of the process for the resolution of customer queries in order to achieve its customer satisfaction goal.

Goal
Resolve all customer queries within 24 h.
Question
How effective is the current customer query resolution process?
What action is required (if any) to achieve this goal?

Fig. 10.30 Histogram

The data class size chosen for the histogram below is six hours, and the data class sizes are of the same in standard histograms (they may be of unequal size for non-standard histograms). The sample mean is 19 h for this example. The histogram shown (Fig. 10.30) is based on query resolution data from 36 samples. The organization goal of customer resolution of all queries within 24 h is not met, and the goal is satisfied in (25/36 = 70% for this particular sample).

Further analysis is needed to determine the reasons why 30% of the goals are outside the target 24-h time period. It may prove to be impossible to meet the goal for all queries, and the organization may need to refine the goal to state that instead all critical and major queries will be resolved within 24 h.

10.6.3   Pareto Chart

The objective of a Pareto chart is to identify and focus on the resolution of problems that have the greatest impact (as *often 20% of the causes are responsible for 80% of the problems*). The problems are classified into various categories, and the frequency of each category of problem is determined. The Pareto chart is displayed in a descending sequence of frequency, with the most significant cause presented first, and the least significant cause presented last.

The Pareto chart is a key problem-solving tool, and a properly constructed chart will enable the organization to resolve the key causes of problems and to verify their resolution. The effectiveness of the improvements may be judged at a later stage from the analysis of new problems and the creation of a new Pareto chart. The results should show tangible improvements, with less problems arising in the category that was the major source of problems.

The construction of a Pareto chart requires the organization to decide on the problem to be investigated; to identify the causes of the problem via brainstorming; to analyse the historical or real time data; to compute the frequency of each cause; and finally to display the frequency in descending order for each cause category.

Fig. 10.31 Pareto chart outages

Example 10.3 An organization wishes to understand the various causes of outages and to minimize their occurrence.

The Pareto chart (Fig. 10.31) below includes data from an analysis of outages, where each outage is classified into a particular cause. The six causal categories identified are hardware, software, operator error, power failure, an act of nature and unknown. The three main causes of outages are hardware, software and operator error, and analysis is needed to identify appropriate actions to address these. The hardware category may indicate that there are problems with the reliability of the system hardware and that existing hardware systems may need improvement or replacement. There may be a need to address availability and reliability concerns with more robust hardware solutions.

The software category may be due to the release of poor-quality software, or to usability issues in the software, and this requires further investigation. Finally, operator issues may be due to lack of knowledge or inadequate training of the operators. An improvement plan needs to be prepared and implemented, and its effectiveness will be judged by a reduction in outages and reductions of problems in the targeted category.

10.6.4   Trend Graphs

A trend graph monitors the performance of a variable over time, and it allows trends in performance to be identified, as well as allowing predictions of future trends to be made (assuming that the future resembles the past). Its construction involves deciding on the variable to measure and to gather the data points to plot the data.

Example 10.4 An organization plans to deploy an enhanced estimation process and wishes to determine whether estimation is actually improving with the new process.

The estimation accuracy determines the extent to which the actual effort differs from the estimated effort. A reading of 25% indicates that the project effort was

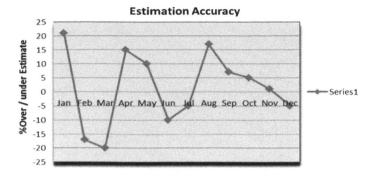

Fig. 10.32 Trend chart estimation accuracy

25% more than estimated, whereas a reading of −10% indicates that the actual effort was 10% less than estimated.

The trend chart (Fig. 10.32) indicates that initially that estimation accuracy is very poor, but then, there is a gradual improvement coinciding with the implementation of the new estimation process.

It is important to analyse the performance trends in the chart. For example, the estimation accuracy for August (17% in the chart) needs to be investigated to determine the reasons why it occurred. It could potentially indicate that a project is using the old estimation process or that a new project manager received no training on the new process). A trend graph is useful for noting positive or negative trends in performance, with negative trends analysed and actions identified to correct performance.

10.6.5   Scatter Graphs

The scatter diagram is used to determine whether there is a relationship or correlation between two variables, and where there is to measure the relationship between them. The results may be a positive correlation, negative correlation, or no correlation. Correlation has a precise statistical definition, and it provides a precise mathematical understanding of the extent to which the two variables are related or unrelated.

The scatter graph provides a graphical way to determine the extent that two variables are related, and it is often used to determine whether there is a connection between an identified cause and the effect. The construction of a scatter diagram requires the collection of paired samples of data, and the drawing of one variable as the x-axis, and the other as the y-axis. The data is then plotted and interpreted.

Example 10.5 An organization wishes to determine whether there is a relationship between the inspection rate and the error density of defects identified.

Fig. 10.33 Scatter graph amount inspected rate/error density

The scatter graph (Fig. 10.33) provides evidence for the hypothesis that there is a relationship between the lines of code inspected and the error density recorded (per KLOC). The graph suggests that the error density of defects identified during inspections is low if the speed of inspection is too fast, and the error density is high if the speed of inspection is below 300 lines of code per hour. A line can be drawn through the data that indicates a linear relationship.

10.6.6 Metrics and Statistical Process Control

The principles of statistical process control (SPC) are important in the monitoring and control of a process. It involves developing a control chart, which is a tool that may be used to control the process, with upper and lower limits for process performance specified. The process is under control if it is performing within the lower and upper control limits.

Figure 10.34 presents an example on breakthrough in performance of an estimation process, and is adapted from [6]. The initial upper and lower control limits

Fig. 10.34 Estimation accuracy and control charts

for estimation accuracy are set at ±40%, and the performance of the process is within the defined upper and control limits.

However, the organization will wish to improve its estimation accuracy and this leads to the organization's revising the upper and lower control limits to ±25%. The organization will need to analyse the slippage data to determine the reasons for the wide variance in the estimation, and part of the solution will be the use of enhanced estimation methods in the organization. In this chart, the organization succeeds in performing within the revised control limit of ±25%, and the limit is revised again to ±15%.

This requires further analysis to determine the causes for slippage and further improvement actions are needed to ensure that the organization performs within the ±15% control limit.

10.7   Review Questions

1. Describe the Goal, Question, Metric model.
2. Explain how the Balanced Scorecard may be used in the implementation of organization strategy.
3. Describe various problem-solving techniques.
4. What is a fishbone diagram?
5. What is a histogram and describe its applications?
6. What is a scatter graph?
7. What is a Pareto chart? Describe its applications.
8. Discuss how a metrics programme may be implemented.
9. What is statistical process control?

10.8   Summary

Measurement is an essential part of mathematics and the physical sciences, and it has been successfully applied to the software engineering field. The purpose of a software measurement programme is to establish and use quantitative measurements to manage the software development processes in the organization, and to assist the organization in understanding its current software capability and to confirm that improvements have been successful.

This chapter includes a collection of sample metrics to give visibility into the various functional areas in the organization, including customer satisfaction metrics, process improvement metrics, project management metrics, HR metrics, development and quality metrics, and customer care metrics.

The Balanced Scorecard assists the organization in selecting appropriate measurements to indicate the success or failure of the organization's strategy. Each of the four scorecard perspectives includes objectives that need to be achieved for the strategy to succeed, and measurements indicate the extent to which the objectives are being met.

The Goal, Question, Metric paradigm is a rigorous, goal-oriented approach to measurement in which goals, questions, and measurements are closely integrated. The business goals are first defined, and then, the questions that relate to the achievement of the goal are identified, and for each question, a metric that gives an objective answer to the particular question is defined.

Metrics play a key role in problem-solving, and various problem-solving techniques were discussed. These include histograms, Pareto charts, trend charts and scatter graphs. The measurement data is used to assist the analysis, to determine the root cause of a particular problem and to verify that the actions taken to correct the problem have been effective. Trends may be seen over time, and the analysis of the trends allows action plans to be prepared for continuous improvement.

Metrics may be employed to track the quality, timeliness, cost, schedule and effort of software projects. They provide an internal view of the quality of the software product, but care is needed before deducing the behaviour that a product will exhibit externally.

References

1. N. Fenton, *Software metrics: A Rigorous Approach* (Thompson Computer Press, 1995)
2. Victor Basili and H. Rombach, The TAME project. Towards improvement-oriented software environments. IEEE Trans. Softw. Eng. **14**(6) (1988)
3. R.S. Kaplan, D.P. Norton, *The Balanced Scorecard. Translating Strategy into Action* (Harvard Business School Press, 1996)
4. P. Crosby, *Quality is Free. The Art of Making Quality Certain* (McGraw Hill, 1979)
5. B. Michael, R. Diane, *The Memory Jogger. A Pocket Guide of Tools for Continuous Improvement and Effective Planning* (Goal *I* QPC, Methuen, MA, 1994)
6. G. Keeni et al., The evolution of quality processes at Tate Consulting Services. IEEE Softw. **17**(4) (2000)

Software Reliability and Dependability

11

Abstract

This chapter discusses software reliability and dependability and covers topics such as software reliability and software reliability models, the Cleanroom methodology, system availability, safety and security critical systems and dependability engineering.

Key Words

Software reliability · Software reliability models · System availability · Dependability · Computer security · Safety critical systems · Cleanroom

11.1 Introduction

This chapter gives an introduction to the important area of software reliability and dependability, and it introduces important topics in software engineering such as software reliability and availability; software reliability models; the Cleanroom methodology; dependability and its various dimensions; security engineering; and safety critical systems.

Software reliability is the probability that the program works without failure for a period of time, and it is usually expressed as the mean time to failure. It is different from hardware reliability, in that hardware is characterized by components that physically wear out, whereas software is intangible and software failures are due to design and implementation errors. In another words, software is either correct or incorrect when it is designed and developed, and it does not physically deteriorate over time.

Harlan Mills and others at IBM developed the Cleanroom approach to software development, and the process is described in [1]. It involves the application of statistical techniques to calculate a software reliability measure based on the

© Springer International Publishing AG 2017

G. O'Regan, *Concise Guide to Software Engineering*, Undergraduate Topics in Computer Science, DOI 10.1007/978-3-319-57750-0_11

expected usage of the software.[1] This involves executing tests chosen from the population of all possible uses of the software in accordance with the probability of its expected use. Statistical usage testing is more effective at finding defects that lead to failure than coverage testing.

Models are simplifications of the reality, and a good model allows accurate predictions of future behaviour to be made. A model is judged effective if there is good empirical evidence to support it, and a good software reliability model will have good theoretical foundations and realistic assumptions. The extent to which the software reliability model can be trusted depends on the accuracy of its predictions, and empirical data will need to be gathered to judge its accuracy.

It is essential that software that is widely used is dependable, which means that the software is available whenever required and that it operates safely and reliably without any adverse side effects. Today, billions of computers are connected to the Internet, and this has led to a growth in attacks on computers. It is essential that computer security is carefully considered and that developers are aware of the threats facing a system and techniques to eliminate them. The developers need to be able to develop secure dependable systems that are able to deal with and recover from external attacks.

11.2   Software Reliability

The design and development of high-quality software has become increasingly important for society. The hardware field has been very successful in developing sound reliability models, which allow useful predictions of how long a hardware component (or product) will function reliably. This has led to a growing interest in the software field in the development of a sound software reliability model. An effective software reliability model would provide a sound mechanism to predict the reliability of the software prior to its deployment at the customer site, as well as confidence that the software is fit for purpose and safe to use.

Definition 11.1 *(Software Reliability)*

Software reliability is the probability that the program works without failure for a specified length of time, and it is a statement of the future behaviour of the software. It is generally expressed in terms of the *mean time to failure* (MTTF) or the *mean time between failure* (MTBF).

Statistical sampling techniques are often employed to predict the reliability of hardware, as it is not feasible to test all items in a production environment. The quality of the sample is then used to make inferences on the quality of the entire

---

[1]The expected usage of the software (or operational profile) is a quantitative characterization (usually based on probability) of how the system will be used.

population, and this approach is effective in manufacturing environments where variations in the manufacturing process often lead to defects in the physical products.

There are similarities and differences between hardware and software reliability. A hardware failure generally arises due to a component wearing out due to its age, and often, a replacement component is required. Many hardware components are expected to last for a certain period of time, and the variation in the failure rate of a hardware component is often due to variations in the manufacturing process or to the operating environment of the component. Good hardware reliability predictors have been developed, and each hardware component has an expected mean time to failure. The reliability of a product may be determined from the reliability of the individual components of the hardware.

Software is an intellectual undertaking involving a team of designers and programmers. It does not physically wear out as such, and software failures manifest themselves from particular user inputs. Each copy of the software code is identical, and the software code is either correct or incorrect. That is, software failures are due to design and implementation errors, rather than due to the software physically wearing out over time. A number of software reliability models (e.g. the software reliability growth models) have been developed, but the software engineering community has not yet developed a sound software reliability predictor model that can be trusted.

The software population to be sampled consists of all possible execution paths of the software, and since this is potentially infinite, it is generally not possible to perform exhaustive testing. The way in which the software is used (i.e. the inputs entered by the users) will impact upon its perceived reliability. Let I_f represent the fault set of inputs (i.e. $i_f \in I_f$ if and only if the input of i_f by the user leads to failure). The randomness of the time to software failure is due to the unpredictability in the selection of an input $i_f \in I_f$. It may be that the elements in I_f are inputs that are rarely used, and therefore, the software will be perceived as being reliable.

Statistical usage testing may be used to make predictions on the future performance and reliability of the software. This requires an understanding of the expected usage profile of the system, as well as the population of all possible usages of the software. The sampling is done in accordance with the expected usage profile, and a software reliability measure is calculated.

11.2.1   Software Reliability and Defects

The release of an unreliable software product may result in damage to property or injury (including loss of life) to a third party. Consequently, companies need to be confident that their software products are fit for purpose prior to their release. The project team needs to conduct extensive inspections and testing of the software, as well as considering all associated risks prior to its release.

Objective product quality criteria may be set (e.g. 100% of tests performed and passed) to be satisfied prior to release. This provides a degree of confidence that the software has achieved the desired quality and is safe and fit for to use at the customer site. However, these results are historical in the sense that they are a statement of past quality and present quality. The question is whether the past behaviour and performance provides a sound indication of future behaviour.

Software reliability models are an attempt to predict the future reliability of the software and to assist in deciding on whether the software is ready for release. A defect does not always result in a failure, as it may occur on a rarely used execution path. Studies indicate that many observed failures arise from a small proportion of the existing defects.

Adam's 1984 case study [2] indicates that over 33% of the defects led to an observed failure with mean time to failure greater than 5000 years, whereas less than 2% of defects led to an observed failure with a mean time to failure less than 50 years. This suggests that a small proportion of defects often lead to almost all of the observed failures (Table 11.1).

The analysis shows that 61.6% of all fixes (Group 1 and 2) were for failures that will be observed less than once in 1580 years of expected use and that these constitute only 2.9% of the failures observed by typical users. On the other hand, groups 7 and 8 constitute 53.7% of the failures observed by typical users and only 1.4% of fixes.

This case study showed that *coverage testing* is not cost-effective in increasing MTTF. *Usage testing*, in contrast, would allocate 53.7% of the test effort to fixes that will occur 53.7% of the time for a typical user. Harlan Mills has argued [3] that the data in the table shows that usage testing is 21 times more effective than coverage testing

There is a need to be careful with *reliability growth models*, as there is no tangible growth in reliability unless the corrected defects are likely to manifest themselves as a failure.[2] Many existing software reliability growth models assume that all remaining defects in the software have an equal probability of failure and that the correction of a defect leads to an increase in software reliability. These assumptions are questionable.

The defect count and defect density may be poor predictors of operational reliability, and an emphasis on removing a large number of defects from the software may not be sufficient to achieve high reliability.

The correction of defects in the software leads to a newer version of the software, and reliability models assume reliability growth; i.e., the new version is more reliable than the older version as several identified defects have been corrected. However, in some sectors (such as the safety critical field), the view is that the new version of a program is a new entity and that no inferences may be drawn until further investigation has been done. There are a number of ways to interpret the relationship between the new version of the software and the older version as shown by Table 11.2.

---

[2]We are assuming that the defect has been corrected perfectly with no new defects introduced by the changes made.

Table 11.1 Adam's 1984 study of software failures of IBM products

	Rare				Frequent			
	1	2	3	4	5	6	7	8
MTTF (years)	5000	1580	500	158	50	15.8	5	1.58
Avg % fixes	33.4	28.2	18.7	10.6	5.2	2.5	1.0	0.4
Prob failure	0.008	0.021	0.044	0.079	0.123	0.187	0.237	0.300

Table 11.2 New and old version of software

Similarities and differences between new/old version
• The new version of the software is identical to the previous version except that the identified defects have been corrected
• The new version of the software is identical to the previous version, except that the identified defects have been corrected, but the developers have introduced some new defects • No assumptions can be made about the behaviour of the new version of the software until further data is obtained

The safety critical industry (e.g. the nuclear power industry) takes the conservative viewpoint that any change to a program creates a new program. The new program is therefore required to demonstrate its reliability, and so extensive testing needs to be performed before any conclusions may be made.

11.2.2 Cleanroom Methodology

Harlan Mills and others at IBM developed the Cleanroom methodology as a way to develop high-quality software [3]. Cleanroom helps to ensure that the software is released only when it has achieved the desired quality level, and the probability of zero defects is very high.

The way in which the software is used will impact on its perceived quality and reliability. Failures will manifest themselves on certain input sequences only, and as users often employ different input sequences, each user may have a different perception of the reliability of the software. The knowledge of how the software will be used allows the software testing to focus on verifying the correctness of common everyday tasks carried out by users.

This means that it is important to determine the operational profile of users to enable effective software testing to be performed. The operational profile may be difficult to determine, and it could change over time, as users may change their behaviour as their needs evolve over time. The determination of the operational profile involves identifying the common operations to be performed and the probability of each operation being performed.

Cleanroom employs *statistical usage testing* rather than coverage testing, and it applies statistical quality control to certify the mean time to failure of the software. This software reliability measure is calculated by statistical techniques based on the

Table 11.3 Cleanroom results in IBM

Project	Results
Flight control project (1987) 33 KLOC	Completed ahead of schedule Error-fix effort reduced by factor of five
Commercial product (1988)	Deployment failures of 0.1/KLOC Certification testing failures 3.4/KLOC Productivity 740 LOC/month
Satellite control (1989) 80 KLOC (partial Cleanroom)	50% improvement in quality Certification testing failures of 3.3/KLOC Productivity 780 LOC/month 80% improvement in productivity
Research project (1990) 12 KLOC	Certified to 0.9978 with 989 test cases

expected usage of the software, and the statistical usage testing involves executing tests chosen from the population of all possible uses of the software in accordance with the probability of expected use.

Coverage testing involves designing tests that cover every path through the program, and this type of testing is as likely to find a rare execution failure as well as a frequent execution failure. It is highly desirable to find failures that occur on frequently used parts of the system.

The advantage of statistical usage testing (that matches the actual execution profile of the software) is that it has a better chance of finding execution failures on frequently used parts of the system. This helps to maximize the expected mean time to failure of the software.

The Cleanroom software development process and calculation of the software reliability measure are described in [1], and the Cleanroom development process enables engineers to deliver high-quality software on time and on budget. Some of the successes and benefits of the use of Cleanroom on projects at IBM are described in [3] and summarized in Table 11.3.

11.2.3   Software Reliability Models

Models are simplifications of the reality, and a good model allows accurate predictions of future behaviour to be made. It is important to determine the adequacy of the model, and this is done by model exploration and determining the extent to which it explains the actual manifested behaviour, as well as the accuracy of its predictions.

A model is judged effective if there is good empirical evidence to support it, and more accurate models are sought to replace inadequate models. Models are often modified (or replaced) over time, as further facts and observations are identified that cannot be explained with the current model. A good software reliability model will have the following characteristics (Table 11.4):

Table 11.4 Characteristics of good software reliability model

Characteristics of good software reliability model
Good theoretical foundation
Realistic assumptions
Good empirical support
As simple as possible (Ockham's Razor)
Trustworthy and accurate

There are several software reliability predictor models employed (Table 11.5) with varying degrees of success. Some of them just compute defect counts rather than estimating software reliability in terms of mean time to failure. They may be categorized into:

- *Size and Complexity Metrics*
  These are used to predict the number of defects that a system will reveal in operation or testing.

Table 11.5 Software reliability models

Model	Description	Comments
Jelinski/Moranda model	The failure rate is a Poisson process[a] and is proportional to the current defect content of program. The initial defect count is N; the initial failure rate is $N\varphi$; it decreases to $(N-1)\varphi$ after the first fault is detected and eliminated, and so on. The constant φ is termed the proportionality constant	Assumes defects corrected perfectly and no new defects are introduced Assumes each fault contributes the same amount to failure rate
Littlewood/Verrall model	Successive execution time between failures is independent exponentially distributed random variables[b]. Software failures are the result of the particular inputs and faults introduced from the correction of defects	Does not assume perfect correction of defects
Seeding and tagging	This is analogous to estimating the fish population of a lake (Mills). A known number of defects is inserted into a software program and the proportion of these identified during testing determined Another approach (Hyman) is to regard the defects found by one tester as tagged and then to determine the proportion of tagged defects found by a 2nd independent tester	Estimate of the total number of defects in the software but not a not s/w reliability predictor Assumes all faults equally likely to be found and introduced faults representative of existing

(continued)

Table 11.5 (continued)

Model	Description	Comments
Generalized Poisson model	The number of failures observed in ith time interval τ_i has a Poisson distribution with mean $\phi(N - M_{i-1})\tau_i^\alpha$ where N is the initial number of faults; M_{i-1} is the total number of faults removed up to the end of the $(i - 1)$th time interval; and ϕ is the proportionality constant	Assumes faults removed perfectly at end of time interval

[a]The Poisson process is a widely used counting process (especially in counting the occurrence of certain events that appear to happen at a certain rate but at random). A Poisson random variable is of the form $P\{X = i\} = e^{-\lambda}\lambda^i/i!$

[b]The exponential distribution is used to model the time between the occurrence of events in an interval of time. Its probability density function is given by $f(x) = \lambda e^{-\lambda x}$

- *Operational Usage Profile*
  These predict failure rates based on the expected operational usage profile of the system. The number of failures encountered is determined, and the software reliability is predicted (e.g. Cleanroom and its prediction of the MTTF).
- *Quality of the Development Process*
  These predict failure rates based on the process maturity of the software development process in the organization (e.g. CMMI maturity).

The extent to which the software reliability model can be trusted depends on the accuracy of its predictions, and empirical data will need to be gathered to make a judgment. It may be acceptable to have a little inaccuracy during the early stages of prediction, provided the predictions of operational reliability are close to the observations. A model that gives overly optimistic results is termed "optimistic", whereas a model that gives overly pessimistic results is termed "pessimistic".

The assumptions in the reliability model need to be examined to determine whether they are realistic. Several software reliability models have questionable assumptions such as:

- All defects are corrected perfectly,
- Defects are independent of one another,
- Failure rate decreases as defects are corrected,
- Each fault contributes the same amount to the failure rate.

11.3 Dependability

Software is ubiquitous and is important to all sections of society, and so it is essential that widely used software is dependable (or trustworthy). In other words, the software should be available whenever required, as well as operating properly, safely and reliably, without any adverse side effects or security concerns. It is essential that the software used in the safety critical and security critical fields is dependable, as the consequence of failure (e.g. the failure of a nuclear power plant) could be massive damage leading to loss of life or endangering the lives of the public.

Dependability engineering is concerned with techniques to improve the dependability of systems, and it involves the use of a rigorous design and development process to minimize the number of defects in the software. A dependable system is generally designed for fault tolerance, where the system can deal with (and recover from) faults that occur during software execution. Such a system needs to be secure and able to protect itself from accidental or deliberate external attacks. Table 11.6 lists a number of dimensions to dependability.

Modern software systems are subject to attack by malicious software such as viruses that may change its behaviour or corrupt data causing the system to become unreliable. Other malicious attacks include a denial of service attack that negatively impacts the system's availability.

The design and development of dependable software needs to include protection measures to prevent against such external attacks that compromise the availability and security of the system. Further, a dependable system needs to include recovery mechanisms to enable normal service to be restored as quickly as possible following an attack.

Dependability engineering is concerned with techniques to improve the dependability of systems and in designing dependable systems. A dependable system will generally be developed using an explicitly defined repeatable process, and it may employ redundancy (spare capacity) and diversity (different types) to achieve reliability.

There is a trade-off between dependability and performance of the system, as dependable systems will need to carry out extra checks to monitor themselves and to check for erroneous states, and to recover from faults before failure occurs. This inevitably leads to increased costs in the design and development of dependable systems.

Software availability is the percentage of the time that the software system is running and is a measure of the uptime/downtime of the software during a particular time period. The downtime refers to a period of time when the software is unavailable for use (including planned and unplanned outages), and many companies aim to develop software that is available for using 99.999% of the time in the year (i.e. an annual downtime of less than 5 min per annum). This goal is known as *five nines*, and it is a common goal in the telecommunications sector. We discussed availability metrics in Chap. 10.

Safety-critical systems are systems where it is essential that the system is safe for the public and that people or the environment are not harmed in the event of system failure. These include aircraft control systems and process control systems for chemical and nuclear power plants. The failure of a safety critical system could in some situations lead to loss of life or serious economic damage.

Table 11.6 Dimensions of dependability

Dimension	Description
Availability	The system is available for use at any time
Reliability	The system operates correctly and is trustworthy
Safety	The system operates safely and does not injure people or damage the environment
Security	The system is secure and prevents unauthorized intrusions

Formal methods are discussed in Chap. 12, and they provide a precise way of specifying the requirements and demonstrating (using mathematics) that key properties are satisfied in the formal specification. Further, they may be used to show that the implemented program satisfies its specification. The use of formal methods leads to increased confidence in the correctness of safety critical and security critical systems.

The security of the system refers to its ability to protect itself from accidental or deliberate external attacks, which are common today since most computers are networked and connected to the Internet. There are various security threats in any networked system including threats to the confidentiality and integrity of the system and its data and threats to the availability of the system.

Therefore, controls are required to enhance security and to ensure that attacks are unsuccessful. Encryption is one way to reduce system vulnerability, as encrypted data is unreadable to the attacker. There may be controls that detect and repel attacks, and these controls are used to monitor the system and to take action to shut down parts of the system or restrict access in the event of an attack. There may be controls that limit exposure (e.g. insurance policies and automated backup strategies) that allows recovery from the problems introduced.

It is important to have a reasonable level of security as otherwise all of the other dimensions of dependability (reliability, availability and safety) are compromised. Security loopholes may be introduced in the development of the system, and so care needs to be taken to prevent hackers from exploiting security vulnerabilities.

Risk analysis plays a key role in the specification of security and dependability requirements, and this involves identifying risks that can result in serious incidents. This leads to the generation of specific security requirements as part of the system requirements to ensure that these risks do not materialize, or if they do materialize, then serious incidents will not materialize.

11.4   Computer Security

The introduction of the Internet in the early 1990s has transformed the world of computing, and it has led inexorably to more and more computers being connected to the Internet. This has subsequently led to an explosive growth in attacks on computers and systems, as hackers and malicious software seek to exploit known security vulnerabilities. It is therefore essential to develop secure systems that can deal with and recover from such external attacks.

Hackers will often attempt to steal confidential data and to disrupt the services being offered by a system. Security engineering is concerned with the development of systems that can prevent such malicious attacks and recover from them. It has become an important part of software and system engineering, and software developers need to be aware of the threats facing a system and develop solutions to eliminate them.

Hackers may probe parts of the system for weaknesses, and system vulnerabilities may lead to attackers gaining unauthorized access to the system. There is a need to conduct a risk assessment of the security threats facing a system early in the software development process, and this will lead to several security requirements for the system.

The system needs to be designed for security, as it is difficult to add security after it has been implemented. Security loopholes may be introduced in the development of the system, and so care needs to be taken to prevent these as well as preventing hackers from exploiting security vulnerabilities. Encryption is one way to reduce system vulnerability, as encrypted data is unreadable to the attacker. There may be controls that detect and repel attacks, and these controls are used to monitor the system and to take action to shut down parts of the system or restrict access in the event of an attack.

The choice of architecture and how the system is organized are fundamental to the security of the system, and different types of systems will require different technical solutions to provide an acceptable level of security to its users. The following guidelines for designing secure systems are described in [4]:

- Security decisions should be based on the security policy,
- A security critical system should fail securely,
- A secure system should be designed for recoverability,
- A balance is needed between security and usability,
- A single point of failure should be avoided,
- A log of user actions should be maintained,
- Redundancy and diversity should be employed,
- Organization information in system into compartments.

It is important to have a reasonable level of security, as otherwise all of the other dimensions of dependability (reliability, availability and safety) are compromised.

11.5 System Availability

System availability is the percentage of time that the software system is running without downtime, and robust systems will generally aim to achieve 5-nine availability (i.e. 99.999% availability). This is equivalent to approximately 5 min of downtime (including planned/unplanned outages) per year. The availability of a system is measured by its performance when a subsystem fails, and its ability to resume service in a state close to the original state. A fault-tolerant system continues to operate correctly (possibly at a reduced level) after some part of the system fails, and it aims to achieve 100% availability.

System availability and software reliability are related with availability measuring the percentage of time that the system is operational and reliability measuring the probability of failure-free operation over a period of time. The consequence of a system failure may be to freeze or crash the system, and system availability is measured by how long it takes to recover and restart after a failure. A system may be unreliable and yet have good availability metrics (fast restart after failure), or it may be highly reliable with poor availability metrics (taking a long time to recover after a failure).

Software that satisfies strict availability constraints is usually reliable. The downtime generally includes the time needed for activities such as rebooting a machine, upgrading to a new version of software and planned and unplanned outages. It is theoretically possible for software to be highly unreliable but yet to be highly available. Consider, for example, software that fails consistently for 0.5 s every day. Then, the total failure time is 183 s or approximately 3 min, and such a system would satisfy 5-nine availability. However, this scenario is highly unlikely for almost all systems, and the satisfaction of strict availability constraints usually means that the software is also highly reliable.

It is also theoretically possible that software that is highly reliable may satisfy poor availability metrics. Consider the upgrade version of software at a customer site to a new version, where the upgrade path is complex or poorly designed (e.g. taking 2 days). Then, the availability measure is very poor even though the product may be highly reliable. Further, the time that system unavailability occurs is relevant, as a system that is unavailable at 03:00 in the morning may have minimal impacts on users. Consequently, care is required before drawing conclusions between software reliability and software availability metrics.

11.6 Safety Critical Systems

A safety critical system is a system whose failure could result in significant economic damage or loss of life. There are many examples of safety critical systems including aircraft flight control systems and missile systems. It is therefore essential to employ rigorous processes in their design and development of safety critical systems, and software testing alone is usually insufficient in verifying the correctness of a safety critical system.

The safety critical industry takes the view that any change to safety critical software creates a new program. The new program is therefore required to demonstrate that it is reliable and safe to the public, and so extensive testing needs to be performed. Other techniques such as formal verification and model checking may be employed to provide an extra level of assurance in the correctness of the safety critical system.

Safety critical systems need to be dependable and available for use whenever required. Safety critical software must operate correctly and reliably without any adverse side effects. The consequence of failure (e.g. the failure of a weapons system) could be massive damage, leading to loss of life or endangering the lives of the public.

The development of a safety critical system needs to be rigorous and subjects to strict quality assurance to ensure that the system is safe to use and that the public will not be in danger. This involves rigorous design and development processes to minimize the number of defects in the software, as well as comprehensive testing to verify its correctness.

Formal methods consist of a set of mathematical techniques to rigorously state the requirements of the proposed system. They may be employed to derive a program from its mathematical specification, and they may be used to provide a rigorous proof that the implemented program satisfies its specification. Formal methods provide the facility to prove that certain properties are true of the specification, and this is valuable, especially in safety critical and security critical applications. The advantages of a mathematical specification are that it is not subject to the ambiguities inherent in a natural language description of a system, and they may be subjected to a rigorous analysis to demonstrate the presence or absence of key properties. Formal methods are discussed in Chap. 12.

Safety critical systems are generally designed for fault tolerance, where the system can deal with (and recover from) faults that occur during execution. Fault tolerance is achieved by anticipating exceptional events and in designing the system to handle them. A fault-tolerant system is designed to fail safely, and programs are designed to continue working (possibly at a reduced level of performance) rather than crashing after the occurrence of an error or exception. Many fault-tolerant systems mirror all operations, where each operation is performed on two or more duplicate systems, and so if one fails, then the other system can take over.

11.7   Review Questions

1. Explain the difference between software reliability and system availability.
2. What is software dependability?
3. Explain the significance of Adam's 1984 study of software defects at IBM.
4. Describe the Cleanroom methodology.

5. Describe the characteristics of a good software reliability model.
6. Explain the relevance of security engineering.
7. What is a safety critical system?

11.8   Summary

This chapter gave an introduction to some important topics in software engineering including software reliability and the Cleanroom methodology; dependability; availability; security; and safety critical systems.

Software reliability is the probability that the program works without failure for a period of time, and it is usually expressed as the mean time to failure. Cleanroom involves the application of statistical techniques to calculate software reliability, and it is based on the expected usage of the software.

It is essential that software used in the safety and security critical fields is dependable, with the software available when required, as well as operating safely and reliably without any adverse side effects. Many of these systems are fault tolerant and are designed to deal with (and recover) from faults that occur during execution.

Such a system needs to be secure and able to protect itself from external attacks and needs to include recovery mechanisms to enable normal service to be restored as quickly as possible. In another words, it is essential that if the system fails, then it fails safely.

Today, billions of computers are connected to the Internet, and this has led to a growth in attacks on computers. It is essential that developers are aware of the threats facing a system and are familiar with techniques to eliminate them.

References

1. G. O'Regan, *Mathematical Approaches to Software Quality* (Springer Verlag, London, 2006)
2. E. Adams, Optimizing preventive service of software products. *IBM Res. J.* **28**(1), 2–14 (1984)
3. R.H. Cobb, H.D. Mills, Engineering software under statistical quality control. IEEE Software **7**(6) (1990)
4. I. Sommerville, *Software Engineering*, 9th edn. (Pearson, 2011)

Formal Methods

12

Abstract

This chapter discusses formal methods, which consist of a set of mathematic techniques that provide an extra level of confidence in the correctness of the software. They consist of a formal specification language and employ a collection of tools to support the syntax checking of the specification, as well as the proof of properties of the specification. They allow questions to be asked about what the system does independently of the implementation, and they may be employed to formally state the requirements of the proposed system and to derive a program from its mathematical specification. They may be employed to provide a rigorous proof that the implemented program satisfies its specification, and they have been applied mainly to the safety-critical field.

Keywords

Formal specification · Vienna development method · Z specification language · B-method · Model-oriented approach · Axiomatic approach · Process calculus · Refinement · Finite state machines · Usability of formal methods

12.1 Introduction

The term *"formal methods"* refers to various mathematical techniques used for the formal specification and development of software. They consist of a formal specification language and employ a collection of tools to support the syntax checking of the specification, as well as the proof of properties of the specification. They allow questions to be asked about what the system does independently of the implementation.

© Springer International Publishing AG 2017
G. O'Regan, *Concise Guide to Software Engineering*, Undergraduate Topics in Computer Science, DOI 10.1007/978-3-319-57750-0_12

The use of mathematical notation avoids speculation about the meaning of phrases in an imprecisely worded natural language description of a system. Natural language is inherently ambiguous, whereas mathematics employs a precise rigorous notation. Spivey [1] defines formal specification as follows:

Definition 12.1(*Formal Specification*) Formal specification is the use of mathematical notation to describe in a precise way the properties that an information system must have, without unduly constraining the way in which these properties are achieved.

The formal specification thus becomes the key reference point for the different parties involved in the construction of the system. It may be used as the reference point for the requirements; program implementation; testing and program documentation. It promotes a common understanding for all those concerned with the system. The term "*formal methods*" is used to describe a formal specification language and a method for the design and implementation of a computer system. Formal methods may be employed at a number of levels:

– Formal specification only (program developed informally);
– Formal specification, refinement and verification (some proofs);
– Formal specification, refinement and verification (with extensive theorem proving).

The specification is written in a mathematical language, and the implementation may be derived from the specification via stepwise refinement.[1] The refinement step makes the specification more concrete and closer to the actual implementation. There is an associated proof obligation to demonstrate that the refinement is valid and that the concrete state preserves the properties of the abstract state. Thus, assuming that the original specification is correct and the proofs of correctness of each refinement step are valid, then there is a very high degree of confidence in the correctness of the implemented software.

Stepwise refinement is illustrated as follows: the initial specification S is the initial model M_0; it is then refined into the more concrete model M_1, and M_1 is then refined into M_2, and so on until the eventual implementation $M_n = E$ is produced.

$$S = M_0 \sqsubseteq M_1 \sqsubseteq M_2 \sqsubseteq M_3 \sqsubseteq \ldots \sqsubseteq M_n = E$$

Requirements are the foundation of the system to be built, and irrespective of the best design and development practices, the product will be incorrect if the requirements are incorrect. The objective of requirements validation is to ensure

---

[1]It is questionable whether stepwise refinement is cost-effective in mainstream software engineering, as it involves rewriting a specification ad nauseum. It is time-consuming to proceed in refinement steps with significant time also required to prove that the refinement step is valid. It is more relevant to the safety-critical field. Others in the formal methods field may disagree with this position.

that the requirements reflect what is actually required by the customer (in order to build the right system). Formal methods may be employed to model the requirements, and the model exploration yields further desirable or undesirable properties.

Formal methods provide the facility to prove that certain properties are true of the specification, and this is valuable, especially in safety-critical and security-critical applications. The properties are a logical consequence of the mathematical requirements, and the requirements may be amended where appropriate. Thus, formal methods may be employed in a sense to debug the requirements during requirements validation.

The use of formal methods generally leads to more robust software and to increased confidence in its correctness. Formal methods may be employed at different levels (e.g. it may just be used for specification with the program developed informally). The challenges involved in the deployment of formal methods in an organization include the education of staff in formal specification, as the use of these mathematical techniques may be a culture shock to many staff.

Formal methods have been applied to a diverse range of applications, including the safety and security-critical fields to develop dependable software. The applications include the railway sector, microprocessor verification, the specification of standards, and the specification and verification of programs. Parnas and others have criticized formal methods on the following grounds (Table 12.1).

However, formal methods are potentially quite useful and reasonably easy to use. The use of a formal method such as Z or VDM forces the software engineer to be precise and helps to avoid ambiguities present in natural language. Clearly, a formal specification should be subject to peer review to provide confidence in its correctness. New formalisms need to be intuitive to be usable by practitioners, and an advantage of classical mathematics is that it is familiar to students.

12.2 Why Should We Use Formal Methods?

There is a strong motivation to use best practice in software engineering in order to produce software adhering to high-quality standards. Quality problems with software may cause minor irritations or major damage to a customer's business including loss of life. Formal methods are a leading-edge technology that may be of benefit to companies in reducing the occurrence of defects in software products. Brown [2] argues that for the safety-critical field that:

Comment 12.1 (Missile Safety)*Missile systems must be presumed dangerous until shown to be safe, and that the absence of evidence for the existence of dangerous errors does not amount to evidence for the absence of danger.*

This suggests that companies in the safety-critical field will need to demonstrate that every reasonable practice was taken to prevent the occurrence of defects. One such practice is the use of formal methods, and its exclusion may need to be

Table 12.1 Criticisms of formal methods

No.	Criticism
1.	Often the formal specification is as difficult to read as the program[a]
2.	Many formal specifications are wrong[b]
3.	Formal methods are strong on syntax but provide little assistance in deciding on what technical information should be recorded using the syntax[c]
4.	Formal specifications provide a model of the proposed system. However, a precise unambiguous mathematical statement of the requirements is what is needed[d]
5.	Stepwise refinement is unrealistic.[e] It is like, for example, deriving a bridge from the description of a river and the expected traffic on the bridge. There is always a need for the creative step in design
6.	Much unnecessary mathematical formalisms have been developed rather than using the available classical mathematics[f]

[a]Of course, others might reply by saying that some of Parnas's tables are not exactly intuitive and that the notation he employs in some of his tables is quite unfriendly. The usability of all of the mathematical approaches needs to be enhanced if they are to be taken seriously by industrialists
[b]Obviously, the formal specification must be analysed using mathematical reasoning and tools to provide confidence in its correctness. The validation of a formal specification can be carried out using mathematical proof of key properties of the specification; software inspections; or specification animation
[c]Approaches such as VDM include a method for software development as well as the specification language
[d]Models are extremely valuable as they allow simplification of the reality. A mathematical study of the model demonstrates whether it is a suitable representation of the system. Models allow properties of the proposed requirements to be studied prior to implementation
[e]Stepwise refinement involves rewriting a specification with each refinement step producing a more concrete specification (that includes code and formal specification) until eventually the detailed code is produced. It is difficult and time-consuming, but tool support may make refinement easier
[f]Approaches such as VDM or Z are useful in that they add greater rigour to the software development process. They are reasonably easy to learn, and there have been some good results obtained by their use. Classical mathematics is familiar to students, and therefore, it is desirable that new formalisms are introduced only where absolutely necessary

justified in some domains. It is quite possible that a software company may be sued for software which injures a third party, and this suggests that companies will need a rigorous quality assurance system to prevent the occurrence of defects.

There is some evidence to suggest that the use of formal methods provides savings in the cost of the project. For example, a 9% cost saving is attributed to the use of formal methods during the CICS project; the T800 project attributes a 12-month reduction in testing time to the use of formal methods. These are discussed in more detail in chapter one of [3].

The use of formal methods is mandatory in certain circumstances. The Ministry of Defence (MOD) in the UK issued two safety-critical standards[2] in the early 1990s related to the use of formal methods in the software development lifecycle.

---

[2]The UK Defence Standards 0055 and 0056 were later revised to be less prescriptive on the use of formal methods.

The first is Defence Standard 00-55, *"The Procurement of safety-critical software in defense equipment"* [4] which makes it mandatory to employ formal methods in the development of safety-critical software in the UK. The standard mandates the use of formal proof that the most crucial programs correctly implement their specifications.

The other is Def. Stan 00-56 *"Hazard analysis and safety classification of the computer and programmable electronic system elements of defense equipment"* [5]. The objective of this standard is to provide guidance to identify which systems or parts of systems being developed are safety-critical and thereby require the use of formal methods. This proposed system is subject to an initial hazard analysis to determine whether there are safety-critical parts.

The reaction to these defence standards 00-55 and 00-56 was quite hostile initially, as most suppliers were unlikely to meet the technical and organization requirements of the standard. This is described in [6].

12.3 Applications of Formal Methods

Formal methods have been employed to verify the correctness of software in several domains such as the safety and security-critical fields. This includes applications to the nuclear power industry, the aerospace industry, the security technology area and the railroad domain. These sectors are subject to stringent regulatory controls to ensure that safety and security are properly addressed.

Several organizations have piloted formal methods in their organizations (with varying degrees of success). IBM developed the VDM specification language at its laboratory in Vienna, and it piloted the Z formal specification language on the CICS (Customer Information Control System) project at its plant in Hursley, England (with a 9% cost saving).

The mathematical techniques developed by Parnas (i.e. his requirements model and tabular expressions) have been employed to specify the requirements of the A-7 aircraft as part of a research project for the US Navy.[3] Tabular expressions were also employed for the software inspection of the automated shutdown software of the Darlington Nuclear power plant in Canada.[4] These were two successful uses of mathematical techniques in software engineering.

There are examples of the use of formal methods in the railway domain, and examples dealing with the modelling and verification of a railroad gate controller and railway signalling are described in [3]. Clearly, it is essential to verify safety-critical properties such as *"when the train goes through the level crossing then the gate is closed"*.

---

[3]However, the resulting software was never actually deployed on the A-7 aircraft.

[4]This was an impressive use of mathematical techniques and it has been acknowledged that formal methods must play an important role in future developments at Darlington. However, given the time and cost involved in the software inspection of the shutdown software some managers have less enthusiasm in shifting from hardware to software controllers [7].

12.4   Tools for Formal Methods

Formal methods have been criticized for the limited availability of tools to support the software engineer in writing the formal specification and in conducting proof. Many of the early tools were criticized as not being of industrial strength. However, in recent years, more advanced tools have become available to support the software engineer's work in formal specification and formal proof, and this is likely to continue in the coming years.

The tools include syntax checkers that determine whether the specification is syntactically correct; specialized editors which ensure that the written specification is syntactically correct; tools to support refinement; automated code generators that generate a high-level language corresponding to the specification; theorem provers to demonstrate the correctness of refinement steps, and to identify and resolve proof obligations, as well as proving the presence or absence of key properties; and specification animation tools where the execution of the specification can be simulated.

The *B*-Toolkit from *B*-Core is an integrated set of tools that supports the *B*-Method. It provides functionality for syntax and type checking, specification animation, proof obligation generator, an auto-prover, a proof assistor and code generation. This, in theory, allows the complete formal development from the initial specification to the final implementation, with every proof obligation justified, leading to a provably correct program.

The IFAD Toolbox[5] is a support tool for the VDM-SL specification language, and it provides support for syntax and type checking, an interpreter and debugger to execute and debug the specification, and a code generator to convert from VDM-SL to C++. The Overture Integrated Development Environment (IDE) is an open-source tool for formal modelling and analysis of VDM-SL specifications.

12.5   Approaches to Formal Methods

There are two key approaches to formal methods, namely the *model-oriented approach* of VDM or *Z*, and the *algebraic* or *axiomatic approach* of the process calculi such as the calculus communicating systems (CCS) or communicating sequential processes (CSP).

12.5.1   Model-Oriented Approach

The model-oriented approach to specification is based on mathematical models, where a model is a simplification or abstraction of the real world that contains only

---

[5]The IFAD Toolbox has been renamed to VDM Tools as IFAD sold the VDM Tools to CSK in Japan.

the essential details. For example, the model of an aircraft will not include the colour of the aircraft, and the objective would be to model the aerodynamics of the aircraft. There are many models employed in the physical world, such as meteorological models that allow weather forecasts to be given.

The importance of models is that they serve to explain the behaviour of a particular entity and may also be used to predict future behaviour. Models may vary in their ability to explain aspects of the entity under study. One model may be good at explaining some aspects of the behaviour, whereas another model might be good at explaining other aspects. The *adequacy* of a model is a key concept in modelling, and it is determined by the effectiveness of the model in representing the underlying behaviour and in its ability to predict future behaviour. Model exploration consists of asking questions and determining the extent to which the model is able to give an effective answer to the particular question. A good model is chosen as a representation of the real world and is referred to whenever there are questions in relation to the aspect of the real world.

It is fundamental to explore the model to determine its adequacy, and to determine the extent to which it explains the underlying physical behaviour, and allows accurate predictions of future behaviour to be made. There may be more than one possible model of a particular entity; for example, the Ptolemaic model and the Copernican model are different models of the solar system. This leads to the question as to which is the best or most appropriate model to use, and on the criteria to use to determine which is more suitable. The ability of the model to explain the behaviour, its simplicity and its elegance will be part of the criteria. The principle of "*Ockham's Razor*" (law of parsimony) is often used in modelling, and it suggests that the simplest model with the least number of assumptions required should be selected.

The adequacy of the model will determine its acceptability as a representation of the physical world. Models that are ineffective will be replaced with models that offer a better explanation of the manifested physical behaviour. There are many examples in science of the replacement of one theory by a newer one. For example, the Copernican model of the universe replaced the older Ptolemaic model, and Newtonian physics was replaced by Einstein's theories of relativity. The structure of the revolutions that take place in science is described in [8].

Modelling can play a key role in computer science, as computer systems tend to be highly complex, whereas a model allows simplification or an abstraction of the underlying complexity, and it enables a richer understanding of the underlying reality to be gained. We discussed system modelling in Chap. 3, and it provides an abstraction of the existing and proposed system, and it helps in clarifying what the existing system does, and in communicating and clarifying the requirements of the proposed system.

The model-oriented approach to software development involves defining an abstract model of the proposed software system, and the model is then explored to determine its suitability as a representation of the system. This takes the form of model interrogation, i.e. asking questions and determining the extent to which the model can answer the questions. The modelling in formal methods is typically performed via elementary discrete mathematics, including set theory, sequences, functions and relations.

Various models have been applied to assist with the complexities in software development. These include the Capability Maturity Model (CMM), which is employed as a framework to enhance the capability of the organization in software development; UML, which has various graphical diagrams that are employed to model the requirements and design; and mathematical models that are employed for formal specification.

VDM and *Z* are model-oriented approaches to formal methods. VDM arose from work done at the IBM laboratory in Vienna in formalizing the semantics for the PL/1 compiler in the early 1970s, and it was later applied to the specification of software systems. The origin of the *Z* specification language is in work done at Oxford University in the early 1980s.

12.5.2   Axiomatic Approach

The axiomatic approach focuses on the properties that the proposed system is to satisfy, and there is no intention to produce an abstract model of the system. The required properties and behaviour of the system are stated in mathematical notation. The difference between the axiomatic specification and a model-based approach may be seen in the example of a stack.

The stack includes operators for pushing an element onto the stack and popping an element from the stack. The properties of *pop* and *push* are explicitly defined in the axiomatic approach. The model-oriented approach constructs an explicit model of the stack, and the operations are defined in terms of the effect that they have on the model. The axiomatic specification of the *pop* operation on a stack is given by properties, for example $pop(push(s, x)) = s$.

Comment 12.2 (Axiomatic Approach)*The property-oriented approach has the advantage that the implementer is not constrained to a particular choice of implementation, and the only constraint is that the implementation must satisfy the stipulated properties.*

The emphasis is on specifying the required properties of the system, and implementation issues are avoided. The properties are typically stated using mathematical logic (or higher-order logics). Mechanized theorem-proving techniques may be employed to prove results.

One potential problem with the axiomatic approach is that the properties specified may not be realized in any implementation. Thus, whenever a "formal axiomatic theory" is developed, a corresponding "model" of the theory must be identified, in order to ensure that the properties may be realized in practice. That is, when proposing a system that is to satisfy some set of properties, there is a need to prove that there is at least one system that will satisfy the set of properties.

12.6   Proof and Formal Methods

A mathematical proof typically includes natural language and mathematical symbols, and often many of the tedious details of the proof are omitted. The proof may employ a "*divide and conquer*" technique, i.e. breaking the conjecture down into subgoals and then attempting to prove each of the subgoals.

Many proofs in formal methods are concerned with cross-checking the details of the specification, or in checking the validity of the refinement steps, or checking that certain properties are satisfied by the specification. There are often many tedious lemmas to be proved, and theorem provers[6] are essential in dealing with these. Machine proof is explicit, and reliance on some brilliant insight is avoided. Proofs by hand are notorious for containing errors or jumps in reasoning, while machine proofs are explicit but are often extremely lengthy and unreadable. The infamous machine proof of the correctness of the VIPER microprocessor[7] consisted of several million formulae [6].

A formal mathematical proof consists of a sequence of formulae, where each element is either an axiom or derived from a previous element in the series by applying a fixed set of mechanical rules.

The application of formal methods in an industrial environment requires the use of machine-assisted proof, since thousands of proof obligations arise from a formal specification, and theorem provers are essential in resolving these efficiently. Automated theorem proving is difficult, as often mathematicians prove a theorem with an initial intuitive feeling that the theorem is true. Human intervention to provide guidance or intuition improves the effectiveness of the theorem prover.

The proof of various properties about a program increases confidence in its correctness. However, an absolute proof of correctness[8] is unlikely except for the most trivial of programs. A program may consist of legacy software that is assumed to work; a compiler that is assumed to work correctly creates it. Theorem provers

---

[6]Many existing theorem provers are difficult to use and are for specialist use only. There is a need to improve the usability of theorem provers.

[7]This verification was controversial with RSRE and Charter overselling VIPER as a chip design that conforms to its formal specification.

[8]This position is controversial with others arguing that if correctness is defined mathematically then the mathematical definition (i.e. formal specification) is a theorem, and the task is to prove that the program satisfies the theorem. They argue that the proofs for non-trivial programs exist and that the reason why there are not many examples of such proofs is due to a lack of mathematical specifications.

are programs that are assumed to function correctly. The best that formal methods can claim is increased confidence in correctness of the software, rather than an absolute proof of correctness.

12.7   The Future of Formal Methods

The debate concerning the level of use of mathematics in software engineering is still ongoing. Many practitioners are against the use of mathematics and avoid its use. They tend to employ methodologies such as software inspections and testing (or more recently, the Agile approach has become popular) to improve confidence in the correctness of the software. They argue that in the current competitive industrial environment, where time to market is a key driver, that the use of such formal mathematical techniques would seriously impact the market opportunity. Industrialists often need to balance conflicting needs such as quality, cost and delivering on time. They argue that the commercial realities require methodologies and techniques that allow them to achieve their business goals effectively.

The other camp argues that the use of mathematics is essential in the delivery of high-quality and reliable software and that if a company does not place sufficient emphasis on quality, then it will pay the price in terms of poor quality and the loss of its reputation in the marketplace.

It is generally accepted that mathematics and formal methods must play a role in the safety-critical and security-critical fields. Apart from that, the extent of the use of mathematics is a hotly disputed topic. The pace of change in the world is extraordinary, and companies face significant competitive forces in a global marketplace. It is unrealistic to expect companies to deploy formal methods unless they have clear evidence that it will support them in delivering commercial products to the marketplace ahead of their competition, at the right price and with the right quality. Formal methods need to prove that it can do this if it wishes to be taken seriously in mainstream software engineering. The issue of technology transfer of formal methods to industry is discussed in [9].

12.8   The Vienna Development Method

VDM dates from work done by the IBM research laboratory in Vienna. This group was specifying the semantics of the PL/1 programming language using an operational semantic approach. That is, the semantics of the language were defined in terms of a hypothetical machine which interprets the programs of that language [10, 11]. Later work led to the Vienna Development Method (VDM) with its specification language, Meta IV. This was used to give the denotational semantics of programming languages; i.e. a mathematical object (set, function, etc.) is associated with each phrase of the language [11]. The mathematical object is termed the *denotation* of the phrase.

VDM is a *model-oriented approach,* and this means that an explicit model of the state of an abstract machine is given, and operations are defined in terms of the state. Operations may act on the system state, taking inputs, and producing outputs as well as a new system state. Operations are defined in a precondition and post-condition style. Each operation has an associated proof obligation to ensure that if the precondition is true, then the operation preserves the system invariant. The initial state itself is, of course, required to satisfy the system invariant.

VDM uses keywords to distinguish different parts of the specification, e.g. preconditions, post-conditions, as introduced by the keywords *pre* and *post,* respectively. In keeping with the philosophy that formal methods specify *what* a system does as distinct from *how,* VDM employs post-conditions to stipulate the effect of the operation on the state. The previous state is then distinguished by employing *hooked variables,* e.g. v^-, and the post-condition specifies the new state which is defined by a logical predicate relating the prestate to the post-state.

VDM is more than its specification language VDM-SL, and is, in fact, a software development method, with rules to verify the steps of development. The rules enable the executable specification, i.e. the detailed code, to be obtained from the initial specification via refinement steps. Thus, we have a sequence $S = S_0, S_1, ...,$ $S_n = E$ of specifications, where S is the initial specification and E is the final (executable) specification.

Retrieval functions enable a return from a more concrete specification to the more abstract specification. The initial specification consists of an initial state, a system state, and a set of operations. The system state is a particular domain, where a domain is built out of primitive domains such as the set of natural numbers and integers, or constructed from primitive domains using domain constructors such as Cartesian product and disjoint union. A domain-invariant predicate may further constrain the domain, and a *type* in VDM reflects a domain obtained in this way. Thus, a type in VDM is more specific than the signature of the type and thus represents values in the domain defined by the signature, which satisfy the domain invariant. In view of this approach to types, it is clear that VDM types may not be "statically type checked".

VDM specifications are structured into modules, with a module containing the module name, parameters, types, operations, etc. Partial functions occur frequently in computer science as many functions, may be undefined or fail to terminate for some arguments in their domain. VDM addresses partial functions by employing non-standard logical operators, namely the logic of partial functions (LPFs), which is discussed in [12].

VDM has been used in industrial projects, and its tool support includes the IFAD Toolbox.[9] VDM is described in more detail in [9]. There are several variants of VDM, including VDM++, the object-oriented extension of VDM, and the Irish school of the VDM, which is discussed in the next section.

---

[9]The VDM Tools are now available from the CSK Group in Japan.

12.9 VDM⁺, The Irish School of VDM

The Irish School of VDM is a variant of standard VDM and is characterized by its constructive approach, classical mathematical style, and its terse notation [13]. This method aims to combine the *what* and *how* of formal methods in that its terse specification style stipulates in concise form *what* the system should do; furthermore, the fact that its specifications are constructive (or functional) means that the *how* is included with the *what*.

However, it is important to qualify this by stating that the how as presented by VDM⁺ is not directly executable, as several of its mathematical data types have no corresponding structure in high-level or functional programming languages. Thus, a conversion or reification of the specification into a functional or high-level language must take place to ensure a successful execution. Further, the fact that a specification is constructive is no guarantee that it is a good implementation strategy, if the construction itself is naive.

The Irish school follows a similar development methodology to standard VDM, and it is a model-oriented approach. The initial specification is presented, with the initial state and operations defined. The operations are presented with preconditions; however, no post-condition is necessary as the operation is "functionally" (i.e. explicitly) constructed.

There are proof obligations to demonstrate that the operations preserve the invariant. That is, if the precondition for the operation is true, and the operation is performed, then the system invariant remains true after the operation. The philosophy is to exhibit existence *constructively* rather than providing a theoretical proof of existence that demonstrates the existence of a solution without presenting an algorithm to construct the solution.

The school avoids the existential quantifier of predicate calculus, and reliance on logic in proof is kept to a minimum, with emphasis instead placed on equational reasoning. Structures with nice algebraic properties are sought, and one nice algebraic structure employed is the monoid, which has closure, associative, and a unit element. The concept of isomorphism is powerful, reflecting that two structures are essentially identical, and thus, we may choose to work with either, depending on which is more convenient for the task in hand.

The school has been influenced by the work of Polya and Lakatos. The former [14] advocated a style of problem-solving characterized by first considering an easier subproblem and considering several examples. This generally leads to a clearer insight into solving the main problem. Lakatos's approach to mathematical discovery [15] is characterized by heuristic methods. A primitive conjecture is proposed, and if global counterexamples to the statement of the conjecture are discovered, then the corresponding *hidden lemma* for which this global counterexample is a local counter example is identified and added to the statement of the primitive conjecture. The process repeats, until no more global counterexamples are found. A sceptical view of absolute truth or certainty is inherent in this.

Partial functions are the norm in VDM⁺, and as in standard VDM, the problem is that functions may be undefined or fail to terminate for several of the arguments in their domain. The LPFs is avoided, and instead care is taken with recursive definitions to ensure termination is achieved for each argument. Academic and industrial projects have been conducted using the method of the Irish school, but tool support is limited.

12.10   The *Z* Specification Language

Z is a formal specification language founded on Zermelo set theory, and it was developed by Abrial at Oxford University in the early 1980s. It is used for the formal specification of software and is a model-oriented approach. An explicit model of the state of an abstract machine is given, and the operations are defined in terms of the effect on the state. It includes a mathematical notation that is similar to VDM and the visually striking schema calculus. The latter consists essentially of boxes (or schemas), and these are used to describe operations and states. The schema calculus enables schemas to be used as building blocks and combined with other schemas. The Z specification language was published as an ISO standard (ISO/IEC 13568:2002) in 2002.

The schema calculus is a powerful means of decomposing a specification into smaller pieces or schemas. This helps to make Z specification highly readable, as each individual schema is small in size and self-contained. Exception handling is done by defining schemas for the exception cases, and these are then combined with the original operation schema. Mathematical data types are used to model the data in a system, and these data types obey mathematical laws. These laws enable simplification of expressions and are useful with proofs.

Operations are defined in a precondition/post-condition style. However, the precondition is implicitly defined within the operation; i.e. it is not separated out as in standard VDM. Each operation has an associated proof obligation to ensure that if the precondition is true, then the operation preserves the system invariant. The initial state itself is, of course, required to satisfy the system invariant. Post-conditions employ a logical predicate which relates the prestate to the post-state, and the post-state of a variable v is given by priming, e.g. v'. Various conventions are employed; e.g. $v?$ indicates that v is an input variable and $v!$ indicates that v is an output variable. The symbol Ξ Op operation indicates that this operation does not affect the state, whereas Δ Op indicates that this operation affects the state.

Many data types employed in Z have no counterpart in standard programming languages. It is therefore important to identify and describe the concrete data structures that will ultimately represent the abstract mathematical structures. The operations on the abstract data structures may need to be refined to yield operations on the concrete data structure that yield equivalent results. For simple systems, direct refinement (i.e. one step from abstract specification to implementation) may be possible; in more complex systems, deferred refinement is employed, where a sequence of increasingly concrete specifications are produced to eventually yield the executable specification.

Z has been successfully applied in industry, and one of its well-known successes is the CICS project at IBM Hursley in England. Z is described in more detail in Chap. 13.

12.11   The *B*-Method

The *B-Technologies* [16] consist of three components: a method for software development, namely the *B*-Method; a supporting set of tools, namely the *B*-Toolkit; and a generic program for symbol manipulation, namely the *B*-Tool (from which the *B*-Toolkit is derived). The *B*-Method is a model-oriented approach and is closely related to the Z specification language. Abrial developed the B specification language, and every construct in the language has a set-theoretic counterpart, and the method is founded on Zermelo set theory. Each operation has an explicit precondition.

A key role of the *abstract machine* in the *B*-Method is to provide encapsulation of variables representing the state of the machine and operations that manipulate the state. Machines may refer to other machines, and a machine may be introduced as a refinement of another machine. The abstract machines are specification machines, refinement machines, or implementable machines. The *B*-Method adopts a layered approach to design where the design is gradually made more concrete by a sequence of design layers. Each design layer is a refinement that involves a more detailed implementation in terms of the abstract machines of the previous layer. The design refinement ends when the final layer is implemented purely in terms of library machines. Any refinement of a machine by another has associated proof obligations, and proof is required to verify the validity of the refinement step.

Specification animation of the Abstract Machine Notation (AMN) specification is possible with the *B*-Toolkit, and this enables typical usage scenarios to be explored for requirements validation. This is, in effect, an early form of testing, and it may be used to demonstrate the presence or absence of desirable or undesirable behaviour. Verification takes the form of a proof to demonstrate that the invariant is preserved when the operation is executed within its precondition, and this is performed on the AMN specification with the *B*-Toolkit.

The *B*-Toolkit provides several tools that support the *B*-Method, and these include syntax and type checking; specification animation, proof obligation generator, auto-prover, proof assistor, and code generation. Thus, in theory, a complete formal development from initial specification to final implementation may be achieved, with every proof obligation justified, leading to a provably correct program.

The *B*-Method and toolkit have been successfully applied in industrial applications, including the CICS project at IBM Hursley in the UK [17]. The automated support provided has been cited as a major benefit of the application of the *B*-Method and the *B*-Toolkit.

12.12   Predicate Transformers and Weakest Preconditions

The precondition of a program S is a predicate, i.e. a statement that may be true or false, and it is usually required to prove that if the precondition Q is true, then execution of S is guaranteed to terminate in a finite amount of time in a state satisfying R. This is written as $\{Q\}S\{R\}$.

The weakest precondition of a command S with respect to a post-condition R [18] represents the set of all states such that if execution begins in any one of these states, then execution will terminate in a finite amount of time in a state with R true. These set of states may be represented by a predicate Q', so that $wp(S, R) = wp_S(R) = Q'$, and so wp_S is a predicate transformer; i.e. it may be regarded as a function on predicates. The weakest precondition is the precondition that places the fewest constraints on the state than all of the other preconditions of (S,R). That is, all of the other preconditions are stronger than the weakest precondition.

The notation $Q\{S\}R$ is used to denote partial correctness, and indicates that if execution of S commences in any state satisfying Q, and if execution terminates, then the final state will satisfy R. Often, a predicate Q which is stronger than the weakest precondition $wp(S,R)$ is employed, especially where the calculation of the weakest precondition is non-trivial. Thus, a stronger predicate Q such that $Q \Rightarrow wp(S,R)$ is often employed.

There are many properties associated with the weakest preconditions, and these may be used to simplify expressions involving weakest preconditions, and in determining the weakest preconditions of various program commands such as assignments and iterations. Weakest preconditions may be used in developing a proof of correctness of a program in parallel with its development [9].

An imperative program F may be regarded as a predicate transformer. This is since a predicate P characterizes the set of states in which the predicate P is true, and an imperative program may be regarded as a binary relation on states, which leads to the Hoare triple $P\{F\}Q$. That is, the program F acts as a predicate transformer with the predicate P regarded as an input assertion, i.e. a Boolean expression that must be true before the program F is executed, and the predicate Q is the output assertion, which is true if the program F terminates (where F commenced in a state satisfying P).

12.13   The Process Calculii

The objectives of the process calculi [19] are to provide mathematical models which provide insight into the diverse issues involved in the specification, design and implementation of computer systems which continuously act and interact with their environment. These systems may be decomposed into subsystems that interact with each other and their environment.

The basic building block is the *process*, which is a mathematical abstraction of the interactions between a system and its environment. A process that lasts indefinitely may be specified recursively. Processes may be assembled into systems; they may execute concurrently or communicate with each other. Process communication may be synchronized, and this takes the form of one process outputting a message simultaneously to another process inputting a message. Resources may be shared among several processes. Process calculi such as CSP [19] and CCS [20] have been developed, and they enrich the understanding of communication and concurrency, and they obey several mathematical laws.

The expression $(a\ ?\ P)$ in CSP describes a process which first engages in event a, and then behaves as process P. A recursive definition is written as $(\mu X) \cdot F(X)$, and an example of a simple chocolate vending machine is:

$$\text{VMS} = \mu X : \{\text{coin}, \text{choc}\} \cdot (\text{coin?}(\text{choc?}X))$$

The simple vending machine has an alphabet of two symbols, namely *coin* and *choc*. The behaviour of the machine is that a coin is entered into the machine; then, a chocolate is selected and provided; and finally, the machine is ready for further use. CSP processes use channels to communicate values with their environment, and input on channel c is denoted by $(c?.x\ P_x)$. This describes a process that accepts any value x on channel c and then behaves as process P_x. In contrast, $(c!e\ P)$ defines a process which outputs the expression e on channel c and then behaves as process P.

The π calculus is a process calculus based on names. Communication between processes takes place between known channels, and the name of a channel may be passed over a channel. There is no distinction between channel names and data values in the π-calculus. The output of a value v on channel a is given by $\bar{a}v$; i.e. output is a negative prefix. Input on a channel a is given by $a(x)$ and is a positive prefix. Private links or restrictions are denoted by $(x)P$.

12.14   Finite State Machines

Warren McCulloch and Walter Pitts published early work on finite state automata in 1943. They were interested in modelling the thought process for humans and machines. Moore and Mealy developed this work further, and these machines are referred to as the "*Moore machine*" and the "*Mealy machine*". The Mealy machine determines its outputs through the current state and the input, whereas the output of Moore's machine is based upon the current state alone.

Definition 12.2(*Finite State Machine*) A finite state machine (FSM) is an abstract mathematical machine that consists of a finite number of states. It includes a start state q_0 in which the machine is in initially; a finite set of states Q; an input alphabet Σ; a state transition function δ; and a set of final accepting states F (where $F \subseteq, Q$).

The state transition function takes the current state and an input and returns the next state. That is, the transition function is of the form:

$$\delta : Q \times \Sigma \rightarrow Q$$

The transition function provides rules that define the action of the machine for each input, and it may be extended to provide output as well as a state transition. State diagrams are used to represent finite state machines, and each state accepts a finite number of inputs. A FSM may be deterministic or non-deterministic, and a *deterministic machine* (Fig. 12.1) changes to exactly one state for each input transition, whereas a *non-deterministic machine* may have a choice of states to move to for a particular input.

Finite state automata can compute only very primitive functions and are not an adequate model for computing. There are more powerful automata such as the *Turing machine* [12] that is essentially a finite state automaton with a potentially infinite storage (memory). Anything that is computable by a Turing machine.

The memory of the Turing machine is a tape that consists of a potentially infinite number of one-dimensional cells. The Turing machine provides a mathematical abstraction of computer execution and storage, as well as provides a mathematical definition of an algorithm.

12.15   The Parnas Way

Parnas has been influential in the computing field, and his ideas on the specification, design, implementation, maintenance, and documentation of computer software remain important. He advocates a solid engineering approach and argues that the role of the engineer is to apply scientific principles and mathematics to design and develop products. He argues that computer scientists need to be educated as engineers to ensure that they have the appropriate background to build software correctly. His contributions to software engineering include (Table 12.2).

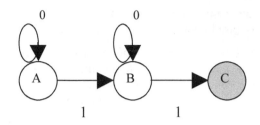

Fig. 12.1 Deterministic finite state machine

Table 12.2 Parnas's contributions to software engineering

Area	Contribution
Tabular expressions	These are mathematical tables for specifying requirements and enable complex predicate logic expressions to be represented in a simpler form
Mathematical documentation	He advocates the use of precise mathematical documentation for requirements and design
Requirements specification	He advocates the use of mathematical relations to specify the requirements precisely
Software design	He developed *information hiding* that is used in object-oriented design[a] and allows software to be designed for change. Every information-hiding module has an interface that provides the only means to access the services provided by the modules. The interface hides the module's implementation
Software inspections	His approach requires the reviewers to take an active part in the inspection. They are provided with a list of questions by the author, and their analysis involves the production of mathematical table to justify the answers
Predicate logic	He developed an extension of the predicate calculus to deal with partial functions, and it preserves the classical two-valued logic when dealing with undefined values

[a]It is surprising that many in the object-oriented world seem unaware that information hiding goes back to the early 1970s and many have never heard of Parnas

12.16 Usability of Formal Methods

There are practical difficulties associated with the industrial use of formal methods. It seems to be assumed that programmers and customers are willing to become familiar with the mathematics used in formal methods, but this is true in only some domains.[10] Customers are concerned with their own domain and speak the technical

---

[10]The domain in which the software is being used will influence the willingness or otherwise of the customers to become familiar with the mathematics required. There appears to be little interest in mainstream software engineering, and their perception is that formal methods are unusable. However, in there is a greater interest in the mathematical approach in the safety-critical field.

language of that domain.[11] Often, the use of mathematics is an alien activity that bears little resemblance to their normal work. Programmers are interested in programming rather than in mathematics and are generally are not interested in becoming mathematicians.[12]

However, the mathematics involved in most formal methods is reasonably elementary, and, in theory, if both customers and programmers are willing to learn the formal mathematical notation, then a rigorous validation of the formal specification can take place to verify its correctness. It is usually possible to get a developer to learn a formal method, as a programmer has some experience of mathematics and logic; however, in practice, it is more difficult to get a customer to learn a formal method.

This often means that often a formal specification of the requirements and an informal definition of the requirements using a natural language are maintained. It is essential that both of these are consistent and that there is a rigorous validation of the formal specification. Otherwise, if the programmer proves the correctness of the code with respect to the formal specification, and the formal specification is incorrect, then the formal development of the software is incorrect. There are several techniques to validate a formal specification (Table 12.3), and these are described in more detail in [21]:

Why are Formal Methods difficult?
Formal methods are perceived as being difficult to use and of providing limited value in mainstream software engineering. Programmers receive education in mathematics as part of their studies, but many never use formal methods or mathematics again once they take an industrial position.

It may well be that the very nature of formal methods is such that it is suited only for specialists with a strong background in mathematics. Some of the reasons why formal methods are perceived as being difficult are listed in Table 12.4.

Characteristics of a Usable Formal Method
It is important to investigate ways by which formal methods can be made more usable to software engineers. This may involve designing more usable notations and better tools to support the process. Practical training and coaching to employees can help. Some of the characteristics of a usable formal method are listed in Table 12.5.

---

[11]Most customers have a very limited interest and even less willingness to use mathematics. There are exceptions to this especially in the regulated sector.

[12]Mathematics that is potentially useful to software engineers is discussed in [11].

Table 12.3 Techniques for validation of formal specification

Technique	Description
Proof	This involves demonstrating that the formal specification satisfies key properties of the requirements. The implementation will need to preserve these properties
Software inspections	This involves a Fagan-like inspection to compare an informal set of requirements (unless the customer has learned the formal method) with the formal specification and to ensure consistency between them
Specification animation	This involves program (or specification) execution as a way to validate the formal specification. It is similar to testing
Tools	Tools provide some limited support in validating a formal specification

Table 12.4 Why are formal methods difficult?

Factor	Description
Notation/intuition	The notation employed differs from that employed in mathematics. Many programmers find the notation in formal methods to be unintuitive
Formal specification	It is easier to read a formal specification than to write one
Validation of formal specification	The validation of a formal specification using proof techniques or a Fagan-like inspection is difficult
Refinement[a]	The refinement of a formal specification into more concrete specifications with proof of each refinement step is difficult and time-consuming
Proof	Proof can be difficult and time-consuming
Tool support	Many of the existing tools are difficult to use

[a]The author doubts that refinement is cost-effective for mainstream software engineering. However, it may be useful in the regulated environment

Table 12.5 Characteristics of a usable formal method

Characteristic	Description
Intuitive	A formal method should be intuitive
Teachable	A formal method needs to be teachable to the average software engineer. The training should include writing practical formal specifications
Tool support	Good tools to support formal specification, validation, refinement and proof are required
Adaptable to change	Change is common in a software engineering environment. A usable formal method should be adaptable to change
Technology transfer path	The process for software development needs to be defined to include formal methods. The migration to formal methods needs to be managed
Cost[a]	The use of formal methods should be cost-effective with a return on investment (e.g. benefits in time, quality and productivity)

[a]A commercial company will expect a return on investment from the use of a new technology. This may be reduced software development costs, improved quality and improved timeliness of projects, and improvements in productivity. A company does not go to the trouble of deploying a new technology just to satisfy academic interest

12.17   Review Questions

1. What are formal methods and describe their potential benefits? How essential is tool support?
2. What is stepwise refinement and how realistic is it in mainstream software engineering?
3. Discuss Parnas's criticisms of formal methods and discuss whether his views are valid.
4. Discuss the applications of formal methods and which areas have benefited most from their use? What problems have arisen?
5. Describe a technology transfer path for the deployment of formal methods in an organization.
6. Explain the difference between the model-oriented approach and the axiomatic approach.
7. Discuss the nature of proof in formal methods and tools to support proof.
8. Discuss the VDM and explain the difference between standard VDM and VDM$^{\clubsuit}$.
9. Discuss Z and B. Describe the tools in the B-Toolkit.
10. Discuss process calculi such as CSP, CCS or π–calculus.

12.18   Summary

This chapter discussed formal methods which offer a mathematical approach to the development of high-quality software. Formal methods employ mathematical techniques for the specification and development of software and are useful in the safety-critical field. They consist of a formal specification language; a methodology for formal software development; and a set of tools to support the syntax checking of the specification, as well as the proof of properties of the specification.

The model-oriented approach includes formal methods such as VDM, Z and B, whereas the axiomatic approach includes the process calculi such as CSP, CCS and the π calculus. VDM was developed at the IBM laboratory in Vienna, and it has been used in academia and industry. CSP was developed by C.A.R Hoare and CCS by Robin Milner.

Formal methods allow questions to be asked and answered about what the system does independently of the implementation. They offer a way to debug the requirements and to show that certain desirable properties are true of the specification, whereas certain undesirable properties are absent.

The use of formal methods generally leads to more robust software and to increased confidence in its correctness. There are challenges involved in the deployment of formal methods, as the use of these mathematical techniques may be a culture shock to many staff.

The usability of existing formal methods was considered, and the reasons for their perceived difficulty were considered. The characteristics of a usable formal method were explored.

There are various tools to support formal methods including syntax checkers; specialized editors; tools to support refinement; automated code generators that generate a high-level language corresponding to the specification; theorem provers; and specification animation tools where the execution of the specification can be simulated.

References

1. J.M. Spivey, *The Z Notation. A Reference Manual*. Prentice Hall International Series in Computer Science (Prentice-Hall, Inc., Upper Saddle River, 1992)
2. M.J.D Brown, Rationale for the development of the UK Defence Standards for Safety Critical Software. COMPASS Conference, 1990
3. M. Hinchey, J. Bowen (eds.), *Applications of Formal Methods*. Prentice Hall International Series in Computer Science (Prentice-Hall, Inc., Upper Saddle River, 1995)
4. Ministry of Defence-55 (PART 1), *I* Issue 1, The Procurement of Safety Critical software in Defence Equipment, PART 1: Requirements. Interim Defence Standard, U.K., 1991a
5. Ministry of Defence-55 (PART 2), *I* Issue 1, The Procurement of Safety Critical software in Defence Equipment, PART 2: Guidance. Interim Defence Standard, UK., 1991b
6. T. Kuhn, *The Structure of Scientific Revolutions* (University of Chicago Press, Chicago, 1970)
7. S. Gerhart, D. Craighen, T. Ralston, Experience with formal methods in critical systems. IEEE Softw. **11**, 21 (1994)
8. M. Tierney, The Evolution of Def Stan 00-55 and 00-56: An Intensification of the "Formal Methods debate" in the UK. Research Centre for Social Sciences, University of Edinburgh, 1991
9. G. O'Regan, *Mathematical Approaches to Software Quality* (Springer, London, 2006)
10. D. Bjorner, C. Jones, The Vienna Development Method. The meta language. *Lecture Notes in Computer Science*, vol. 61 (Springer, New York, 1978)
11. D. Bjorner, C. Jones, *Formal Specification and software Development*. Prentice Hall International Series in Computer Science (Prentice-Hall, Inc., Upper Saddle River, 1982)
12. G. O'Regan, *Guide to Discrete Mathematics* (Springer, Switzerland, 2016)
13. M.M.A. Airchinnigh, Conceptual Models and Computing. PhD Thesis. Department of Computer Science, University of Dublin, Trinity College, Dublin, 1990
14. G. Polya, *How to Solve It. A New Aspect of Mathematical Method* (Princeton University Press, Princeton, 1957)
15. I. Lakatos, *Proof and Refutations. The Logic of Mathematical Discovery* (Cambridge University Press, Cambridge, 1976)
16. E. McDonnell, MSc Thesis. Department of Computer Science, Trinity College, Dublin, 1994
17. J.P. Hoare, Application of the B-Method to CICS, in *Applications of Formal Methods*, ed. By M. Hinchey, J.P. Bowen. Prentice Hall International Series in Computer Science (Prentice-Hall, Inc., Upper Saddle River, 1995)

18. D. Gries, *The Science of Programming* (Springer, Berlin, 1981)
19. C.A.R. Hoare, *Communicating Sequential Processes*. Prentice Hall International Series in Computer Science (Prentice-Hall, Inc., Upper Saddle River, 1985)
20. R. Milner et al., A Calculus of Mobile Processes (Part 1). LFCS Report Series. ECS-LFCS-89-85. Department of Computer Science, University of Edinburgh, 1989
21. B.A. Wickmann, A Personal View of Formal Methods. National Physical Laboratory, 2000

Z Formal Specification Language

13

Abstract

This chapter presents the Z specification language, which is one of the most widely used formal methods. Z is a formal specification language based on Zermelo set theory. It was developed at the Programming Research Group at Oxford University in the early 1980s. Z specifications are mathematical and employ a classical two-valued logic. The use of mathematics ensures precision and allows inconsistencies and gaps in the specification to be identified. Theorem provers may be employed to demonstrate that the software implementation meets its specification.

Keywords

Sets, relations and functions · Bags and sequences · Precondition · Post-condition · Invariant · Data reification · Refinement · Schema calculus · Proof in Z

13.1 Introduction

Z is a formal specification language based on Zermelo set theory. It was developed at the Programming Research Group at Oxford University in the early 1980s [1] and became an ISO standard in 2002. Z specifications are mathematical and employ a classical two-valued logic. The use of mathematics ensures precision and allows inconsistencies and gaps in the specification to be identified. Theorem provers may be employed to prove properties of the specification and to demonstrate that the software implementation meets its specification.

Z is a *"and an explicit model"* approach with an explicit model of the state of an abstract machine given, and operations are defined in terms of this state. Its mathematical notation is used for formal specification, and its schema calculus is used to structure the specification. The schema calculus is visually striking and consists essentially of boxes, with these boxes or schemas used to describe operations and states. The schemas may be used as building blocks and combined with other schemas. The simple schema below (Fig. 13.1) is the specification of the positive square root of a real number.

The schema calculus is a powerful means of decomposing a specification into smaller pieces or schemas. This helps to make Z specifications highly readable, as each individual schema is small in size and self-contained. Exception handling is addressed by defining schemas for the exception cases. These are then combined with the original operation schema. Mathematical data types are used to model the data in a system, and these data types obey mathematical laws. These laws enable simplification of expressions and are useful with proofs.

Operations are defined in a precondition/post-condition style. A precondition must be true before the operation is executed, and the post-condition must be true after the operation has executed. The *precondition is implicitly defined* within the operation. Each operation has an associated proof obligation to ensure that if the precondition is true, then the operation preserves the system invariant. The system invariant is a property of the system that must be true at all times. The initial state itself is, of course, required to satisfy the system invariant.

The precondition for the specification of the square root function above is that $num? \geq 0$; i.e., the function *SqRoot* may be applied to positive real numbers only. The post-condition for the square root function is $root!^2 = num?$ and $root! \geq 0$. That is, the square root of a number is positive and its square gives the number. Post-conditions employ a logical predicate which relates the prestate to the post-state, with the post-state of a variable being distinguished by priming the variable, e.g. v'.

Z is a typed language, and whenever a variable is introduced, its type must be given. A type is simply a collection of objects, and there are several standard types in Z. These include the natural numbers $\mathbb{N}$, the integers $\mathbb{Z}$ and the real numbers $\mathbb{R}$. The declaration of a variable x of type X is written as $x{:}X$. It is also possible to create your own types in Z.

$$
\begin{array}{|l}
\hline
-SqRoot\text{\rule{2cm}{0.4pt}} \\
\text{num?, } root! : \mathbb{R} \\
\hline
num? \geq 0 \\
root!^2 = num? \\
root! \geq 0 \\
\hline
\end{array}
$$

Fig. 13.1 Specification of positive square root

Various conventions are employed within Z specification: for example, v? indicates that v is an input variable, and v! indicates that v is an output variable. The variable num? is an input variable, and $root$! is an output variable in the square root schema above. The notation Ξ Op in a schema indicates that the operation Op does not affect the state, whereas the notation ΔOp in the schema indicates that Op is an operation that affects the state.

Many of the data types employed in Z have no counterpart in standard programming languages. It is therefore important to identify and describe the concrete data structures that ultimately will represent the abstract mathematical structures. As the concrete structures may differ from the abstract, the operations on the abstract data structures may need to be refined to yield operations on the concrete data that yield equivalent results. For simple systems, direct refinement (i.e. one step from abstract specification to implementation) may be possible; in more complex systems, deferred refinement[1] is employed, where a sequence of increasingly concrete specifications are produced to yield the executable specification. There is a calculus for combining schemas to make larger specifications, and this is discussed later in the chapter.

Example 13.1 The following is a Z specification to borrow a book from a library system. The library is made up of books that are on the shelf; books that are borrowed; and books that are missing. The specification models a library with sets representing books on the shelf, on loan or missing. These are three mutually disjoint subsets of the set of books *Bkd-Id*. The system state is defined in the *Library* schema (Fig. 13.2), and operations such as *Borrow* and *Return* affect the state. The *Borrow* operation is specified in Fig. 13.3.

The notation $\mathbb{P}Bkd\text{-}Id$ is used to represent the power set of *Bkd-Id* (i.e. the set of all subsets of *Bkd-Id*). The disjointness condition for the library is expressed by the requirement that the pairwise intersection of the subsets *on-shelf, borrowed and missing* is the empty set.

The precondition for the *Borrow* operation is that this book must be available on the shelf to borrow. The post-condition is that the borrowed book is added to the set of borrowed books and is removed from the books on the shelf.

Z has been successfully applied in industry including the CICS project at IBM Hursley in the UK.[2] Next, we describe key parts of Z including sets, relations, functions, sequences and bags.

---

[1]Stepwise refinement involves producing a sequence of increasingly more concrete specifications until eventually the executable code is produced. Each refinement step has associated proof obligations to prove that the refinement step is valid.

[2]This project claimed a 9% increase in productivity attributed to the use of formal methods.

```
┌─Library──────
│ on-shelf, missing, borrowed : ℙ Bkd-Id
├──────────────
│ on-shelf ∩ missing = ∅
│ on-shelf ∩ borrowed = ∅
│ borrowed ∩ missing = ∅
└──────────────
```

Fig. 13.2 Specification of a library system

```
┌─Borrow──────
│ Δ Library
│ b? :Bkd-Id
├──────────────
│ b? ∈ on-shelf
│ on-shelf' = on-shelf \ {b?}
│ borrowed' = borrowed ∪ {b?}
└──────────────
```

Fig. 13.3 Specification of borrow operation

13.2 Sets

A set is a collection of well-defined objects, and this section focuses on their use in Z. Sets may be enumerated by listing all of their elements. Thus, the set of all even natural numbers less than or equal to 10 is as follows:

$$\{2, 4, 6, 8, 10\}$$

Sets may be created from other sets using set comprehension, i.e. stating the properties that its members must satisfy. For example, the set of even natural numbers less than or equal to 10 is given by set comprehension as follows:

$$\{n : \mathbb{N} | n \neq 0 \wedge n \leq 10 \wedge n \bmod 2 = 0 \cdot n\}$$

There are three main parts to the set comprehension above. The first part is the signature of the set, and this is given by n:$\mathbb{N}$. The first part is separated from the second part by a vertical line. The second part is given by a predicate, and for this example, the predicate is $n \neq 0 \wedge n \leq 10 \wedge n \bmod 2 = 0$. The second part is separated from the third part by a bullet. The third part is a term, and for this example, it is simply n. The term is often a more complex expression, e.g. $\log(n^2)$.

In mathematics, there is just one empty set ∅. However, there is an empty set for each type of set in Z (as Z is a typed language), and so there are an infinite number of empty sets in Z. The empty set is written as ∅ [X] where X is the type of the empty set. However, in practice, X is omitted when the type is clear.

Various set operations such as union, intersection, set difference and symmetric difference are employed in Z. The power set of a set X is the set of all subsets of X, and it is denoted by $\mathbb{P}X$. The set of non-empty subsets of X is denoted by $\mathbb{P}_1X$ where

$$\mathbb{P}_1X == \{U : \mathbb{P}X | U \neq \varnothing\,[X]\}$$

A finite set of elements of type X (denoted by F X) is a subset of X that cannot be put into a one to one correspondence with a proper subset of itself. That is:

$$F\,X == \{U : \mathbb{P}\,X \mid \neg \exists V : \mathbb{P}\,U \bullet V \neq U \wedge (\exists f{:}V \rightarrowtail U)\}$$

The expression $f{:}V \rightarrowtail U$ denotes that f is a bijection from U to V, and injective, surjective and bijective functions are discussed in [2].

The fact that Z is a typed language means that whenever a variable is introduced (e.g. in quantification with $\forall$ and $\exists$), it is first declared. For example, $\forall j{:}J \cdot P \Rightarrow Q$. There is also the unique existential quantifier $\exists_1 j{:}J|P$ which states that there is exactly one j of type J that has property P.

13.3 Relations

Relations are used extensively in Z, and a relation R between X and Y is any subset of the Cartesian product of X and Y, i.e., $R \subseteq (X \times Y)$. A relation in Z is denoted by R: $X \leftrightarrow Y$, and the notation $x \mapsto y$ indicates that the pair $(x, y) \in R$.

Consider the relation *home_owner: Person* $\leftrightarrow$ *Home* that exists between people and their homes. An entry *daphne* $\mapsto$ *mandalay* $\in$ *home_owner* if *daphne* is the owner of *mandalay*. It is possible for a person to own more than one home:

$$rebecca \mapsto nirvana \in home\_owner$$
$$rebecca \mapsto tivoli \in home\_owner$$

It is possible for two people to share ownership of a home:

$$rebecca \mapsto nirvana \in home\_owner$$
$$lawrence \mapsto nirvana \in home\_owner$$

There may be some people who do not own a home, and there is no entry for these people in the relation *home_owner*. The type *Person* includes every possible person, and the type *Home* includes every possible home. The domain of the relation *home_owner* is given by:

$$x \in \text{dom } home\_owner \Leftrightarrow \exists h : Home \cdot x \mapsto h \in home\_owner.$$

The range of the relation *home_owner* is given by:

$$h \in \text{ran} \, home\_owner \Leftrightarrow \exists x : Person \cdot x \mapsto h \in home\_owner.$$

The composition of two relations *home_owner*: *Person* ↔ *Home* and *home_-value*: *Home* ↔ *Value* yields the relation *owner_wealth*: *Person* ↔ *Value* and is given by the relational composition *home_owner; home_value* where

$$p \mapsto v \in home\_owner; home\_value \Leftrightarrow$$
$$(\exists h : Home \cdot p \mapsto h \in home\_owner \wedge h \mapsto v \in home\_value)$$

The relational composition may also be expressed as:

$$owner\_wealth = home\_value \circ home\_owner$$

The union of two relations often arises in practice. Suppose a new entry *aisling* ↦ *muckross* is to be added. Then, this is given by

$$home\_owner' = home\_owner \cup \{aisling \mapsto muckross\}$$

Suppose that we are interested in knowing all females who are house owners. Then, we restrict the relation *home_owner* so that the first element of all ordered pairs has to be female. Consider *female*: $\mathbb{P}$ *Person* with $\{aisling, rebecca\} \subseteq$ *female*.

$$home\_owner = \{aisling \mapsto muckross, rebecca \mapsto nirvana,$$
$$lawrence \mapsto nirvana\}$$

$$female \lhd home\_owner = \{aisling \mapsto muckross, \ rebecca \mapsto nirvana\}$$

That is, *female* ⊲ *home_owner* is a relation that is a subset of *home_owner*, such that the first element of each ordered pair in the relation is female. The operation ⊲ is termed domain restriction, and its fundamental property is:

$$x \mapsto y \in U \lhd R \Leftrightarrow (x \in U \wedge x \mapsto y \in R\}$$

where R: X ↔ Y and *U*: $\mathbb{P}$X.

There is also a domain anti-restriction (subtraction) operation, and its fundamental property is:

$$x \mapsto y \in U \ntriangleleft R \Leftrightarrow (x \notin U \wedge x \mapsto y \in R\}$$

where R: X ↔ Y and *U*: $\mathbb{P}$X.

There are also range restriction (the ▷ operator) and the range anti-restriction operator (the ⋫operator). These are discussed in [1].

13.4 Functions

A function is an association between objects of some type X and objects of another type Y such that given an object of type X, there exists only one object in Y associated with that object [1]. A function is a set of ordered pairs where the first element of the ordered pair has at most one element associated with it. A function is therefore a special type of relation, and a function may be *total* or *partial*.

A total function has exactly one element in Y associated with each element of X, whereas a partial function has at most one element of Y associated with each element of X (there may be elements of X that have no element of Y associated with them). A partial function from X to Y ($f: X \nrightarrow Y$) is a relation $f: X \leftrightarrow Y$ such that:

$$\forall x : X; y, z : Y \cdot (x \mapsto y \in f \wedge x \mapsto z \in f \Rightarrow y = z)$$

The association between x and y is denoted by $f(x) = y$, and this indicates that the value of the partial function f at x is y. A total function from X to Y (denoted $f: X \rightarrow Y$) is a partial function such that every element in X is associated with some value of Y.

$$f : X \rightarrow Y \Leftrightarrow f : X \nrightarrow Y \wedge \mathrm{dom} f = X$$

Clearly, every total function is a partial function but not vice versa.

```
-TempMap-----------
CityList : PCity
temp : City ⇸ Z
-------------------
dom temp = CityList
```

One operation that arises quite frequently in specifications is the function override operation. Consider the specification of a temperature map above and an example temperature map given by $temp = \{Cork \mapsto 17,\ Dublin \mapsto 19,\ London \mapsto 15\}$. Then, consider the problem of updating the temperature map if a new temperature reading is made in Cork, e.g. $\{Cork \mapsto 18\}$. Then, the new temperature chart is obtained from the old temperature chart by function override to yield $\{Cork \mapsto 18,\ Dublin \mapsto 19,\ London \mapsto 15\}$. This is written as follows:

$$temp' = temp \oplus \{Cork \mapsto 18\}$$

The function override operation combines two functions of the same type to give a new function of the same type. The effect of the override operation is that the entry $\{Cork \mapsto 17\}$ is removed from the temperature chart and replaced with the entry $\{Cork \mapsto 18\}$.

Suppose $f, g: X \nrightarrow Y$ are partial functions, then $f \oplus g$ is defined and indicates that f is overridden by g. It is defined as follows:

$$(f \oplus g)(x) = g(x) \text{where} \, x \in \operatorname{dom} g$$
$$(f \oplus g)(x) = f(x) \text{where} \, x \notin \operatorname{dom} g \wedge x \in \operatorname{dom} f$$

This may also be expressed (using domain anti-restriction) as follows:

$$f \oplus g = ((\operatorname{dom} g) \lhd f) \cup g$$

There is notation in Z for injective, surjective and bijective functions. An injective function is one to one, i.e.

$$f(x) = f(y) \Rightarrow x = y$$

A surjective function is onto, i.e.

Given $y \in Y$, $\exists x \in X$ such that $f(x) = y$

A bijective function is one to one and onto, and it indicates that the sets X and Y can be put into one to one correspondence with one another. Z includes lambda calculus notation (λ calculus is discussed in [2]) to define functions. For example, the function cube $= \lambda x{:}\mathbf{N} \cdot x * x * x$. Function composition is $f; g$ is similar to relational composition.

13.5 Sequences

The type of all sequences of elements drawn from a set X is denoted by seq X. Sequences are written as $\langle x_1, x_2, \ldots x_n \rangle$, and the empty sequence is denoted by $\langle \rangle$. Sequences may be used to specify the changing state of a variable over time, with each element of the sequence representing the value of the variable at a discrete time instance.

Sequences are functions, and a sequence of elements drawn from a set X is a finite function from the set of natural numbers to X. A finite partial function f from X to Y is denoted by $f{:} X \nrightarrow Y$.

A finite sequence of elements of X is given by $f{:} \mathbf{N} \nrightarrow X$, and the domain of the function consists of all numbers between 1 and $\#f$ (where $\#f$ is the cardinality of f). It is defined formally as follows:

$$\operatorname{seq} X == \{f{:} \mathbf{N} \nrightarrow X \mid \operatorname{dom} f = 1 .. \#f \bullet f\}$$

The sequence $\langle x_1, x_2, \ldots x_n \rangle$ above is given by:

$$\{1 \mapsto x_1, 2 \mapsto x_2, \ldots n \mapsto x_n\}$$

There are various functions to manipulate sequences. These include the sequence concatenation operation. Suppose $\sigma = \langle x_1, x_2, \ldots x_n \rangle$ and $\tau = \langle y_1, y_2, \ldots y_m \rangle$, then:

$$\sigma \cap \tau = \langle x_1, x_2, \ldots x_n, y_1, y_2, \ldots y_m \rangle$$

The head of a non-empty sequence gives the first element of the sequence:

$$\text{heads } \sigma = \text{head}\langle x_1, x_2, \ldots x_n \rangle = x_1$$

The tail of a non-empty sequence is the same sequence except that the first element of the sequence is removed:

$$\text{tail } \sigma = \text{tail}\langle x_1, x_2, \ldots x_n \rangle = \langle x_2, \ldots x_n \rangle$$

Suppose $f\colon X \to Y$ and a sequence $\sigma\colon \text{seq } X$, then the function map applies f to each element of σ:

$$\text{map} f \sigma = \text{map} f \langle x_1, x_2, \ldots x_n \rangle = \langle f(x_1), f(x_2), \ldots f(x_n) \rangle$$

The map function may also be expressed via function composition as:

$$\text{map} f \; \sigma = \sigma; f$$

The reverse order of a sequence is given by the rev function:

$$\text{rev } \sigma = \text{rev}\langle x_1, x_2, \ldots x_n \rangle = \langle x_n, \ldots x_2, x_1 \rangle$$

13.6 Bags

A bag is similar to a set except that there may be multiple occurrences of each element in the bag. A bag of elements of type X is defined as a partial function from the type of the elements of the bag to positive whole numbers. The definition of a bag of type X is:

$$\text{bag } X = X \nrightarrow \mathbb{N}_1.$$

For example, a bag of marbles may contain 3 blue marbles, 2 red marbles and 1 green marble. This is denoted by B = [−b, b, b, g, r, r]. The bag of marbles is thus denoted by:

$$\text{bag } Marble = Marble \nrightarrow \mathbb{N}_1.$$

The function count determines the number of occurrences of an element in a bag. For the example above, count *Marble b* = 3 and count *Marble y* = 0 since there are no yellow marbles in the bag. This is defined formally as follows:

$$\text{count bag}\,X\,y = 0 \qquad\qquad y \notin \text{bag X}$$
$$\text{count bag}\,X\,y = (\text{bag}\,X)(y) \quad y \in \text{bag X}$$

An element y is in bag X if and only if y is in the domain of bag X:

$$y \text{ in bag}\,X \Leftrightarrow y \in \text{dom}(\text{bag}\,X)$$

The union of two bags of marbles $B_1 = [b, b, b, g, r, r]$ and $B_2 = [b, g, r, y]$ is given by $B_1 \uplus B_2 = [b, b, b, b, g, g, r, r, y]$. It is defined formally as follows:

$$(B_1 \uplus B_2)(y) = B_2(y) \qquad y \notin \text{dom}\,B_1 \wedge y \in \text{dom}\,B_2$$
$$(B_1 \uplus B_2)(y) = B_1(y) \qquad y \in \text{dom}\,B_1 \wedge y \notin \text{dom}\,B_2$$
$$(B_1 \uplus B_2)(y) = B_1(y) + B_2(y) \quad y \in \text{dom}\,B_1 \wedge y \in \text{dom}\,B_2$$

A bag may be used to record the number of occurrences of each product in a warehouse as part of an inventory system. It may model the number of items remaining for each product in a vending machine (Fig. 13.4).

The operation of a vending machine would require other operations such as identifying the set of acceptable coins, checking that the customer has entered sufficient coins to cover the cost of the good, returning change to the customer and updating the quantity on hand of each good after a purchase. A detailed account is in [1].

13.7   Schemas and Schema Composition

The Z specification is presented in visually striking boxes called schemas. These are used for specifying states and state transitions, and they employ notation to represent the before and after state (e.g. s and s' where s' represents the after state of s). They group all relevant information that belongs to a state description.

There are a number of useful schema operations such as schema inclusion, schema composition and the use of propositional connectives to link schemas together. The Δ convention indicates that the operation affects the state, whereas the Ξ convention indicates that the state is not affected. These conventions allow complex operations to be specified concisely and assist with the readability of the

$$
\begin{array}{|l}
\hline
-\Delta Vending\ Machine\text{------} \\
stock : \text{bag}\ Good \\
price : Good \rightarrow \mathbb{N}_1 \\
\hline
\text{dom}\ stock \subseteq \text{dom}\ price \\
\hline
\end{array}
$$

Fig. 13.4 Specification of vending machine using bags

specification. Schema composition is analogous to relational composition and allows new schemas to be derived from existing schemas.

A schema name S_1 may be included in the declaration part of another schema S_2. The effect of the inclusion is that the declarations in S_1 are now part of S_2 and the predicates of S_1 are S_2 are joined together by conjunction. If the same variable is defined in both S_1 and S_2, then it must be of the same type in both.

$$
\begin{array}{|l}
\hline
-S_1\text{---} \\
x, y : \mathbb{N} \\
\hline
x + y > 2 \\
\hline
\end{array}
\qquad
\begin{array}{|l}
\hline
-S_2\text{---} \\
S_1 \, ; z : \mathbb{N} \\
\hline
z = x + y \\
\hline
\end{array}
$$

The result is that S_2 includes the declarations and predicates of S_1 (Fig. 13.5):

Two schemas may be linked by propositional connectives such as $S_1 \wedge S_2$, $S_1 \vee S_2$, $S_1 \Rightarrow S_2$, and $S_1 \Leftrightarrow S_2$. The schema $S_1 \vee S_2$ is formed by merging the declaration parts of S_1 and S_2 and then combining their predicates by the logical $\vee$ operator. For example, $S = S_1 \vee S_2$ yields as shown in Fig. 13.6.

Schema inclusion and the linking of schemas use normalization to convert subtypes to maximal types, and predicates are employed to restrict the maximal type to the subtype. This involves replacing declarations of variables (e.g. u: 1.35 with u:Z, and adding the predicate $u > 0$ and $u < 36$ to the predicate part). The Δ and Ξ conventions are used extensively, where the notation $\Delta TempMap$ is used in the specification of schemas that involve a change of state.

$$\Delta TempMap = TempMap \wedge TempMap'$$

The longer form of $\Delta TempMap$ is written as follows:

$$
\begin{array}{|l}
\hline
-\Delta TempMap\text{---} \\
CityList,\ CityList' : \mathbb{P}\ City \\
temp,\ temp' : City \nrightarrow Z \\
\hline
\mathrm{dom}\ temp = CityList \\
\mathrm{dom}\ temp' = CityList' \\
\hline
\end{array}
$$

The notation $\Xi\ TempMap$ is used in the specification of operations that do not involve a change to the state.

$$
\begin{array}{|l}
\hline
-\Xi\ TempMap\text{---} \\
\Delta TempMap \\
\hline
CityList = CityList' \\
temp = temp' \\
\hline
\end{array}
$$

$$
\begin{array}{|l}
\hline
-S_2\text{---}\\
x,y : \mathbb{N}\\
z : \mathbb{N}\\
\hline
x + y > 2\\
z = x + y\\
\hline
\end{array}
$$

Fig. 13.5 Schema inclusion

$$
\begin{array}{|l}
\hline
-S\text{---}\\
x,y : \mathbb{N}\\
z : \mathbb{N}\\
\hline
x + y > 2 \vee z = x + y\\
\hline
\end{array}
$$

Fig. 13.6 Merging schemas ($S_1 \vee S_2$)

Schema composition is analogous to relational composition, and it allows new specifications to be built from existing ones. It allows the after state variables of one schema to be related with the before variables of another schema. The composition of two schemas S and T (S; T) is described in detail in [1] and involves 4 steps (Table 13.1):

The example below should make schema composition clearer. Consider the composition of S and T where S and T are defined as follows:

$$
\begin{array}{|l}
\hline
-S\text{---}\\
x,x',y? : \mathbb{N}\\
\hline
x' = y? - 2\\
\hline
\end{array}
\qquad
\begin{array}{|l}
\hline
-T\text{---}\\
x,x' : \mathbb{N}\\
\hline
x' = x + 1\\
\hline
\end{array}
$$

$$
\begin{array}{|l}
\hline
-S_1\text{---}\\
x,x^+,y? : \mathbb{N}\\
\hline
x^+ = y? - 2\\
\hline
\end{array}
\qquad
\begin{array}{|l}
\hline
-T_1\text{---}\\
x^+,x' : \mathbb{N}\\
\hline
x' = x^+ + 1\\
\hline
\end{array}
$$

Table 13.1 Schema composition

Step	Procedure
1.	Rename all *after* state variables in S to something new: S $[s^+/s']$
2.	Rename all *before* state variables in T to the same new thing, i.e. T $[s^+/s]$
3.	Form the conjunction of the two new schemas: S $[s^+/s'] \wedge$ T $[s^+/s]$
4.	Hide the variable introduced in step 1 and 2. S; T = (S $[s^+/s'] \wedge$ T $[s^+/s])\backslash(s^+)$

$$
\left|
\begin{array}{l}
\text{-}S_1 \wedge T_1 \underline{\quad\quad} \\
x,x^+,x\,',y? : \mathbb{N} \\
\hline
x^+ = y? - 2 \\
x\,' = x^+ + 1 \\
\hline
\end{array}
\right.
\qquad
\left|
\begin{array}{l}
\text{-}S ; T\underline{\quad\quad} \\
x, x\,',\, y? \ : \mathbb{N} \\
\hline
\exists x^+ : \mathbb{N} \bullet \\
\quad (x^+ = y? - 2 \\
\quad\;\; x\,' = x^+ + 1) \\
\hline
\end{array}
\right.
$$

Fig. 13.7 Schema composition

S_1 and T_1 represent the results of step 1 and step 2, with x' renamed to x^+ in S, and x renamed to x^+ in T. Step 3 and step 4 yield as shown in Fig. 13.7.

Schema composition is useful as it allows new specifications to be created from existing ones.

13.8 Reification and Decomposition

A Z specification involves defining the state of the system and then specifying the required operations. The Z specification language employs many constructs that are not part of conventional programming languages, and a Z specification is therefore not directly executable on a computer. A programmer implements the formal specification, and mathematical proof may be employed to prove that a program meets its specification.

Often, there is a need to write an intermediate specification that is between the original Z specification and the eventual program code. This intermediate specification is more algorithmic and uses less abstract data types than the Z specification. The intermediate specification needs to be correct with respect to the specification, and the program needs to be correct with respect to the intermediate specification. The intermediate specification is a refinement (reification) of the state of the specification, and the operations of the specification have been decomposed into those of the intermediate specification.

The representation of an abstract data type such as a set by a sequence is termed data reification, and data reification is concerned with the process of transforming an abstract data type into a concrete data type. The abstract and concrete data types are related by the retrieve function, and the retrieve function maps the concrete data type to the abstract data type. There are typically several possible concrete data types for a particular abstract data type (i.e. refinement is a relation), whereas there is one abstract data type for a concrete data type (i.e. retrieval is a function). For example, sets are often refined to unique sequences; however, more than one unique sequence can represent a set, whereas a unique sequence represents exactly one set.

The operations defined on the concrete data type are related to the operations defined on the abstract data type. That is, the commuting diagram property is required to hold (Fig. 13.8). That is, for an operation □ on the concrete data type to

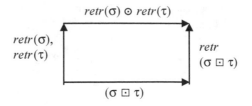

Fig. 13.8 Refinement commuting diagram

correctly model the operation ⊙ on the abstract data type, the commuting diagram property must hold. That is, it is required to prove that:

$$ret(\sigma\Box\tau) = (ret\ \sigma) \odot (ret\ \tau)$$

In Z, the refinement and decomposition are done with schemas. It is required to prove that the concrete schema is a valid refinement of the abstract schema, and this gives rise to a number of proof obligations. It needs to be proved that the initial states correspond to one another; that each operation in the concrete schema is correct with respect to the operation in the abstract schema; and also that it is applicable (i.e. whenever the abstract operation may be performed, the concrete operation may also be performed).

13.9   Proof in Z

Mathematicians perform rigorous proof of theorems using technical and natural language. Logicians employ formal proofs to prove theorems using propositional and predicate calculus. Formal proofs generally involve a long chain of reasoning with every step of the proof justified. Rigorous proofs involve precise reasoning using a mixture of natural and mathematical language. Rigorous proofs [1] have been described as being analogous to high-level programming languages, with formal proofs analogous to machine language.

A mathematical proof includes natural language and mathematical symbols, and often many of the tedious details of the proof are omitted. Many proofs in formal methods such as Z are concerned with cross-checking on the details of the specification, or on the validity of the refinement step, or proofs that certain properties are satisfied by the specification. There are often many tedious lemmas to be proved, and tool support is essential as proof by hand often contains errors or jumps in reasoning. Machine proofs are lengthy and largely unreadable; however, they provide extra confidence as every step in the proof is justified. The proof of various properties about the programs increases confidence in its correctness.

13.10   Review Questions

1. Describe the main features of the Z specification language.
2. Explain the difference between $\mathbb{P}_1 X$, $\mathbb{P}X$ and FX.
3. Explain the three main parts of set comprehension in Z. Give examples.
4. Discuss the applications of Z. What problems have arisen?
5. Give examples to illustrate the use of domain and range restriction operators and domain and range anti-restriction operators with relations in Z.
6. Give examples to illustrate relational composition.
7. Explain the difference between a partial and total function, and give examples to illustrate function override.
8. Give examples to illustrate the various operations on sequences including concatenation, head, tail, map and reverse operations.
9. Give examples to illustrate the various operations on bags.
10. Discuss the nature of proof in Z and tools to support proof.
11. Explain the process of refining an abstract schema to a more concrete representation, the proof obligations and the commuting diagram property.

13.11   Summary

Z is a formal specification language that was developed in the early 1980s at Oxford University in England. It has been employed in both industry and academia, and it was used successfully on the IBM's CICS project at Hursley. Its specifications are mathematical, and this allows properties to be proved about the specification, and any gaps or inconsistencies in the specification may be identified.

Z is a "and an explicit model" approach and an explicit model of the state of an abstract machine is given, and the operations are defined in terms of their effect on the state. Its main features include a mathematical notation that is similar to VDM and the schema calculus. The latter consists essentially of boxes that are used to describe operations and states.

The schemas are used as building blocks to form larger specifications, and they are a powerful means of decomposing a specification into smaller pieces. This helps with the readability of Z specifications, since each schema is small in size and self-contained.

Z is a highly expressive specification language, and it includes notation for sets, functions, relations, bags, sequences, predicate calculus, and schema calculus. Z specifications are not directly executable, as many of its data types and constructs are not part of modern programming languages. A programmer implements the formal specification, and mathematical proof may be employed to prove that a program meets its specification.

Often, there is a need to write an intermediate specification that is between the original Z specification and the eventual program code. This intermediate specification is more algorithmic and uses less abstract data types than the Z specification. The intermediate specification needs to be correct with respect to the specification, and the program needs to be correct with respect to the intermediate specification. The intermediate specification is a refinement (reification) of the state of the specification, and the operations of the specification have been decomposed into those of the intermediate specification.

Therefore, there is a need to refine the Z specification into a more concrete representation and prove that the refinement is valid. The refinement and decomposition are done with schemas, and it is required to prove that the concrete schema is a valid refinement of the abstract schema. This gives rise to a number of proof obligations, and it needs to be shown that each operation in the concrete schema is correct with respect to the operation in the abstract schema.

References

1. A. Diller, Z. *An Introduction to Formal Methods* (John Wiley and Sons, England, 1990)
2. G. O'Regan, *Guide to Discrete Mathematics* (Springer, 2016)

Unified Modelling Language

14

Abstract

This chapter presents the unified modelling language (UML), which is a visual modelling language for software systems, and it is used to present several views of the system architecture. It was developed at rational corporation as a notation for modelling object-oriented systems. We present various UML diagrams such as use case diagrams, sequence diagrams and activity diagrams.

Keywords

Use case diagrams · Classes and objects · Sequence diagrams · Activity diagrams · State diagrams · Collaboration diagrams · Object constraint language · Rational unified process

14.1 Introduction

The unified modelling language (UML) is a visual modelling language for software systems. It was developed by Jim Rumbaugh, Grady Booch and Ivar Jacobson [1] at rational corporation (now part of IBM), as a notation for modelling object-oriented systems. It provides a visual means of specifying, constructing and documenting object-oriented systems, and it facilitates the understanding of the architecture of the system, and in managing the complexity of a large system.

The language was strongly influenced by three existing methods: the object modelling technique (OMT) developed by Rumbaught, the *Booch Method* developed by Booch and object-oriented software engineering (OOSE) developed by Jacobson. UML unifies and improves upon these methods, and it has become a popular formal approach to modelling software systems.

© Springer International Publishing AG 2017
G. O'Regan, *Concise Guide to Software Engineering*, Undergraduate Topics in Computer Science, DOI 10.1007/978-3-319-57750-0_14

Models provide a better understanding of the system to be developed, and a UML model allows the system to be visualized prior to its implementation, and it simplifies the underlying reality. Large complex systems are difficult to understand in their entirety, and the use of a UML model is an aid to abstracting and simplifying complexity. The choice of the model is fundamental, and a good model will provide a good insight into the system. Models need to be explored and tested to ensure their adequacy as a representation of the system. Models simplify the reality, but it is important to ensure that the simplification does not exclude any important details. The chosen model affects the view of the system, and different roles require different viewpoints of the proposed system.

An architect will design a house prior to its construction, and the blueprints will contain details of the plan of each room, as well as plans for electricity and plumbing. That is, the plans for a house include floor plans, electrical plans and plumping plans. These plans provide different viewpoints of the house to be constructed and are used to provide estimates of the time and materials required to construct it.

A database developer will often focus on entity-relationship models, whereas a systems analyst may focus on algorithmic models. An object-oriented developer will focus on classes and on the interactions of classes. Often, there is a need to view the system at different levels of detail, and no single model in itself is sufficient for this. This leads to the development of a small number of interrelated models.

UML provides a formal model to the system, and it allows the same information to be presented in several ways, and at different levels of detail. The requirements of the system are expressed in terms of use cases; the design view captures the problem space and solution space; the process view models the systems processes; the implementation view addresses the implementation of the system, and the deployment view models the physical deployment of the system.

There are several UML diagrams providing different viewpoints of the system, and these provide the blueprint of the software.

14.2   Overview of UML

UML is an expressive graphical modelling language for visualizing, specifying, constructing and documenting a software system. It provides several views of the software's architecture, and it has a clearly defined syntax and semantics. Each stakeholder (e.g. project manager, developers and testers) has a different perspective and looks at the system in different ways at different times during the project. UML is a way to model the software system before implementing it in a programming language.

A UML specification consists of precise, complete and unambiguous models. The models may be employed to generate code in a programming language such as Java or C++. The reverse is also possible, and so it is possible to work with either the graphical notation of UML or the textual notation of a programming language. UML expresses things that are best expressed graphically, whereas a programming language expresses things that are best expressed textually, and tools are employed to keep both views consistent. UML may be employed to document the software system, and it has been employed in several domains including the banking sector, defence and telecommunications.

The use of UML requires an understanding of its basic building blocks, the rules for combining the building blocks and the common mechanisms that apply throughout the language. There are three kinds of building blocks employed:

- Things
- Relationships
- Diagrams

Things are the object-oriented building blocks of the UML. They include *structural things, behavioural things, grouping things* and *annotational things* (Table 14.1). Structural things are the nouns of the UML models, behavioural things are the dynamic parts and represent behaviour and their interactions over time, grouping things are the organization parts of UML, and annotation things are the explanatory parts. Things, relationships and diagrams are all described graphically and are discussed in detail in [1].

Table 14.1 Classification of UML things

Thing	Kind	Description
Structural	Class	A class is a description of a set of objects that share the same attributes and operations
	Interface	An interface is a collection of operations that specify a service of a class or component. It specifies externally visible behaviour of the element
	Collaboration	A collaboration defines an interaction between software objects
	Use case	A use case is a set of actions that define the interaction between an actor and the system to achieve a particular goal
	Active class	An active class is used to describe concurrent behaviour of a system
	Component	A component is used to represent any part of a system for which UML diagrams are made
	Node	A node is used to represent a physical part of the system (e.g. server and network)
Behavioural	Interaction	These comprise interactions (message exchange between components) expressed as sequence diagrams or collaboration diagrams
	State machine	A state machine is used to describe different states of system components
Grouping	Packages	These are the organization parts of UML models. A package organizes elements into groups and is a way to organize a UML model
Annotation		These are the explanatory parts (notes) of UML

There are four kinds of relationship in UML:

- Dependency
- Association
- Generalization
- Extensibility

Dependency is used to represent a relationship between two elements of a system, in which a change to one thing affects the other thing (dependent thing). *Association* describes how elements in the UML diagram are associated and describes a set of connections among elements in a system. *Aggregation* is an association that represents a structural relationship between a whole and its parts. A *generalization* is a parent–child relationship in which the objects of the specialized element (child) are substituted for objects of the generalized element (the parent). *Extensibility* refers to a mechanism to extend the power of the language to represent extra behaviour of the system. Next, we describe the key UML diagrams.

14.3   UML Diagrams

The UML diagrams provide a graphical visualization of the system from different viewpoints, and we present several key UML diagrams in Table 14.2.

Table 14.2 UML diagrams

Diagram	Description
Class	A class is a key building block of any objected-oriented system. The class diagram shows the classes, their attributes and operations, and the relationships between them
Object	This shows a set of objects and their relationships. An object diagram is an instance of a class diagram
Use case	These show the actors in the system and the different functions that they require from the system
Sequence	These diagrams show how objects interact with each other, and the order in which the interactions occur
Collaboration	This is an interaction diagram that emphasizes the structural organization of objects that send and receive messages
State chart	These describe the behaviour of objects that act differently according to the state that they are in
Activity	This diagram is used to illustrate the flow of control in a system (it is similar to a flow chart)
Component	This diagram shows the structural relationship of components of a software system and their relationships/interfaces
Deployment	This diagram is used for visualizing the deployment view of a system and shows the hardware of the system and the software on the hardware

The concept of class and objects are taken from object-oriented design, and classes are the most important building block of any object-oriented system. A class is a set of objects that share the same attributes, operations, relationships and semantics [1]. Classes may represent software things and hardware things. For example, walls, doors and windows are all classes, whereas individual doors and windows are objects. A class represents a set of objects rather than an individual object.

Automated bank teller machines (ATMs) include two key classes: Customers and Accounts. The class definition includes both the data structure for Customers and Accounts, and the operations on Customers and Accounts. These include operations to add or remove a Customer, operations to debit or credit an Account, or to transfer from one Account to another. There are several instances of Customers and Accounts, and these are the actual Customers of the bank and their Accounts.

Every class has a name (e.g. Customer and Account) to distinguish it from other classes. There will generally be several objects associated with the class. The class diagram describes the name of the class, its attributes and its operations. An attribute represents some property of the class that is shared by all objects; for example, the attributes of the class "Customer" are name and address. Attributes are listed below the class name, and the operations are listed below the attributes. The operations may be applied to any object in the class. The responsibilities of a class may also be included in the definition (Table 14.3).

Class diagrams typically include various relationships between classes. In practice, very few classes are stand alone, and most collaborate with others in various ways. The relationship between classes needs to be considered, and these provide different ways of combining classes to form new classes. The relationships include dependencies (a change to one thing affects the dependent thing), generalizations (these link generalized classes to their specializations in a subclass/superclass relationship) and associations (these represent structural relationships among objects).

A dependency is a relationship that states that a change in the specification of one thing affects the dependent thing. It is indicated by a dashed line (——— >). Generalizations allow a child class to be created from one or more parent classes (single inheritance or multiple inheritance). A class that has no parents is termed a base class (e.g. consider the base class Shape with three children: Rectangle, Circle and Polygon, and where Rectangle has one child namely Square). Generalization is indicated by a solid directed line that points to the parent (——— ►). Association is a

Table 14.3 Simple class diagram	Customer	Account
	Name: String	Balance:Real
	Address: String	Type:String
	Add()	Debit()
	Remove()	Credit()
		CheckBal()
		Transfer()

Fig. 14.1 Simple object
diagram

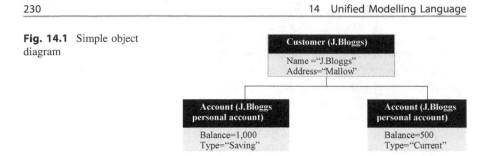

structural relationship that specifies that objects of one thing are connected to objects of another thing. It is indicated by a solid line connecting the same or different classes.

The object diagram (Fig. 14.1) shows a set of objects and their relationships at a point of time. It is related to the class diagram in that the object is an instance of the class. The ATM example above had two classes (Customers and Accounts), and the objects of these classes are the actual Customers and their corresponding Accounts. Each Customer may have several Accounts, and the names and addresses of the Customers are detailed as well as the corresponding balance in the Customer's Accounts. There is one instance of the Customer class and two instances of the Account class in this example.

An object has a state that has a given value at each time instance. Operations on the object will typically (with the exception of query operations) change its state. An object diagram contains objects and links to other objects and gives a snapshot of the system at a particular moment of time.

A use case diagram models the dynamic aspects of the system, and it shows a set of use cases and actors and their relationships. It describes scenarios (or sequences of actions) in the system from the user's viewpoint (actor) and shows how the actor interacts with the system. An actor represents the set of roles that a user can play, and the actor may be human or an automated system. Actors are connected to use cases by association, and they may communicate by sending and receiving messages.

A use case diagram shows a set of use cases, with each use case representing a functional requirement. Use cases are employed to model the visible services that the system provides within the context of its environment, and for specifying the requirements of the system as a black box. Each use case carries out some work that is of value to the actor, and the behaviour of the use case is described by the flow of events in text. The description includes the main flow of events for the use case and the exceptional flow of events. These flows may also be represented graphically. There may also be alternate flows and the main flow of the use case. Each sequence is termed a scenario, and a scenario is one instance of a use case.

Use cases provide a way for the end-users and developers to share a common understanding of the system. They may be applied to all or part of the system (subsystem), and the use cases are the basis for development and testing. A use case is represented graphically by an ellipse. The benefits of use cases include:

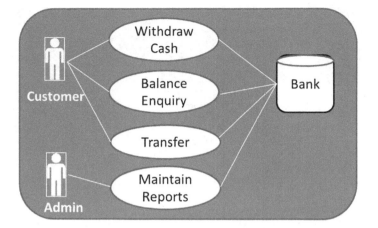

Fig. 14.2 Use case diagram of ATM machine

- Enables the stakeholders (e.g. domain experts, developers, testers and end-users) to share a common understanding of the functional requirements.
- Models the requirements (specifies what the system should do).
- Models the context of a system (identifies actors and their roles)
- May be used for development and testing.

Figure 14.2 presents a simple example of the definition of the use cases for an ATM application. The typical user operations at an ATM machine include the balance enquiry operation, cash withdrawal and the transfer of funds from one Account to another. The actors for the system include "Customer" and "admin," and these actors have different needs and expectations of the system.

The behaviour from the user's viewpoint is described, and the use cases include "withdraw cash," "balance enquiry," "transfer" and "maintain/reports." The use case view includes the actors who are performing the sequence of actions.

The next UML diagram considered is the sequence diagram which models the dynamic aspects of the system and shows the interaction between objects/classes in the system for each use case. The interactions model the flow of control that characterizes the behaviour of the system, and the objects that play a role in the interaction are identified. A sequence diagram emphasizes the time ordering of messages, and the interactions may include messages that are dispatched from object to object, with the messages ordered in sequence by time.

The example in Fig. 14.3 considers the sequences of interactions between objects for the "Balance Enquiry" use case. This sequence diagram is specific to the case of a valid balance enquiry, and a sequence diagram is also needed to handle the exception cases.

The behaviour of the "balance enquiry" operation is evident from the diagram. The Customer inserts the card into the ATM machine, and the PIN number is requested by the ATM. The Customer then enters the number, and the ATM

Fig. 14.3 UML sequence diagram for balance enquiry

machine contacts the bank for verification of the number. The bank confirms the validity of the number, and the Customer then selects the balance enquiry operation. The ATM contacts the bank to request the balance of the particular Account, and the bank sends the details to the ATM machine. The balance is displayed on the screen of the ATM machine. The Customer then withdraws the card. The actual sequence of interactions is evident from the sequence diagram.

The example above has four objects (Customer, ATM, Bank and Account), and these are laid out from left to right at the top of the sequence diagram. Collaboration diagrams are interaction diagrams that consist of objects and their relationships. However, while sequence diagrams emphasize the time ordering of messages, a collaboration diagram emphasizes the structural organization of the objects that send and receive messages. Sequence diagrams and collaboration diagrams may be converted to the other without loss of information. Collaboration diagrams are described in more detail in [1].

The activity diagram is considered in Fig. 14.4, and this diagram is essentially a flow chart showing the flow of control from one activity to another. It is used to model the dynamic aspects of a system, and this involves modelling the sequential and possibly concurrent steps in a computational process. It is different from a sequence diagram in that it shows the flow from activity to activity, whereas a sequence diagram shows the flow from object to object.

State diagrams (also known as state machine diagrams or state charts) show the dynamic behaviour of a class and how an object behaves differently depending on the state that it is in. There is an initial state and a final state, and the operation generally results in a change of state, with the operations resulting in different states being entered and exited. A state diagram is an enhanced version of a finite state machine (as discussed in Chap. 12) Fig. 14.5.

Fig. 14.4 UML activity diagram

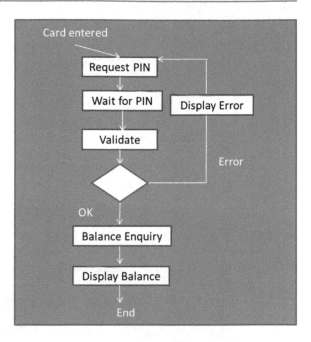

There are several other UML diagrams including component and deployment diagrams. The reader is referred to [1].

Advantages of UML UML offers a rich notation to model software systems and to understand the proposed system from different viewpoints. Its main advantages are shown in Table 14.4.

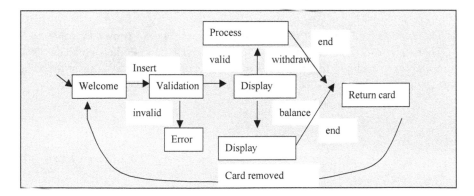

Fig. 14.5 UML state diagram

Table 14.4 Advantages of
UML

Advantages of UML
Visual modelling language with a rich expressive notation
Mechanism to manage complexity of a large system Enables the proposed system to be studied before implementation
Visualization of architecture design of the system
It provides different views of the system
Visualization of system from different viewpoints
Use cases allow the description of typical user behaviour Better understanding of implications of user behaviour
Use cases provide a mechanism to communicate the proposed behaviour of the software system Use cases are the basis of development and testing

14.4   Object Constraint Language

The object constraint language (OCL) is a declarative language that provides a
precise way of describing rules (or expressing constraints) on the UML models.
OCL was originally developed as a business modelling language by Jos Warmer at
IBM, and it was developed further by the Object Management Group (OMG), as
part of a formal specification language extension to UML. It was initially used as
part of UML, but it is now used independently of UML.

OCL is a pure expression language, i.e., there are no side effects as in imperative
programming languages, and the OCL expressions can be used in various places in
the UML model including:

- Specify the initial value of an attribute.
- Specify the body of an operation.
- Specify a condition.

There are several types of OCL constraints including are shown in Table 14.5.

There are various tools available to support OCL, and these include OCL
compilers (or checkers) that provide syntax and consistency checking of the OCL
constraints, and the USE specification environment is based on UML/OCL.

Table 14.5 OCL constraints

OCL constraint	Description
Invariant	A condition that must always be true. An invariant may be placed on an attribute in a class, and this has the effect of restricting the value of the attribute. All instances of the class are required to satisfy the invariant. An invariant is a predicate and is introduced after the keyword **inv**
Precondition	A condition that must be true before the operation is executed. A precondition is a predicate and is introduced after the keyword **pre**
Postcondition	A condition that must be true when the operation has just completed execution. A post-condition is a predicate and is introduced after the keyword **post**
Guard	A condition that must be true before the state transition occurs

14.5 Tools for UML

There are many tools that support UML (mainly developed by IBM/Rational), and a small selection is listed in Table 14.6.

14.6 Rational Unified Process

Software projects need a well-structured software development process to achieve their objectives, and the *Rational Unified Development Software Process* (RUP) [2] is a way to mitigate risk in software development projects. RUP and UML are often used together, and RUP is

- Use case driven
- Architecture centric
- Iterative and incremental

Table 14.6 UML tools

Tool	Description
Requisite pro	Requirements and use case management tool. It provides requirements management and traceability
Rational software modeller (RSM)	Visual modelling and design tool that is used by systems architects/systems analysts to communicate processes, flows and designs
Rational software architect (RSA)	RSA is a tool that enables good architectures to be created
ClearCase/ClearQuest	These are configuration management/change control tools that are used to manage change in the project

It includes iterations, phases, workflows, risk mitigation, quality control, project management and configuration control. Software projects may be complex, and there are risks that requirements may be missed in the process, or that the interpretation of a requirement may differ between the Customer and developer. RUP gathers requirements as use cases, which describe the functional requirements from the point of view of the users of the system.

The use case model describes what the system will do at a high level, and there is a focus on the users in defining the scope the project. Use cases drive the development process, and the developers create a series of design and implementation models that realize the use cases. The developers review each successive model for conformance to the use case model. The testers verify that the implementation model correctly implements the use cases.

The software architecture concept embodies the most significant static and dynamic aspects of the system. The architecture grows out of the use cases and factors such as the platform that the software is to run on, deployment considerations, legacy systems and non-functional requirements.

A commercial software product is a large undertaking, and the work is decomposed into smaller slices or mini-projects, where each mini-project is a manageable chunk. Each mini-project is an iteration that results in an increment to the product (Fig. 14.6).

Iterations refer to the steps in the workflow, and an increment leads to the growth of the product. If the developers need to repeat the iteration, then the organization loses only the misdirected effort of a single iteration, rather than the entire product. Therefore, the unified process is a way to reduce risk in software engineering. The early iterations implement the areas of greatest risk to the project.

RUP consists of four phases, and these are inception, elaboration, construction and transition (Fig. 14.7). Each phase consists of one or more iterations, where each iteration consists of several workflows. The workflows may be requirements,

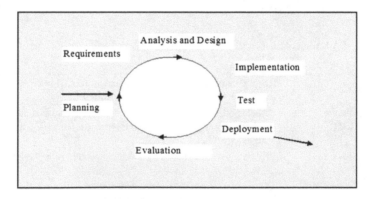

Fig. 14.6 Iteration in rational unified process

Fig. 14.7 Phases and workflows in rational unified process

analysis, design, implementation and test. Each phase terminates in a milestone with one or more project deliverables.

The inception identifies and prioritizes the most important project risks, and it is concerned with initial project planning, cost estimation and early work on the architecture and functional requirements for the product. The elaboration phase specifies most of the use cases in detail. The construction phase is concerned with building the product and implements all agreed use cases. The transition phase covers the period during which the product moves into the Customer site and includes activities such as training Customer personnel, providing helpline assistance and correcting defects found after delivery.

The waterfall lifecycle has the disadvantage that the risk is greater towards the end of the project, where it is costly to undo mistakes from earlier phases. The iterative process develops an increment (i.e. a subset of the system functionality with the waterfall steps applied in the iteration), then another, and so on, and avoids developing the whole system in one step as in the waterfall methodology. That is, the RUP approach is a way to mitigate risk in software development projects.

14.7 Review Questions

1. What is UML? Explain its main features.
2. Explain the difference between an object and a class.
3. Describe the various UML diagrams.
4. What are the advantages and disadvantages of UML?
5. What is the Rational Unified Process?
6. Describe the workflows in a typical iteration of RUP.
7. Describe the phases in the Rational Unified Process.

8. Describe OCL and explain how it is used with UML.
9. Investigate and describe tools to support UML.

14.8   Summary

The unified modelling language is a visual modelling language for software systems, and it facilitates the understanding of the architecture, and management of the complexity of large systems. It was developed by Rumbaugh, Booch and Jacobson as a notation for modelling object-oriented systems and it provides a visual means of specifying, constructing and documenting such systems. It facilitates the understanding of the architecture of the system and in managing its complexity.

UML allows the same information to be presented in several different ways and at different levels of detail. The requirements of the system are expressed in use cases, and other views include the design view that captures the problem space and solution space, the process view which models the systems processes, the implementation view and the deployment view.

The UML diagrams provide different viewpoints of the system and provide the blueprint of the software. These include class and object diagrams, use case diagrams, sequence diagrams, collaboration diagrams, activity diagrams, state charts, collaboration diagrams and deployment diagrams.

The OCL is an expression language, and the OCL expressions may be used in various places in a UML model to specify the initial value of an attribute, the body of an operation or a condition.

RUP consists of four phases, and these are inception, elaboration, construction and transition. Each phase consists of one or more iterations, and the iteration consists of several workflows. The workflows may be requirements, analysis, design, implementation and test. Each phase terminates in a milestone with one or more project deliverables. The RUP approach is a way to mitigate risk in software development project.

References

1. G. Booch, J. Rumbaugh, and I. Jacobson. *The Unified Software Modelling Language User Guide* (Addison-Wesley, New York, 1999)
2. J. Rumbaugh et al., *The Unified Software Development Process* (Addison Wesley, New York, 1999)

Software Process Improvement

15

Abstract

This chapter discusses software process improvement. It begins with a discussion of a software process and discusses the benefits that may be gained from a software process improvement initiative. Various models that support software process improvement are discussed, and these include the Capability Maturity Model Integration (CMMI), ISO 9000, Personal Software Process (PSP) and Team Software Process (TSP).

Keywords

Software process · Software process improvement · Process mapping · Benefits of software process improvement · CMMI · ISO/IEC 15504 (SPICE) · ISO 9000 · PSP and TSP · Root cause analysis · Six sigma

15.1 Introduction

The success of business today is highly influenced by the functionality and quality of the software that it uses. It is essential that the software is safe, reliable, of a high quality and fit for purpose. Companies may develop their own software internally, or they may acquire software solutions off-the-shelf or from bespoke software development. Software development companies need to deliver high-quality and reliable software consistently on time to their customers.

Cost is a key driver in most organizations, and it is essential that software is produced as cheaply and efficiently as possible, and that waste is reduced or eliminated in the software development process. In a nutshell, companies need to produce software that is *better, faster and cheaper* than their competitors in order to survive in the marketplace. Another words, companies need to continuously work

© Springer International Publishing AG 2017
G. O'Regan, *Concise Guide to Software Engineering*, Undergraduate Topics in Computer Science, DOI 10.1007/978-3-319-57750-0_15

smarter to improve their businesses, and to deliver superior solutions to their customers.

Software process improvement initiatives are aligned to business goals and play a key role in helping companies achieve their strategic goals. It is invaluable in the implementation of best practice in organizations and allows companies to focus on fire prevention rather than firefighting. It allows companies to problem solve key issues to eliminate quality problems, and to critically examine their current processes to determine the extent to which they meet its needs, as well as identifying how the processes may be improved and identifying where waste can be minimized or eliminated.

It allows companies to identify the root causes of problems (e.g. using the *five why tool*) and to determine appropriate solutions to the problems. The benefits of successful process improvement include the consistent delivery of high-quality software, improved financial results and increased customer satisfaction.

Software process improvement initiatives lead to a focus on the process and on ways to improve it. Many problems are caused by a defective process rather than people, and a focus on the process helps to avoid the blame culture that arises when blame is apportioned to individuals rather than the process. The focus on the process leads to a culture of openness in discussing problems and their solutions, and in instilling process ownership among the process practitioners.

Software process improvement (SPI) allows companies to mature their software engineering processes and to achieve their business goals more effectively. It helps software companies to improve performance and to deliver high-quality software on time and on budget, as well, reducing the cost of development and improving customer satisfaction. It has become an indispensable tool for software engineers and managers to achieve their goals, and it provides a return on investment to the organization.

15.2   What Is a Software Process?

A software development process is the process used by software engineers to design and develop computer software. It may be an undocumented ad hoc process as devised by the team for a particular project, or it may be a standardized and documented process used by various teams on similar projects. The process is seen as the glue that ties people, technology and procedures coherently together.

The processes employed in software development include processes to determine the requirements, processes for the design and development of the software, processes to verify that the software is fit for purpose and processes to maintain the software.

A *software process* is a set of activities, methods, practices and transformations that people use to develop and maintain software and the associated work products.

Definition 15.1 (Software Process)

A *process* is a set of practices or tasks performed to achieve a given purpose. It may include tools, methods, material and people.

An organization will typically have many processes in place for doing its work, and the objective of process improvement is to improve these to meet business goals more effectively.

The Software Engineering Institute (SEI) believes that there is a close relationship between the quality of the delivered software and the quality and maturity of the underlying processes employed to create the software. The SEI adopted and applied the principles of process improvement used in the manufacturing field to develop process maturity models such as the Capability Maturity Model (CMM) and its successor the Capability Maturity Model Integration (CMMI). These maturity models are invaluable in maturing the software processes in software-intensive organizations.

The process is an abstraction of the way in which work is done in the organization, and it is seen as the glue (Fig. 15.1) that ties people, procedures and tools together.

A process is often represented by a process map which details the flow of activities and tasks. The process map will typically include the inputs to each activity and the output from an activity. Often, the output from one activity will become an input to the next activity. A simple example of a process map for creating the system requirements specification is described in Fig. 15.2. The input to the activity to create the system requirements specification will typically be the business (user) requirements, whereas the output is the system requirements specification document itself.

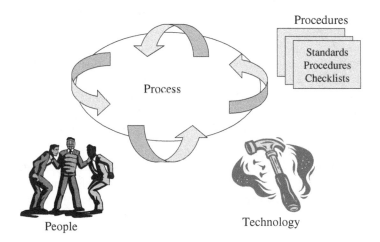

Fig. 15.1 Process as glue for people, procedures and tools

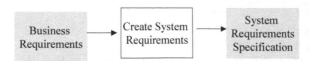

Fig. 15.2 Sample process map

As a process matures, it is defined in more detail and documented. It will have clearly defined entry and exit criteria, inputs and outputs, an explicit description of the tasks, verification of the process and consistent implementation throughout the organization.

15.3   What Is Software Process Improvement?

The origins of the software process improvement field go back to Walter Shewhart's work on statistical process control in the 1930s. Shewhart's work was later refined by Deming and Juran, and they argued that high-quality processes are essential to the delivery of a high-quality product. Deming and Juran argued that the quality of the end product is largely determined by the processes used to produce and support, and that therefore there needs to be an emphasis on the process as well as on the product.

These quality gurus argued that product quality will improve as variability in process performance is reduced [1], and their approach was effective in transforming manufacturing companies with quality problems to companies that would consistently deliver high-quality products. Further, the improvements to quality led to cost reductions and higher productivity, as less time was spent in reworking defective products.

The work of Deming and Juran was later applied to the software quality field by Watts Humphrey and others at the SEI leading to the birth of the software process improvement field. Software process improvement is concerned with practical action to improve the software processes in the organization to improve performance, and to ensure that business goals are achieved more effectively. For example, the business goals may be to deliver projects faster with higher quality.

Definition 15.2 (Software Process Improvement)
A program of activities is designed to improve the performance and maturity of the organization's software processes and the results of such a program.

Software process improvement initiatives (Fig. 15.3) support the organization in achieving its key business goals more effectively, where the business goals could be delivering software faster to the market, improving quality and reducing or eliminating waste. The objective is to work smarter and to build software better, faster and cheaper than competitors. Software process improvement makes business sense, and it provides a return on investment.

Fig. 15.3 Steps in process improvement

There are international standards and models available to support software process improvement. These include the CMMI model, the ISO 90001 standard and ISO 15504 (popularly known as SPICE). The SEI developed the CMMI model, and it includes best practice for processes in software and systems engineering. The ISO 9001 standard is a quality management system that may be employed in hardware, software development or service companies. The ISO 15504 standard is an international standard for software process improvement and process assessment, and it is popular in the automotive sector.

Software process improvement is concerned with defining the right processes and following them consistently. It involves training all staff on the new processes, refining the processes and continuously improving the processes. The need for a process improvement initiative often arises due to the realization that the organization is weak in some areas in software engineering, and that it needs to improve to achieve its business goals more effectively. The starting point of any improvement initiative is an examination of the business needs of the organization, and these may include goals such as delivering high-quality products on time or delivering products faster to the market.

15.4   Benefits of Software Process Improvement

It is a challenge to deliver high-quality software consistently on time and on budget. There are problems with budget and schedule overruns, late delivery of the software, spiralling costs, quality problems with the delivered software, customer complaints and staff morale.

Software process improvement can assist in dealing with these problems. There are costs involved, but it provides a return on the investment made. Specifically, the benefits from software process improvement include as follows:

- Improvements to quality
- Reductions in the cost of poor quality
- Improvements in productivity
- Reductions to the cost of software development
- Improvements in on-time delivery
- Improved consistency in budget and schedule delivery
- Improvements to customer satisfaction
- Improvements to employee morale

The SEI maintains data on the benefits that organizations have achieved from using the CMMI. These include improvements in several categories such as cost, schedule, productivity, quality, customer satisfaction and the return on investment.

Table 15.1 presents results in software process improvement collaborations of twenty-five organizations taken from conference presentations, published papers and individual [2].

For example, *Northrop Grumman Defense Systems* met every milestone (25 in a row) with high quality and customer satisfaction; *Lockheed Martin* reported an 80% increase in software productivity over a five-year period when it achieved CMM level 5 and obtained further increases in productivity as it moved to CMMI level 5. *Siemens (India)* reported an improved defect removal rate from over 50% before testing to over 70% before testing and a post-release defect rate of 0.35 defects per KLOC. *Accenture* reported a 5:1 return on investment from software process improvement activities.

15.5 Software Process Improvement Models

A process model[1] such as the CMMI defines best practice for software processes in an organization. It describes what the processes should do rather than how they should be done, and this allows the organization to use its professional judgment in the implementation of processes to meet its needs. The process model will need to be interpreted and tailored to the particular organization.

A process model provides a place to start an improvement initiative, and it provides a common language and shared vision for improvement. It provides a framework to prioritize actions and it allows the benefits of the experience of other organizations to be shared. The popular process models used in software process improvement include as follows:

---

[1]There is the well-known adage "All models are wrong, some are useful".

Table 15.1 Benefits of software process improvement (CMMI)

Improvements	Median	#Data points	Low	High
Cost	20%	21	3%	87%
Schedule	37%	19	2%	90%
Productivity	62%	17	9%	255%
Quality	50%	20	7%	132%
Customer satisfaction	14%	6	−4%	55%
ROI	4.7:1	16	2:1	27:1

- Capability Maturity Model Integration (CMMI)
- ISO 9001 Standard
- ISO 15504
- PSP and TSP
- Six sigma
- Root cause analysis (RCA)
- Balanced score card

The CMMI was developed by the SEI, and it is the successor to the older software CMM which was released in the early 1990s. The latter is specific to the software field, and it was influenced by Watts Humphrey's work at IBM [3]. The CMMI is a suite of products used for improving processes, and it includes models, appraisal methods and training material. The CMMI models address three areas of interest:

- CMMI for Development (CMMI-DEV)
- CMMI for Services (CMMI-SVC)
- CMMI for Acquisition (CMMI-ACQ)

The CMMI Development Model is discussed in Chap. 16, and it provides a structured approach to improvement, which allows the organization to set its improvement goals and priorities. The CMMI framework allows organizations to improve their maturity by improvements to their underlying processes. It provides a clearly defined road map for improvement, and it allows the organization to improve at its own pace. Its approach is evolutionary rather than revolutionary, and it recognizes that a balance is required between project needs and process improvement needs. It allows the processes to evolve from ad hoc immature activities to disciplined mature processes.

The CMMI practices may be used for the development, acquisition and maintenance of products and services. A SCAMPI appraisal determines the actual process maturity of an organization, and a SCAMPI class A appraisal allows the organization to benchmark itself against other organizations.

ISO 9001 is an internationally recognized quality management standard (Fig. 15.4), and it is customer and process focused. It applies to the processes that an organization uses to create and control products and services, and it emphasizes

Fig. 15.4 ISO 9001 quality management system

continuous improvement.[2] The standard is designed to apply to any product or service that an organization supplies.

The implementation of ISO 9001 involves understanding the requirements of the standard and how the standard applies to the organization. It requires the organization to identify its quality objectives, define a quality policy, produce documented procedures and carry out independent audits to ensure that the processes and procedures are followed. An organization may be certified against the ISO 9001 standard to gain recognition on its commitment to quality and continuous improvement. The certification involves an independent assessment of the organization to verify that it has implemented the ISO 9001 requirements properly, and that the quality management system is effective. It will also verify that the processes and procedures defined are consistently followed and that appropriate records are maintained. The ISO 9004 standard provides guidance for continuous improvement.

The ISO/IEC 15504 standard (popularly known as ISO SPICE) is an international standard for process assessment. It includes guidance for process improvement and for process capability determination, as well as for performing an assessment. It uses the international standard for software and systems lifecycle processes (ISO/IEC 12207) as its process model.

The ISO 12207 standard distinguishes between several categories of software processes including the primary lifecycle processes for developing and maintaining software, supporting processes to support the software development lifecycle and organizing lifecycle processes. There is a version of SPICE termed "*Automotive SPICE*" that is popular in the automotive sector. ISO/IEC 15504 can be used in a similar way to the CMMI, and its process model (i.e. ISO 12207) may be employed

---

[2]The ISO 9004 standard provides guidance on continuous improvement.

to implement best practice in the definition of processes. Assessments may be performed to identify strengths and opportunities for improvement.

The Personal Software Process (PSP) is a disciplined data-driven software development process that is designed to help software engineers understand and to improve their PSP performance. It was developed by Watts Humphrey at the SEI, and it helps engineers to improve their estimation and planning skills and to reduce the number of defects in their work. This enables them to make commitments that they can keep and to manage the quality of their projects.

The Team Software Process (TSP) was developed by Watts Humphrey at the SEI and is a structured approach designed to help software teams understand and improve their quality and productivity. Its focus is on building an effective software development team, and it involves establishing team goals, assigning team roles as well as other teamwork activities. Team members must already be familiar with the PSP.

Six sigma (6σ) was developed by Motorola as a way to improve quality and reduce waste. Its approach is to identify and remove the causes of defects in processes by reducing process variability. It uses quality management techniques and tools such as the five whys, business process mapping, statistical techniques, and the DMAIC and DMADV methodologies. There are several roles involved in six sigma initiatives such as Champions, Black Belts and Green Belts, and each role requires knowledge and experience, and is awarded on merit subject to training and certification. Sponsorship and leadership are required from top management to ensure the success of a 6σ initiative, and 6σ was influenced by earlier quality management techniques developed by Shewhart, Deming and Juran. A 6σ project follows a defined sequence of steps and has quantified targets (e.g. financial, quality, customer satisfaction and cycle time reduction).

15.6   Process Mapping

The starting point for improving a process is first to understand the process as it is currently performed and to determine the extent to which it is effective. The process stakeholders reach a common understanding of how the process is actually performed, and the process (as currently performed) is then sketched pictorially, with the activities and their inputs and outputs recorded graphically. This graphical representation is termed as "*process map,*" and is an abstract description of the process "*as is.*"

The process map is an abstraction of the way that work is done, and it may be critically examined to determine how effective it really is and to identify weaknesses and potential improvements. This critical examination by the process practitioners leads to modifications to its definition, and the proposed definition is sketched in a new process map to yield the process "*to be.*"

Each activity has an input and an output, and these are recorded in the process map. Once the team has agreed the definition of new process, the supporting templates required become clear from an examination of the input and output of the various activities. There may be a need for standards to support the process (e.g. procedures and templates), and the procedures or guidelines will be documented to provide the details on how the process is to be carried out, and they will detail the tasks and activities, and the roles required to perform them.

15.7   Process Improvement Initiatives

The need for a software process improvement initiative often arises from the realization that the organization is weak in some areas in software engineering, and that it needs to improve to achieve its business goals more effectively. The starting point of any improvement initiative is an examination of the business goals of the organization, and these may include as follows:

- Delivering high-quality products on time
- Delivering products faster to the market
- Reducing the cost of software development
- Improving software quality

There is more than one approach to the implementation of an improvement programme. A small organization has fewer resources available, and team members involved in the initiative will typically be working part-time. Larger organizations may be able to assign people full time on the improvement activities. The software process improvement initiative is designed to enable the organization achieve its business goals more effectively.

Once the organization goals have been defined, the improvement initiative commences. This involves conducting an appraisal (Fig. 15.6) to determine the current strengths and weaknesses of the processes, analysing the results to formulate a process improvement plan, implementing the plan, piloting the improved processes and verifying that they are effective, training staff and rolling out the new processes. The improvements are monitored for effectiveness and the cycle repeats. The software process improvement philosophy is as follows:

- The improvement initiative is based on business needs.
- Improvements should be planned based on the strengths and weaknesses of the processes in the organization.
- The CMMI model (or an alternate model) is the vehicle for improvement.
- The improvements are prioritized (it is not possible to do everything at once).
- The improvement initiative needs to be planned and managed as a project.
- The results achieved need to be reviewed at the end of the period, and a new improvement cycle started for continuous improvement

- Software process improvement requires people to change their behaviour, and so organization culture (and training) needs to be considered.
- There needs to be a process champion/project manager to drive the process improvement initiative in the organization.
- Senior management need to be 100% committed to the success of the initiative.
- Staff need to be involved in the improvement initiative, and there needs to be a balance between project needs and the improvement activities.

15.8   Barriers to Success

Software process improvement initiatives are not always successful and occasionally are abandoned. Some of the reasons for failure are as follows:

- Unrealistic expectations
- Trying to do too much at once
- Lack of senior management sponsorship
- Focusing on a maturity level
- Poor project management of the initiative
- Not run as a standard project
- Insufficient involvement of staff
- Insufficient time to work on improvements
- Inadequate training on software process improvement
- Lack of pilots to validate new processes
- Inadequate training/roll-out of new processes

It is essential that a software process improvement initiative be treated as a standard project with a project manager assigned to manage the initiative. Senior management need to be 100% committed to the success of the initiative, and they need to make staff available to work on the improvement activities. It needs to be clear to all staff that the improvement initiative is a priority to the organization. All employees need to receive appropriate training on software process improvement and on the process maturity model.

The CMMI project manager needs to consider the risks of failure of the initiative and to manage them accordingly.

15.9   Setting Up an Improvement Initiative

The implementation of an improvement initiative is a project, and it needs good planning and management to ensure its success. Once an organization makes a decision to embark on such an initiative, a project manager needs to be appointed to manage the project. The project manager will treat the implementation as a standard project, and plans are made to implement the initiative within the approved schedule and budget. The improvement initiative will often consist of several improvement cycles, with each improvement cycle implementing one or more process areas. Small improvement cycles may be employed to implement findings from an appraisal or improvement suggestions from staff.

One of the earliest activities carried out on any improvement initiative is to determine the current maturity of the organization with respect to the model. This will usually involve an appraisal conducted by one or more experienced appraisers. The findings will indicate the current strengths and weaknesses of the processes, as well as gaps with respect to the practices in the model. This initial appraisal is important, as it allows management in the organization to understand its current maturity with respect to the model and to communicate where it wants to be, as well as how it plans to get there. The initial appraisal assists in prioritizing improvements for the first improvement cycle.

The project manager will then prepare a project plan and schedule. The plan will detail the scope of the initiative, the budget, the process areas to be implemented, the teams and resources required, the initial risks identified, the key milestones, the quality and communication plan and so on. The project schedule will detail the deliverables to be produced, the resources required and the associated timeline for delivery. Project management was discussed in Chap. 2.

The software process improvement initiative is designed to support the organization in achieving its business goals more effectively. The steps include examining organization needs, conducting an appraisal to determine the current strengths and weaknesses and analysing the results to formulate an improvement plan. The improvement plan is then implemented; the improvements monitored and confirmed as being effective, and the improvement cycle repeats. The continuous improvement cycle is described in Fig. 15.5 and Table 15.2.

The teams involved in implementation are discussed in Table 15.3.

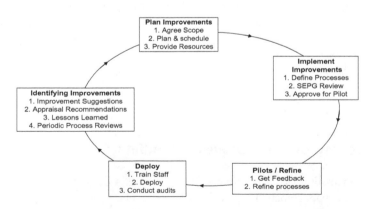

Fig. 15.5 Continuous improvement cycle

Table 15.2 Continuous improvement cycle

Activity	Description
Identify improvements to be made	The improvements to be made during an improvement cycle come from several sources – Improvement suggestions from staff – Lessons learned by projects – Periodic process reviews – Recommendations from appraisals
Plan improvements	A project plan and schedule is prepared for a large improvement cycle (involving the implementation of several process areas). An action plan (with owners and target completion dates) is sufficient for small improvement initiatives
Implement improvements	The improvements will consist of new processes, standards, templates, procedures, guidelines checklists and tools (where appropriate) to support the process
Pilots/refine	Selected new processes and standards will often be piloted[a] prior to their deployment to ensure that they are fit for purpose
Deploy	– Staff are trained on the new processes and standards – Staff receive support during the deployment – Audits are conducted
Do it all again	Improvement is continuous and as soon as an improvement cycle is complete its effectiveness is considered, and a new improvement cycle is ready to commence

[a]The result from the pilot may be that the new process is not suitable to be deployed in the organization or that it needs to be significantly revised prior to deployment

15.10 Appraisals

Appraisals (Fig. 15.6) play an essential role in the software process improvement programme. They allow an organization to understand its current software process maturity, including the strengths and weaknesses in its processes. An initial appraisal is conducted at the start of the initiative to allow the organization to understand its current process maturity, and to plan and prioritize improvements for the first improvement cycle. Improvements are then implemented, and an appraisal is typically conducted at the end of the cycle to confirm that progress has been made in the improvement initiative.

An appraisal is an independent examination of the software engineering and management practices in the organization and is conducted using an appraisal methodology (e.g. SCAMPI). It will identify strengths and weaknesses in the processes and any gaps that exist with respect to the maturity model.

The appraisal leader kicks off the appraisal with an opening presentation, which introduces the appraisal team, and presents the activities that will be carried out during the appraisal. These will include presentations, interviews, reviews of project documentation and detailed analysis to determine the extent to which the practices in the model have been implemented.

Table 15.3 Teams in improvement programme

Role/Team	Members	Responsibility
Project manager	Project manager	Project manage the improvement project Provide leadership on process improvement
Steering group (project board)	Senior manager(s)/ project manager	Provides management sponsorship of initiative Provides resources and funding for the initiative Uses influence to remove any roadblocks that arise with the improvement activities
SEPG team	Managers, technical and project manager	Coordinate day-to-day improvement activities Provides direction and support to improvement terms Review and approve new processes and coordinate pilots, training and roll-out of new processes
Improvement teams	Process users/project manager	Focus on specific process area(s) Review the current process "as is" and define the new process "to be" Obtain feedback on new process, conduct pilots, refine process, provide training and conduct roll-out of new process
Staff	All affected staff	Participate in improvement teams Participate in pilots Participate in training on new processes Adhere to new processes
External consultancy	External consultant	Conduct appraisal to determine initial maturity and assist in planning of first improvement cycle Provide expertise/training on the maturity model Conduct periodic process reviews Conduct appraisal at end of each improvement cycle

Fig. 15.6 Appraisals

Table 15.4 Phases in an Appraisal

Phase	Description
Planning and preparation	This involves identifying the sponsor's objectives and the requirements for the appraisal. A good appraisal plan is essential to its success
Conducting the appraisal	The appraisal team interviews the participants and examines data to judge the extent to which the CMMI is implemented in the organization
Reporting the results	The findings (including a presentation and an appraisal report).are reported to the sponsor

The appraisal leader will present the appraisal findings, and this may include a presentation and an appraisal report. The appraisal output summarizes the strengths and weaknesses, and ratings of the process areas will be provided (where this is part of the appraisal). The appraisal findings are valuable and will allow the project manager to plan and schedule the next improvement cycle. They allow an organization to:

- Understand its current process maturity (including strengths and weaknesses)
- Relate its strengths and weaknesses to the improvement model
- Prioritize its improvements for the next improvement cycle
- Benchmark itself against other organizations

There are three phases in an appraisal (Table 15.4).

15.11   Review Questions

1. What is a software process?
2. What is software process improvement?
3. What are the benefits of software process improvement?
4. Describe the various models available for software process improvement?
5. Draw the process map for the process of cooking your favourite meal.
6. Describe how a process improvement initiative may be run?
7. What are the main barriers to successful software process improvement initiatives and how can they be overcome?
8. Describe the three phases in an appraisal.

15.12   Summary

The success of business is highly influenced by software, and companies may develop their own software internally, or they may acquire software solutions off-the-shelf or from bespoke software development.

Software process improvement plays a key role in helping companies to improve their software engineering capability and to achieve their strategic goals. It enables organizations to implement best practice in software engineering and to achieve improved results. It allows companies to focus on fire prevention rather than fire-fighting, by critically examine their processes to determine the extent to which they are fit for purpose. It helps in identifying how the process may be improved and how waste may be eliminated.

Software process improvement initiatives lead to a focus on the process, which is important since many problems are caused by defective processes rather than by people. This leads to a culture of openness in discussing problems and instills process ownership among the process practitioners.

Software process improvement helps software companies to deliver the agreed software on time and on budget, as well as improving the quality of the delivered software, reducing the cost of development and improving customer satisfaction.

It has become an indispensable tool for software engineers and managers to achieve their goals, and it provides a return on investment to the organization. The next chapter gives an introduction to the CMMI, which has become a useful framework in maturing software engineering processes.

References

1. W. Edwards Deming, *Out of Crisis* (MIT Press, Cambridge, 1986)
2. Software Engineering Institute, in *CMMI Executive Overview*. Presentation by the SEI, 2006
3. W. Humphry, *Managing the Software Process* (Addison Wesley, New York, 1989)

Capability Maturity Model Integration

16

Abstract

This chapter gives an overview of the CMMI model and discusses its five maturity levels and their constituent process areas. We discuss both the staged and continuous representations of the CMMI, and SCAMPI appraisals that indicate the extent to which the CMMI has been implemented in the organization, as well as identifying opportunities for improvement.

Keywords

CMMI maturity levels · CMMI capability levels · CMMI staged representation · CMMI continuous representation · CMMI process areas · Appraisals

16.1 Introduction

The Software Engineering Institute[1] developed the Capability Maturity Model (CMM) in the early 1990s as a framework to help software organizations improve their software process maturity. The CMMI is the successor to the older CMM, and its implementation brings best practice in software and systems engineering into the organization. The SEI and many other quality experts believe that there is a close relationship between the maturity of software processes and the quality of the delivered software product.

---

[1]The SEI was founded by the US Congress in 1984 and has worked successfully in advancing software engineering practices in the US and worldwide. It performs research to find solutions to key software engineering problems, and its proposed solutions are validated through pilots. These solutions are then disseminated to the wider software engineering community through its training programme. The SEI's research and maturity models have played an important role in helping companies to deliver high-quality software consistently on time and on budget.

© Springer International Publishing AG 2017   255
G. O'Regan, *Concise Guide to Software Engineering*, Undergraduate Topics
in Computer Science, DOI 10.1007/978-3-319-57750-0_16

The CMM built upon the work of quality gurus such as Deming [1], Juran [2] and Crosby [3]. These quality gurus were effective in transforming struggling manufacturing companies with quality problem to companies that could consistently produce high-quality products. Their success was due to the focus on improving the manufacturing process and in reducing variability in the process. The work of these quality experts is discussed in [4].

Similarly, software companies need to have quality software processes to deliver high-quality software to their customers. The SEI has collected empirical data to suggest that there is a close relationship between software process maturity and the quality of the delivered software. Therefore, there is a need to focus on the software process as well as on the product.

The CMM was released in 1991 and its successor, the CMMI® model, was released in 2002 [5]. The CMMI is a framework to assist an organization in the implementation of best practice in software and systems engineering. It is an internationally recognized model for process improvement and is used worldwide by thousands of organizations.

The focus of the CMMI is on improvements to the software process to ensure that they meet business needs more effectively. A *process* is a set of practices or tasks performed to achieve a given purpose. It may include tools, methods, materials and people. An organization will typically have many processes in place for doing its work, and the object of process improvement is to improve these to meet business goals more effectively.

The process is an abstraction of the way in which work is done in the organization, and is seen as the glue (Fig. 16.1) that ties people, procedures and tools together.

It may be described by a process map which details the flow of activities and tasks. The process map will include the input to each activity and the output from each activity. Often, the output from one activity will become the input to the next activity. A simple example of a process map for creating the system requirements specification was described in Chap. 15 (Fig. 15.2).

The ISO/IEC 12207 standard for software processes distinguishes between several categories of software processes, including the primary lifecycle processes for developing and maintaining software; supporting processes to support the software development lifecycle, and organization lifecycle processes. These are summarized in Fig. 16.2.

Fig. 16.1 Process as glue for people, procedures and tools

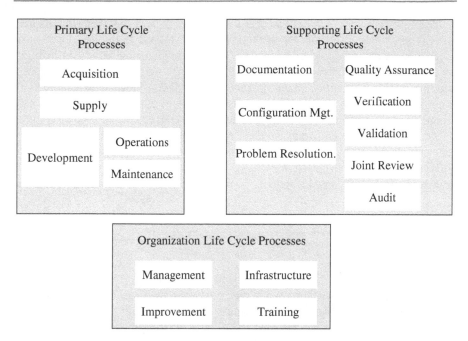

Fig. 16.2 ISO/IEC 12207 standard for software engineering processes

Watts Humphrey began applying the ideas of Deming, Juran and Crosby to software development, and he published the book "*Managing the Software Process*" [6]. He moved to the SEI to work on software process maturity models with the other SEI experts, and the SEI released the Capability Maturity Model in the early 1990s. This process model has proved to be effective in assisting companies in improving their software engineering practices and in achieving consistent results and high-quality software.

The CMM is a process model and it defines the characteristics or best practices of good processes. It does not prescribe how the processes should be defined, and it allows the organization the freedom to interpret the model to suit its particular context and business needs. It also provides a roadmap for an organization to get from where it is today to a higher level of maturity. The advantage of model-based improvement is that it provides a place to start process improvement, as well as a common language and a shared vision.

The CMM consists of five maturity levels with the higher maturity levels representing advanced software engineering capability. The lowest maturity level is level one and the highest is level five. The SEI developed an assessment methodology (CBA IPI) to determine the maturity of software organizations, and initially most organizations were assessed at level one maturity. However, over time companies embarked on improvement initiatives and matured their software processes, and today, many companies are performing at the higher maturity levels.

The first company to be assessed at CMM level 5^2 was the Motorola plant in Bangalore in India. The success of the software CMM led to the development of other process maturity models such as the systems engineering capability maturity model (CMM/SE) which is concerned with maturing systems engineering practices, and the people Capability Maturity Model (P-CMM) which is concerned with improving the ability of the software organizations to attract, develop and retain talented software engineering professionals.

The SEI commenced work on the CMMI® [5] in the late 1990s. This is a replacement for the older CMM model, and its development involved merging the software CMM and the systems CMM, and ensuring that the new model was compatible with ISO 15504 standard.[3] The CMMI is described in the next section.

16.2 The CMMI

The CMMI consists of five maturity levels (Fig. 16.4) with each maturity level (except level one) consisting of a number of process areas. Each process area consists of a set of goals, and these must be implemented by a set of related practices in order for the process area to be satisfied. The practices specify what is to be done rather than how it should be done. Processes are activities associated with carrying out certain tasks, and they need to be defined and documented. The users of the process need to receive appropriate training to enable them to carry out the process, and process discipline need to be enforced by independent audits. Process performance needs to be monitored and improvements made to ineffective processes.

The emphasis on level two of the CMMI is on maturing management practices such as project management, requirements management and configuration management. The emphasis on level three of the CMMI is on maturing engineering and organization practices. Maturity level three is concerned with defining standard organization processes, and it also includes process areas for the various engineering activities needed to design and develop the software. Level four is concerned with ensuring that key processes are performing within strict quantitative limits, and adjusting processes, where necessary, to perform within these limits. Level five is concerned with continuous process improvement. Maturity levels may not be skipped in the staged implementation of the CMMI, as each maturity level is the foundation for work on the next level.

---

[2]Of course, the fact that a company has been appraised at a certain CMM or CMMI rating is no guarantee that it is performing effectively as a commercial organization. For example, the Motorola plant in India was appraised at CMM level 5 in the late 1990s while Motorola lost business opportunities in the GSM market.

[3]ISO 15504 (popularly known as SPICE) is an international standard for software process assessment.

There is also a continuous representation[4] of the CMMI (similar to ISO 15504) that allows the organization to focus its improvements on the key processes that are closely related to its business goals. This allows it the freedom to choose an approach that should result in the greatest business benefit rather than proceeding with the standard improvement roadmap of the staged approach. However, in practice, it is often necessary to implement several of the level two process areas before serious work can be done on maturing a process to a higher capability level. Table 16.1 presents motivations for the implementation of the CMMI.

The CMMI model covers both the software engineering and systems engineering disciplines. Systems engineering is concerned with the development of systems that may or may not include software, whereas software engineering is concerned with the development of software systems. The model contains extra information relevant to a particular discipline, and this is done by discipline amplification.[5] The CMMI has been updated in recent years to provide support for the Agile methodology.

The CMMI allows organizations to benchmark themselves against similar organizations (Fig. 16.3). This is generally done by a formal SEI SCAMPI Class A appraisal[6] conducted by an authorized SCAMPI lead appraiser. The results will generally be reported back to the SEI, and there is a strict qualification process to become an authorized lead appraiser. The qualification process helps to ensure that the appraisals are conducted fairly and objectively and that the results are consistent. An appraisal verifies that an organization has improved, and it enables the organization to prioritize improvements for the next improvement cycle. Small organizations will often prefer a SCAMPI Class B or C appraisal, as these are less expensive and time consuming.[7]

---

[4]Our focus is on the implementation of the staged representation of the CMMI rather than the continuous representation. This provides a clearly defined roadmap to improvement, and it also allows benchmarking of organizations. Appraisals against the staged representation are useful since a CMMI maturity level rating is awarded to the organization, and the company may use this to publicize its software engineering capability.

[5]Discipline amplification is a specialized piece of information that is relevant to a particular discipline. It is introduced in the model by text such as "For Systems Engineering".

[6]A SCAMPI Class An appraisal is a systematic examination of the processes in an organization to determine the maturity of the organization with respect to the CMMI. An appraisal team consists of a SCAMPI lead appraiser, one or more external appraisers, and usually one internal appraiser. It consists of interviews with senior and middle management and reviews with project managers and project teams. The appraisers will review documentation and determine the extent to which the processes defined are effective, as well as the extent to which they are institutionalized in the organization. Data will be gathered and reviewed by the appraisers, ratings produced and the findings presented.

[7]Small organizations may not have the budget for a formal SCAMPI Class A appraisal. They may be more interested in an independent SCAMPI Class B or C appraisal, which is used to provide feedback on their strengths and opportunities for improvement. Feedback allows the organization to focus its improvement efforts for the next improvement cycle.

Table 16.1 Motivation for
CMMI implementation

Motivation for CMMI implementation
Enhances the credibility of the company
Marketing benefit of CMMI maturity level
Implementation of best practice in software and systems engineering
Clearly defined roadmap for improvement
It increases the capability and maturity of an organization
It improves the management of subcontractors
It provides improved technical and management practices
It leads to higher quality of software
It leads to increased timeliness of projects
It reduces the cost of maintenance and incidence of defects
It allows the measurement of processes and products
It allows projects/products to be quantitatively managed
It allows innovative technologies to be rigorously evaluated to enhance process performance
It improves customer satisfaction
It changes the culture from firefighting to fire prevention
It leads to a culture of improvement
It leads to higher morale in company

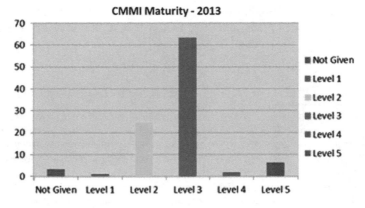

Fig. 16.3 CMMI worldwide maturity 2013

The time required to implement the CMMI in an organization depends on its size and current maturity. It generally takes one to two years to implement maturity level two, and a further one to two years to implement level 3. The implementation of the CMMI needs to be balanced against the day-to-day needs of the organization in delivering products and services to its customers.

The SEI has gathered empirical data (Table 16.2) on the benefits gained from the implementation of the CMMI [7]. The table shows the median results reported to the SEI.

Table 16.2 Benefits of
CMMI implementation

Benefit	Actual saving
Cost	34%
Schedule	50%
Productivity	61%
Quality	48%
Customer satisfaction	14%
Return on investment	4:1

The processes implemented during a CMMI initiative will generally include:

- Developing and Managing Requirements
- Design and Development
- Project Management
- Selecting and managing Subcontractors
- Managing change and Configurations
- Peer reviews
- Risk Management and Decision Analysis
- Testing
- Audits

16.3   CMMI Maturity Levels

The CMMI is divided into five maturity levels (Table 16.3) with each maturity level (except level one) consisting of several process areas. The maturity level is a predictor of the results that will be obtained from following the software process, and the higher the maturity level of the organization, the more capable it is and the more predictable its results. The current maturity level acts as the foundation for the improvements to be made in the move to the next maturity level.

The maturity levels provide a roadmap for improvements in the organization, and maturity levels are not skipped in the staged implementation. A particular maturity level is achieved only when all process areas belonging to that maturity level (and all process areas belonging to lower maturity levels) have been successfully implemented and institutionalized[8] in the organization.

---

[8]Institutionalization is a technical term and means that the process is ingrained in the way in which work is performed in the organization. An institutionalized process is defined, documented and followed in the organization. All employees have been appropriately trained in its use and process discipline is enforced via audits. It is illustrated by the phrase *"That's the way we do things around here"*.

Table 16.3 CMMI maturity levels

Maturity level	Description
Initial	Processes are often ad hoc or chaotic with performance often unpredictable. Success is often due to the heroics of people rather than having high-quality processes in place. The defined process is often abandoned in times of crisis, and there are no audits to enforce the process
	It is difficult to repeat previous success since success is due to heroic efforts of its people rather than processes. These organizations often over-commit, as they often lack an appropriate estimation process on which to base project commitments
	Firefighting is a way of life in these organizations. High-quality software might be produced, but at a cost including long hours, high level of rework, over budget and schedule and unhappy staff and customers. Projects do not perform consistently as their success is dependent on the people involved
	They may have few processes defined and poor change control, poor estimation and project planning and weak enforcement of standards
Managed	A level two organization has good project management practices in place, and planning and managing new projects is based on experience with similar previous projects
	The process is planned, performed and controlled. A level two organization is disciplined in following processes, and the process is enforced with independent audits
	The status of the work products produced by the process is visible to management at major milestones, and changes to work products are controlled. The work products are placed under appropriate configuration management control
	The requirements for a project are managed and changes to the requirements are controlled. Project management practices are in place to manage the project, and a set of measures are defined for the budget, schedule and effort variance. Subcontractors are managed
	Independent audits are conducted to enforce the process. The processes in a level two organization are defined at the project level
Defined	A maturity level three organization has standard processes defined that support the whole organization
	These standard processes ensure consistency in the way that projects are conducted across the organization. There are guidelines defined that allow the organization process to be tailored and applied to each project
	There are standards in place for design and development and procedures defined for effective risk management and decision analysis
	Level 3 processes are generally defined more rigorously than level 2 processes, and the definition includes the purpose of the process, inputs, entry criteria, activities, roles, measures, verification steps, exit criteria and output. There is also an organization-wide training program and improvement data is collected

(continued)

Table 16.3 (continued)

Maturity level	Description
Quantitatively managed	A level 4 organization sets quantitative goals for the performance of key processes, and these processes are controlled using statistical techniques Processes are stable and perform within narrowly defined limits. Software process and product quality goals are set and managed A level 4 organization has predictable process performance, with variation in process performance identified and the causes of variation corrected
Optimizing	A level 5 organization has a continuous process improvement culture in place, and processes are improved based on a quantitative understanding of variation Defect prevention activities are an integral part of the development lifecycle. New technologies are evaluated and introduced (where appropriate) into the organization. Processes may be improved incrementally or through innovative process and technology improvements

The implementation of the CMMI generally starts with improvements to processes at the project level. The focus at level two is on improvements to managing projects and suppliers and improving project management, supplier selection, management practices and so on.

The improvements at level 3 involve a shift from the focus on projects to the organization. It involves defining standard processes for the organization, and projects may then tailor the standard process (using tailoring guidelines) to produce the project's software process. Projects are not required to do everything in the same way as the tailoring of the process allows the project's defined software process to reflect the unique characteristics of the project: i.e., a degree of variation is allowed as per the tailoring guidelines to reflect the unique characteristics of the project.

The implementation of level three involves defining procedures and standards for engineering activities such as design, coding and testing. Procedures are defined for peer reviews, testing, risk management and decision analysis.

The implementation of level four involves achieving process performance within defined quantitative limits. This involves the use of metrics and setting quantitative goals for project and process performance and managing process performance. The implementation of level 5 is concerned with achieving a culture of continuous improvement in the company. The causes of defects are identified and resolution actions implemented to prevent a reoccurrence.

16.3.1   CMMI Representations

The CMMI is available in the staged and continuous representations. Both representations use the same process areas as well as the same specific and generic goals and practices.

The staged representation was described in Fig. 16.4, and it follows the well-known improvement roadmap from maturity level one through improvement cycles until the organization has achieved its desired level of maturity. The staged approach is concerned with organization maturity, and it allows statements of organization maturity to be made, whereas the continuous representation is concerned with individual process capability.

The continuous representation is illustrated in Fig. 16.5, and it has been influenced by ISO 15504 (the standard for software process assessment). It is concerned with improving the capability of those selected processes, and it gives the organization the freedom to choose the order of improvements that best meet its busi-

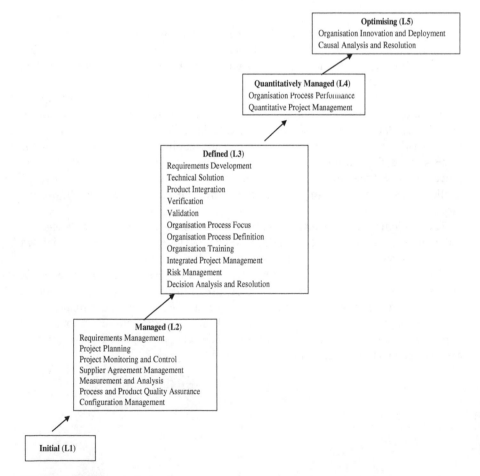

Fig. 16.4 CMMI maturity levels

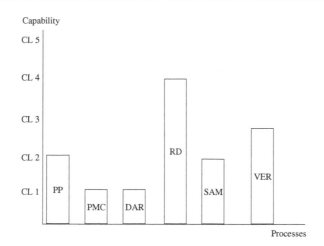

Fig. 16.5 CMMI capability levels

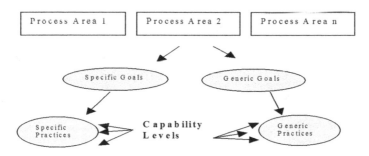

Fig. 16.6 CMMI—continuous representation

ness needs (Fig. 16.6). The continuous representation allows statements of individual process capability to be made. It employs six capability levels and a process is rated at a particular capability level.

Each capability level consists of a set of specific and generic goals and practices, and the capability levels provide a path for process improvement within the process area. Process improvement is achieved by the evolution of a process from its current capability level to a higher capability level. For example, a company may wish to mature its project planning process from its current process rating of capability level 2 to a rating of capability level 3. This requires the implementation of practices to define a standard project planning process as well as collecting improvement data. The capability levels are shown in Table 16.4.

An incomplete process is a process that is either partially performed or not performed at all. A performed process carries out the expected practices and work products. However, such a process may not be adequately planned or enforced. A managed process is planned and executed with appropriately skilled and trained personnel. The process is monitored and controlled and periodically enforced via audits.

Table 16.4 CMMI capability levels for continuous representation

Capability level	Description
Incomplete (0)	The process does not implement all of the capability level one generic and specific practices. The process is either not performed or partially performed
Performed (1)	A process that performs all of the specific practices and satisfies its specific goals. Performance may not be stable
Managed (2)	A process at this level has the infrastructure to support the process. It is managed: i.e., planned and executed in accordance with policy, its users are trained; it is monitored and controlled and audited for adherence to its process description
Defined (3)	A process at this level has a defined process: i.e., a managed process that is tailored from the organization's set of standard processes. It contributes work products, measures and other process improvement information to the organization's process assets
Quantitatively managed (4)	A process at this level is a quantitatively managed process: i.e., a defined process that is controlled by statistical techniques. Quantitative objectives for quality and process performance are established and used to control the process
Optimizing (5)	A process at this level is an optimizing process: i.e., a quantitatively managed process that is continually improved through incremental and innovative improvements

A defined process is a managed process that is tailored from the standard process in the organization using tailoring guidelines. A quantitatively managed process is a defined process that is controlled using quantitative techniques. An optimizing process is a quantitatively managed process that is continuously improved through incremental and innovative improvements.

The process is rated at a particular capability level provided it satisfies all of the specific and generic goals of that capability level, and it also satisfies the specific and generic goals of all lower capability levels.

We shall be concerned with the implementation of the staged representation of the CMMI rather than the continuous representation. The reader is referred to [5] for more information on both representations.

16.4   Categories of CMMI Processes

The process areas on the CMMI can be divided into four categories. These are shown in Table 16.5.

Table 16.5 CMMI process categories

Maturity level	Description
Process management	The process areas in this category are concerned with activities to define, plan, implement, deploy, monitor, control, appraise, measure and improve the processes in the organization: They include: • Organization process focus • Organization process definition • Organization training • Organization process performance • Organization innovation and deployment
Project management	These process areas are concerned with activities to create and maintain a project plan, tailoring the standard process to produce the project's defined process, monitoring progress with respect to the plan, taking corrective action, the selection and management of suppliers, and the management of risk. They include: • Project planning • Project monitoring and control • Risk management • Integrated project management • Supplier agreement management • Quantitative project management
Engineering	These process areas are concerned with engineering activities such as determining and managing requirements, design and development, testing and maintenance of the product. They include: • Requirements development • Requirements management • Technical solution • Product integration • Verification • Validation
Support	This includes activities that support product development and maintenance • Configuration management • Process and product quality assurance • Measurement and analysis • Decision analysis and resolution

16.5   CMMI Process Areas

This section provides a brief overview of the process areas of the CMMI model. All maturity levels (with the exception of level one) contain several process areas. The process areas are described in more detail in [5] (Table 16.6).

Table 16.6 CMMI Process Areas

Maturity level	Process area	Description of process area
Level 2	REQM	**Requirements management** This process area is concerned with managing the requirements for the project and ensuring that the work products are kept consistent with the requirements
	PP	**Project planning** This process area is concerned with estimation for the project, developing and obtaining commitment to the project plan and maintaining the plan
	PMC	**Project monitoring and control** This process area is concerned with monitoring progress against the plan and taking corrective action when project performance deviates from the plan
	SAM	**Supplier agreement management** This process area is concerned with the selection of suppliers, documenting the (legal) agreement/statement of work with the supplier and managing the supplier during the execution of the agreement
	MA	**Measurement and analysis** This process area is concerned with determining management information needs and measurement objectives. Measures are then specified to meet these objectives, and data collection and analysis procedures defined
	PPQA	**Process and product quality assurance** This process area is concerned with providing visibility to management on process compliance. Non-compliance issues are documented and resolved by the project team
	CM	**Configuration management** This process area is concerned with setting up a configuration management system; identifying the items that will be subject to change control, and controlling changes to them
Level 3	RD	**Requirements development** This process area is concerned with specifying the user and system requirements, and analyzing and validating them
	TS	**Technical solution** This process area is concerned with the design, development and implementation of an appropriate solution to the customer requirements
	PI	**Product integration** This process area is concerned with the assembly of the product components to deliver the product and verifying that the assembled components function correctly together
	VER	**Verification** This process area is concerned with ensuring that selected work products satisfy their specified requirements. This is achieved by peer reviews and testing

(continued)

Table 16.6 (continued)

Maturity level	Process area	Description of process area
	VAL	**Validation** This process area is concerned with demonstrating that the product or product component is fit for purpose and satisfies its intended use
	OPF	**Organization process focus** This process area is concerned with planning and implementing process improvements based on a clear understanding of the current strengths and weakness of the organization's processes
	OPD	**Organization process definition** This process area is concerned with creating and maintaining a usable set of organization processes. This allows consistent process performance across the organization
	OT	**Organization training** This process area is concerned with developing the skills and knowledge of people to enable them to perform their roles effectively
	IPM	**Integrated project management** This process area is concerned with tailoring the organization set of standard processes to define the project's defined process. The project is managed according to the project's defined process
	RSKM	**Risk management** This process area is concerned with identifying risks and determining their probability of occurrence and impact should they occur. Risks are identified and managed throughout the project
	DAR	**Decision analysis and resolution** This process area is concerned with formal decision making. It involves identifying options, specifying evaluation criteria and method, performing the evaluation, and recommending a solution
Level 4	OPP	**Organization process performance** This process area is concerned with obtaining a quantitative understanding of the performance of selected organization processes in order to quantitatively manage projects in the organization
	QPM	**Quantitative project management** This process area is concerned with quantitatively managing the project's defined process to achieve the project's quality and performance objectives
Level 5	OID	**Organization innovation and deployment** This process area is concerned with incremental and innovative process improvements
	CAR	**Causal analysis and resolution** This process area is concerned with identifying causes of defects and taking corrective action to prevent a reoccurrence in the future

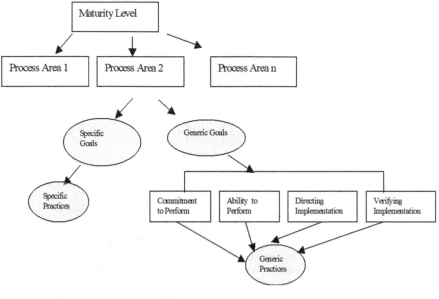

Fig. 16.7 CMMI-staged model

16.6   Components of CMMI Process Areas

The maturity level of an organization indicates the expected results that its projects will achieve and is a predictor of future project performance. Each maturity level consists of a number of process areas, and each process area consists of specific and generic goals, and specific and generic practices. Each maturity level is the foundation for improvements for the next level (Fig. 16.7).

The specific goals and practices are listed first and then followed by the generic goals and practices. The specific goals and practices are unique to the process area being implemented and are concerned with what needs to be done to perform the process. The specific practices are linked to a particular specific goal, and they describe activities that when performed achieve the associated specific goal for the process area.

The generic goals and practices are common to all process areas for that maturity level and are concerned with process institutionalization at that level. The generic practices are organized by four common features:

- Commitment to perform
- Ability to perform
- Directing implementation
- Verifying implementation

Fig. 16.8 Specific practices for SG1—manage requirements

They describe activities that when implemented achieve the associated generic goal(s) for the process area. The commitment to perform practices relate to the creation of policies and sponsorship of process improvement; the ability to perform practices are related to the provision of appropriate resources and training to perform the process; the directing implementation practices relate to activities to control and manage the process; and verifying practices relate to activities to verify adherence to the process.

The implementation of the generic practices institutionalizes the process and makes it ingrained in the way that work is done. Institutionalization means that the process is defined, documented and understood. Process users are appropriately trained and the process is enforced by independent audits. Institutionalization helps to ensure that the process is performed consistently and is more likely to be retained during times of stress. The degree of institutionalization is reflected in the extent to which the generic goals and practices are satisfied. The generic practices ensure the sustainability of the specific practices over time.

There is one specific goal associated with the Requirements Management process area (Fig. 16.8), and it has five associated specific practices:

SG 1—Manage Requirements Requirements are managed and inconsistencies with project plans and work products are identified.

The components of the CMMI model are grouped into three categories, namely required, expected and informative components. The *required category* is essential to achieving goals in a particular area and includes the *specific* and *generic goals* that must be implemented and institutionalized for the process area to be satisfied. The *expected category* includes the *specific and generic practices* that an organization will typically implement to perform the process effectively. These are intended to guide individuals or groups who are implementing improvements, or who are performing appraisals to determine the current maturity of the organization.

Table 16.7 CMMI generic practices

Generic goal	Generic practice	Description of generic practice
GG 1 Performed process	GP 1.1	**Perform base practices** The purpose of this generic practice is to produce the work products and services associated with the process (i.e., as detailed in the specific practices). These practices may be done informally without following a documented process description and success may be dependent on the individuals performing the work. That is, the basic process is performed but it may be immature
GG 2 Managed process	GP 2.1	**Organization policy** The organization policy is established by senior management and defines the management expectations of the organization
	GP 2.2	**Plan the process** A plan is prepared to perform the process and it will assign responsibilities and document the resources needed to perform the process as well as any training requirements. The plan is revised as appropriate
	GP 2.3	**Provide resources** This is concerned with ensuring that the resources required to perform the process (as specified in the plan) are available when required
	GP 2.4	**Assign responsibility** The purpose of this generic practice is to assign responsibility for performing the process
	GP 2.5	**Train people** This generic practice is concerned with ensuring that people receive the appropriate training to enable them to perform and support the process
	GP 2.6	**Manage configurations** This generic practice is concerned with identifying the work products created by the process that will be subject to configuration management control
	GP 2.7	**Identify and involve relevant stakeholders** This is concerned with ensuring that the stakeholders are identified (as described in the plan), and involved appropriately during the execution of the process
	GP 2.8	**Monitor and control the process** This generic practice is concerned with monitoring process performance and taking corrective action
	GP 2.9	**Objectively evaluate adherence** This is concerned with conducting audits to verify that process execution adheres to the process description

(continued)

Table 16.7   (continued)

Generic goal	Generic practice	Description of generic practice
	GP 2.10	**Review status with higher level management** This is concerned with providing higher level management with appropriate visibility into the process
GG 3 Defined process	GP 3.1	**Establish a defined process** This is concerned with tailoring the organization set of standard processes to produce the project's defined process
	GP 3.2	**Collect improvement information** This generic practice is concerned with collecting improvement information and work products to support future improvement of the processes
GG 4 Quantitatively managed process	GP 4.1	**Establish quantitative objectives** This is concerned with agreeing on quantitative objectives (e.g., quality/performance) for the process with the stakeholders
	GP 4.2	**Stabilize subprocess performance** This generic practice is concerned with stabilizing the performance of one or more key subprocesses of the process using statistical techniques. This enables the process to achieve its objectives
GG 5 Optimizing process	GP 5.1	**Ensure continuous process improvement** This generic practice is concerned with systematically improving selected processes to meet quality and process performance targets
	GP 5.2	**Correct root cause of problems** This generic practice is concerned with analyzing defects encountered to correct the root cause of these problems and to prevent reoccurrence

They state what needs to be done rather than how it should be done, thereby giving the organization freedom on the most appropriate implementation.

The informative category includes information to guide the implementer on how best to approach the implementation of the specific and generic goals and practices. These include *subpractices*, *typical work products* and *discipline amplifications*. This information assists with the implementation of the process area.

The implementation and institutionalization of a process area involves the implementation of the specific and generic practices. The specific practices are concerned with process implementation and are described in detail in [8]. The generic practices are concerned with process institutionalization and are summarized in Table 16.7.

The generic goals support an evolution of process maturity, and the implementation of each generic goal provides a foundation for further process improvements. That is, a process rated at a particular maturity level has all of the

Table 16.8 Implementation of generic practices

Generic goal	Generic practice	Process area supporting implementation of generic practice
GG 2 Managed process	GP 2.2 Plan the process	Project planning
	GP 2.5 Train the people	Organization training Project planning
	GP 2.6 Manage configurations	Configuration management
	GP 2.7 Identify/involve relevant stakeholders	Project planning
	GP 2.8 Monitor and control the process	Project monitoring and control
	GP 2.9 Objectively evaluate adherence	Process and product quality assurance
GG 3 Defined process	GP 3.1 Establish defined process	Integrated project management Organization process definition
	GP 3.2 Improvement information	Integrated project management Organization process focus Organization process definition
GG 4 Quantitatively managed process	GP4.1 Establish quantitative objectives for process	Quantitative project management Organization process performance
	GP 4.2 Stabilize subprocess performance	Quantitative project management Organization process performance
GG 5 Optimizing process	GP5.1 Ensure continuous process improvement	Organization innovation and deployment
	GP 5.2 Correct root cause of problems	Causal analysis and resolution

maturity of a process at the lower levels and the additional maturity of its rated level. In other words, a defined process is a managed process; a quantitatively managed process is a defined process, and so on.

Several of the CMMI process areas support the implementation of the generic goals and practices. These process areas contain one or more specific practices that when implemented may either fully implement a generic practice or generate a work product that is used in the implementation of the generic practice. The implementation of the generic practices is supported by the following process areas (Table 16.8).

16.7   SCAMPI Appraisals

SCAMPI appraisals are conducted to enable an organization to understand its current software process maturity, and to prioritize future improvements [9]. The appraisal is an independent examination of the processes used in the organization against the CMMI model, and its objective is to identify strengths and weaknesses in the processes, which are then used to prioritize improvements in the next improvement cycle.

The SCAMPI methodology is the appraisal methodology used with the CMMI, and there are three distinct classes of appraisal (SCAMPI Class A, B and C) [10]. These classes vary in formality, the cost, effort and timescales involved, the rating of the processes and the reporting of results.

The scope of the appraisal includes the process areas to be examined, and the projects and organization unit to be examined. It may be limited to the level 2 process areas, or the level 2 and level 3 process areas, and so on. The scope depends on how active the organization has been in process improvement.

The appraisal will identify any gaps that exist with respect to the implementation of the CMMI practices for each process area within the scope of the appraisal. The appraisal team will conduct interviews and review project documentation, and they will examine the extent to which the practices are implemented.

The appraisal findings are presented and are used to plan and prioritize the next improvement cycle. SCAMPI appraisals are discussed in more detail in [4].

16.8   Review Questions

1. Describe the CMMI Model.
2. Describe the staged and continuous representations of the CMMI.
3. What are the advantages and disadvantages of each CMMI representation?
4. Describe the CMMI maturity levels and the process areas in each level.
5. What is the purpose of the CMMI specific and generic practices?
6. Describe how the generic practices are implemented?
7. What is the difference between implementation and institutionalization?
8. What is the purpose of SCAMPI appraisals?
9. How do appraisals fit into the software process improvement cycle?

16.9 Summary

The Capability Maturity Model Integration is a framework to assist an organization in the implementation of best practice in software and systems engineering. It was developed at the Software Engineering Institute and is used by many organizations around the world.

The SEI and other quality experts believe that there is a close relationship between the quality of the delivered software and the maturity of the processes used to create the software. Therefore, there needs to be a focus on the process as well as on the product, and the CMMI contains best practice in software and systems engineering to assist in the creation of high-quality processes.

The process is seen as the glue that ties people, technology and procedures coherently together. Processes are activities associated with carrying out certain tasks, and they need to be defined and documented. The users of the process need to receive appropriate training on their use, and process discipline needs to be enforced with independent audits. Process performance needs to be monitored and improvements made to ineffective processes.

The CMMI consists of five maturity levels with each maturity level (except level one) consisting of several process areas. Each maturity level acts as a foundation for improvement for the next improvement level, and each increase in maturity level represents more advanced software engineering capability. The higher the maturity level of the organization, the more capable it is, and the more predictable its results. The lowest level of maturity is maturity level 1 and the highest level is maturity level 5.

Each process area consists of a set of specific and generic goals, and these must be implemented by an associated set of specific and generic practices. The practices specify what is to be done rather than how it should be done, and the organization is given freedom in choosing the most appropriate implementation to meet its needs.

The SCAMPI appraisal methodology is used to determine the maturity of software organizations. It is a systematic examination of the processes used in the organization against the CMMI model, and it includes interviews and reviews of documentation. A successful SCAMPI Class A appraisal allows the organization to report its maturity rating to the SEI and to benchmark itself against other companies. Appraisals are a part of the improvement cycle, and improvement plans are prepared after the appraisal to address the findings and to prioritize improvements.

References

1. W. Edwards Deming, *Out of Crisis* (MIT Press, Cambridge, 1986)
2. J. Juran, *Juran's Quality Handbook* (McGraw Hill, New York, 1951)
3. P. Crosby, *Quality is Free. The Art of Making Quality Certain* (McGraw Hill, New York, 1979)
4. G. O'Regan, *Introduction to Software Quality* (Springer, Switzerland, 2014)

5. M.D. Chrissis, M. Conrad, S. Shrum, *CMMI for Development. Guidelines for Process Integration and Product Improvement*, 3rd edn. SEI Series in Software Engineering (Addison Wesley, New York, 2011)
6. W. Humphry, *Managing the Software Process*. (Addison Wesley, New York, 1989)
7. Software Engineering Institute. August 2009 CMMI Impact. Presentation by Anita Carleton
8. G. O'Regan, *Introduction to Software Process Improvement* (Springer, London, 2010)
9. Standard CMMI Appraisal Method for Process Improvement. CMU/SEI-2006-HB-002. V1.2. August 2006
10. Appraisal Requirements for CMMI V1.2. (ARC V1.2). SCAMPI Upgrade Team. TR CMU/SEI-2006-TR-011. August 2006

Software Engineering Tools

17

Abstract

This chapter discusses various tools to support the various software engineering activities. The focus is first to define the process and then to find tools to support the process. Tools to support project management are discussed as well as tools to support requirements engineering, configuration management, design and development activities and software testing.

Keywords

Microsoft project · Cocomo · Planview enterprise · IBM Rational DOORS · Rational software modeler · LDRA testbed · Integrated development environment · Sparx Enterprise Architect · HP Quality Center

17.1 Introduction

The goal of this chapter is to give a flavour of a selection of tools[1] that can support the performance of the various software engineering activities. Tools for project management, requirements management, configuration management, design and development, testing and so on are considered. The approach is generally to choose tools to support the process, rather than choosing a process to support the tool.[2]

Mature organizations will employ a structured approach to the introduction of new tools. First, the requirements for a new tool are specified, and the options to satisfy the requirements are considered. These may include developing a tool

---

[1]The list of tools discussed in this chapter is intended to give a flavour of what tools are available, and the inclusion of a particular tool is not intended as a recommendation of that tool. Similarly, the omission of a particular tool should not be interpreted as disapproval of that tool.

[2]That is, the process normally comes first then the tool rather than the other way around.

© Springer International Publishing AG 2017   279
G. O'Regan, *Concise Guide to Software Engineering*, Undergraduate Topics
in Computer Science, DOI 10.1007/978-3-319-57750-0_17

Table 17.1 Tool evaluation table

	Tool 1	Tool 2	...	Tool k
Requirement 1	8	7		9
Requirement 2	4	6		8
...				
...				
Requirement n	3	6		8
Total	35	38	...	45

internally, outsourcing the development of a tool to a third-party supplier or purchasing an off-the-shelf solution from a vendor.

The sample tool evaluation process below (Table 17.1) lists all of the requirements vertically that the test tool is to satisfy, and the candidate tools that are to be evaluated and rated against each requirement are listed horizontally. Various rating schemes may be employed, and a simple numeric mechanism is employed for the example below. The tool evaluation criteria are used to rate the effectiveness of each candidate tool and to indicate the extent to which the tool satisfies the defined requirements. The chosen tool in this example is Tool k as it is the most highly rated of the evaluated tools.

Several candidate tools will be identified and considered prior to selection, and each candidate tool will be evaluated to determine the extent to which it satisfies the specified requirements. An informed decision is then made, and the proposed tool will be piloted prior to its deployment. The pilot provides feedback on its suitability, and the feedback will be considered prior to a decision on full deployment, and whether any customization is required prior to roll-out.

Finally, the users are trained on the tool, and the tool is rolled out throughout the organization. Support is provided for a period post-deployment. First, we consider a selection of tools for project management.

17.2   Tools for Project Management

There are several tools to support the various project management activities such as estimation and cost prediction, planning and scheduling, monitoring risks and issues, and managing a portfolio of projects. These include tools like Microsoft Project, which is a powerful project planning and scheduling tool that is widely used in industry. Small projects may employ a simpler tool such as Microsoft Excel for their project scheduling activities.

The Constructive Cost Model (Cocomo) is a cost prediction model developed by Boehm [1], and it is used to estimate effort, schedule and cost for small and medium projects. It is based on an effort estimation equation that calculates the software development effort in person-months from the estimated project size. The effort estimation calculation is based on the estimate of a project's size in thousands of *source lines of code* (SLOC[3]). The accuracy of the tool is limited, as there is a great deal of variation among teams due to differences in the expertise and experience of the personnel in the project team.

There are several commercial variants of the tool including the COCOMO Basic, Intermediate and Advanced Models. The Intermediate Model includes several cost drivers to model the project environment, and each cost driver is rated. There are over fifteen cost drivers used, and these include product complexity, reliability and experience of personnel as well as programming language experience. The COCOMO parameters need to be calibrated to reflect the actual project development environment. The effort equation used in COCOMO is given by:

$$\text{Effort} = 2.94 * \text{EAF} * (\text{KSLOC})^{\text{E}} \qquad (17.1)$$

In this equation, EAF refers to the effort adjustment factor that is derived from the cost drivers, and E is the exponent that is derived from the five scale drivers.[4] The Costar tool is a commercial tool that implements the COCOMO Model, and it may be used on small or large projects. It needs to be calibrated to reflect the particular software engineering environment, and this will enable more accurate estimates to be produced.

Microsoft Project (Fig. 2.2) is a project management tool that is used for planning, scheduling and charting project information. It enables a realistic project schedule to be created, and the schedule is updated regularly during the project to reflect the actual progress made, and the project is re-planned as appropriate. We discussed project management in Chap. 2.

A project is defined as a series of steps or tasks to achieve a specific goal. The amount of time that it takes to complete a task is termed its duration, and tasks are performed in a sequence determined by the nature of the project. Resources such as people and equipment are required to perform a task. A project will typically consist of several phases such as planning and requirements, design, implementation, testing and closing the project.

The project schedule (Fig. 2.2) shows the tasks and activities to be carried out during the project, the effort and duration of each task and activity, the percentage complete of each task and the resources needed to carry out the various tasks. The schedule shows how the project will be delivered within the key project parameters such as time, cost and functionality without compromising quality in any way.

The project manager is responsible for managing the schedule and will take corrective action when project performance deviates from expectations. The project schedule will be updated regularly to reflect actual progress made, and the project re-planned appropriately.

---

[3]SLOC includes delivered source lines of code created by project staff (excluding automated code generated and also code comments).

[4]The five scale drivers are factors contributing to duration and cost and they determine the exponent used in the Effort equation. Examples include team cohesion and process maturity.

The project manager may employ tools for recording and managing risks and issues, and this may be as simple as using an excel spreadsheet. The project manager may maintain a lessons learned log to record the lessons learned during a project, and these will be analysed towards the end of a project and the lessons learned report prepared. The project reporting may be done with a tool or with a standard Microsoft Word report.

Project portfolio management (PPM) is concerned with managing a portfolio of projects, and it allows the organization to choose the mix and sequencing of its projects in order to yield the greatest business benefit to the organization.

PPM tools analyse the project's total expected cost, the resources required, the schedule, the benefits that will be realized as well as interdependencies with other projects in the portfolio. This allows project investment decisions to be made methodically to deliver the greatest benefit to the organization. This approach moves away from the normal once off analysis of an individual project proposal, to the analysis of a portfolio of projects. PPM tools aim to manage the continuous flow of projects from concept all the way to completion.

There are several commercial portfolio management tools available from various vendors. These include Clarity PPM from Computer Associates, Change Point from Compuware, RPM from IBM Rational, PPM Center from HP and Planview Enterprise from Planview. We limit our discussion in this section to the Planview Enterprise tool.

Planview Enterprise Portfolio Management allows organizations to manage projects and resources across the enterprise and to align their initiatives for maximum business benefit. It provides visibility into and control of project portfolios and allows the organization to prioritize and manage its projects and resources. This allows it to make better investment decisions and to balance its business strategy against its available resources. Planview helps an organization to optimize its business through eight key capabilities (Table 17.2):

Planview allows key project performance indicators to be closely tracked, and these include dashboard views of variances of cost, effort and schedule, which are used for analysis and reporting (Fig. 17.1).

Planview includes Process Builder (Fig. 17.2), which allows modelling and management of enterprise-wide processes. It provides tracking, control and audit capabilities in key process areas such as requirements management and product development, as well as satisfying key regulatory requirements.

The organization may define and model its processes in Process Builder, and this includes process adoption, compliance and continuous improvement. The functionality includes as follows:

- Process design.
- Process automation.
- Process measurement.
- Process auditing.

Table 17.2 Key capabilities of planview enterprise

Capability	Description
Strategic planning	Define mission, objectives and strategies Allocate funding/staffing for chosen strategy Automate and manage strategic process
Investment analysis	Devise strategic long-term plans Identify key criteria to evaluate initiatives Optimize strategic and project investments to maximize business benefit
Capacity management	Balance resources with business demands Ensure capacity supports business strategy Align top-down and bottom-up planning Forecast resource capacity
Demand management	Request work and check status Review lifecycles
Project management	Scope, schedule and execution of work Track/report time worked against projects Track and manage risks and issues Track/display performance and trend analysis
Financial management	Collaborate to better forecast cost Monitor spending
Resource management	Balance portfolios/assign people efficiently Improve forecasting Keep staff productive
Change management	Determine impact of change on schedule/cost Effectively manage change

Fig. 17.1 Dashboard views in planview enterprise

Fig. 17.2 Planview process builder

Next, we will consider tools to support requirements development and management.

17.3 Tools for Requirements

There are several tools available to assist organizations in carrying out requirements development and management. These tools assist in eliciting requirements from the stakeholders, modelling requirements, verifying and validating the requirements, managing the requirements throughout the lifecycle, and providing traceability of the requirements to the design and test cases. The following is a small selection of some of the tools that are available (Table 17.3):

Doors® (Dynamic Object-Oriented Requirements System) is a requirements management tool developed by IBM Rational. It allows the stakeholders to actively participate in the requirements process and aims to optimize requirements communication, collaboration and verification. High-quality requirements help the organization in reducing costs[5] and in meeting their business objectives.

---

[5]A good requirements process will enable high-quality requirements to be consistently produced, and the cost of poor quality is reduced as wastage and rework are minimized. The requirements are the foundation of the system, and if they are incorrect then the delivered system will not be fit for purpose.

Table 17.3 Tools for requirements development and management

Tool	Description
Doors (IBM/Rational)	This is a requirements management tool developed by Telelogic (which is now part of IBM/Rational)
RequisitePro (IBM/Rational)	This is a requirements management and use case management tool developed by IBM/Rational
Enterprise Architect (Sparx Systems)	This is a UML analysis and design tool that covers requirements gathering, analysis and design, and testing and maintenance. It was developed by Sparx Systems and integrates requirements management with the other software development activities
Core (Vitech)	This is a requirements tool developed by Vitech, which may be used for modelling and simulation
Integrity (MKS)	This tool was developed by MKS and enables organizations to capture and validate software requirements, and to link them to downstream development and testing activities

The tool can capture, link, trace, analyse and manage changes to the requirements. It enhances communication and collaboration to ensure that the project conforms to the customer requirements, as well as compliance to regulations and standards.

Requirements are documented in a way that is easy to interpret and navigate. It is easy to locate information within the database, and the user requirements are recorded in a document style showing each individual requirement. It provides views of the list with assigned identifiers and also an Explorer-like navigation tree.

The tool employs links to support traceability of the requirements, and these are traversed with a simple click of the mouse to the corresponding object. The links are easy to create by dragging and dropping; for example, a new link from the user requirements to the system requirements is created in this way. The tool provides dynamic reporting on traceability, and filters may be employed to ensure that traceability is complete. Traceability is essential in demonstrating that the requirements have been implemented and tested.

The management of change is an important part of the requirements process. The Doors tool supports changes to requirements and allows an impact analysis of the proposed changes to be performed. It allows changes that could impact other requirements or design items and test cases to be tagged. The Doors$^{®}$ tool (Fig. 17.3) provides:

- A comprehensive requirements management environment.
- Web browser access to the requirements database.
- Manages changes to requirements.
- Scalable solution for managing project scope and cost.
- Traceability to design items, Test Plans and test cases.
- Active engagement from stakeholders.
- Integrates with other IBM Rational tools.

There are several other IBM Rational tools that may be integrated with Doors$^{®}$. These include the IBM Rational System Architect, Requirements Composer, Rhapsody and Quality Manager.

Fig. 17.3 IBM Rational DOORS tool

IBM Rational RequisitePro is a requirements management tool that allows requirements to be documented with familiar document-based methods, and it provides capabilities such as requirements traceability and impact analysis. Requirements are managed throughout the lifecycle, and changes to the requirements controlled.

The CORE product suite was developed by Vitech, and it has functionality for requirements management, modelling and simulation, and verification and validation. It supports UML activity and sequence diagrams, which are used to describe the desired behaviour and flow of control, as well as allowing analysis to be carried out. The tool provides:

- Comprehensive end-to-end system traceability.
- Change impact analysis.
- Multiple modelling notations with integrated graphical views.
- System simulation based on behavioural models.
- Generation of documentation from the database.

The Integrity tool was developed by MKS, and it enables organizations to capture and validate software requirements. It enables them to link the requirements to downstream development and testing activities, and to manage changes to the requirements. Next, we will consider tools to support software design and development.

17.4 Tools for Design and Development

Table 17.4 describes various tools to support software design and development activities. The software design includes the high-level architecture of the system, as well as the lower level design and algorithms.

Table 17.4 Tools for software design

Tool	Description
Microsoft Visio	This tool is used to create many types of drawings such as flowcharts, work flow diagrams and network diagrams
IBM Rational Software Modeler	This is a UML-based visual modelling and software design tool
IBM Rational Rhapsody	This modelling environment tool is based on UML and provides a visual development environment for software engineers. It uses graphical models and generates code in C, C++ and Java
IBM Rational Software Architect	This modelling and development tool uses UML for designing architecture for C++ and Java applications
Enterprise Architect (Sparx Systems)	This UML analysis and design tool is used for modelling systems with traceability from requirements to design and testing. It supports code generation

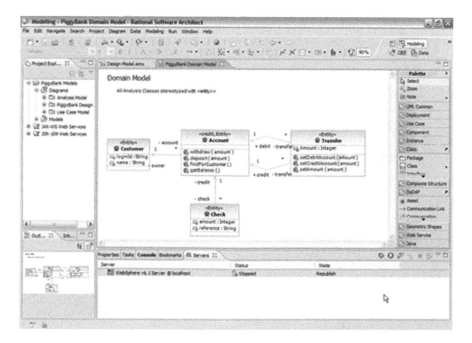

Fig. 17.4 IBM Rational Software Modeler

IBM Rational Software Modeler® (RSM) is a UML-based visual modelling and design tool (Fig. 17.4). It promotes communication and collaboration during design and development and allows information about development projects to be specified and communicated from several perspectives. It is used for model-driven development and aligns the business needs with the product.

It gives the organization control over the evolving architecture and provides an integrated analysis and design platform. Abstract UML specifications may be built with traceability and impact analysis shown.

It has an intuitive user interface and a diagram editor to create expressive and interactive diagrams. The tool may be integrated with other IBM Rational tools such as Clearcase, Clearquest and RequisitePro.

IBM Rational Rhapsody® is a visual development environment used in real-time or embedded systems. It helps teams collaborate to understand and elaborate requirements, abstract complexity using modelling languages such as UML, validate functionality early in development and automate code generation to speed up the development process.

Sparx Enterprise Architect (Fig. 17.5) is a UML analysis and design tool used for modelling business and IT systems. It was developed by the Australian company, Sparx Systems, and it covers the full product development lifecycle, including business modelling, requirements management, software design, code generation and testing. It supports automated document generation, code generation and reverse engineering of source code. Its reverse engineering feature allows a visual representation of the software application to be provided.

Fig. 17.5 Sparx Enterprise Architect

It is a multi-user graphical tool with built-in reporting and documentation. It can model, manage and trace requirements to the design, test cases and deployment, and it can trace the implementation of the system requirements to model elements. It can search and report on requirements and perform an impact analysis on proposed changes to the requirements.

The tool allows deployments scripts to be built, debugged and tested and executed from within its development environment. UML and modelling are integrated into the development process, and debugging capabilities are provided. This includes runtime examination of the executing code for several programming languages, and NUnit and JUnit test classes (used as part of test-driven development) may be generated and integrated directly into the test process.

An integrated development environment (IDE) is a software application that provides comprehensive support facilities to software developers. It includes specialized text editors, a compiler, build automation and debugging capabilities. The features of an IDE are described in Table 17.5 below:

IDEs help to improve programmer productivity. They are usually dedicated to a specific programming language, although there are some multi-language tools such as Eclipse and Microsoft Visual Studio. There are many IDEs for languages such as Pascal, C, C++ and Java. The next section is concerned with tools to support configuration management.

Table 17.5 Integrated development environment

Item	Description
Source code editor	This is a specialized text editor (e.g. Microsoft Visual Studio) designed for editing the source code. It includes features to speed up the input of source code, including syntax checking of the code while the programmer types
Compiler or interpreter	A compiler is a computer program that translates the high-level programming language source code into object code to produce the executable code. A compiler carries out lexical analysis, parsing and code generation An interpreter is a program that executes instructions written in a programming language. It may involve the direction execution of the code, translation of the code into an intermediate representation and immediate direct execution, or execution of stored precompiled code made by a compiler which is part of the Interpreter System
Build automation tools	Build automation involves scripting to automate the build process. This includes tasks such as compiling the source code, linking the object code and building the executable software, performing automated tests and reporting results, reporting the build status and generating release notes
Debugger	A debugger is a software application that is used to debug and test other software programs. Debuggers offer step-by-step execution of the code, or execution to break points in the code. Examples include IBM Rational Purify and Microsoft Visual Studio Debugger

17.5   Tools for Configuration Management and Change Control

Configuration management is concerned with identifying the work products that are subject to change control, and controlling changes to them. It involves creating and releasing baselines, maintaining their integrity, recording and reporting the status of the configuration items and change requests, and verifying the correctness and completeness of the configuration items with configuration audits.

Visual Source Safe (VSS) is a version control management system for source code and binary files. It was developed by the Microsoft Corporation and is used mainly by small software development organizations. It allows multiple users to place their source code and work products under version control management. It is fairly easy to use and may be integrated with the Microsoft Visual Studio tool. Microsoft plans to replace VSS with its Visual Studio Team System tool.

Polytron Version Control System (PVCS) is a version control system for software code and binary files. It was developed by Serena Software Inc. and is suitable for use by large or small teams. It allows multiple users to place their source code and project deliverables under version control management, and it allows files to be checked in and checked out, baselines to be controlled, rollback of code and tracking of check-ins. It includes functionality for branching, merging and labelling. It includes the PV Tracker tool for tracking defects, and the PV Builder tool for performing builds and releases.

The PV Tracker tool automates the capture and communication of issues and change requests. This is done throughout the software development lifecycle for project teams, and the tool allows the developers to link the affected source code files with issues and changes. It allows managers to determine and report on team progress, and to prioritize tasks. PV Builder maintains an audit trail of the files included in the build as well as their versions.

IBM Rational Clearcase and Clearquest are popular configuration management tools with a rich feature set. Clearcase allows software code and other software deliverables to be placed under version control management, and it may be employed in large or medium projects. It can handle a large number of files, and it supports standard configuration management tasks such as checking in and checking out of the software assets as well as labelling and branching. Objects are stored in repositories called VOBs.

Clearquest may be linked to Clearcase and to other IBM Rational tools. It allows the defects in a project to be tracked, and it allows the versions of source code modules that were changed to be linked to a defect number in Clearquest.

17.6   Tools for Code Analysis and Code Inspections

Static code analysis is the analysis of software code without the actual execution of the code. It is usually performed with automated tools, and the analysis performed depends on the sophistication of the tools. Some tools may analyse individual statements or declarations, whereas others may analyse the whole source code. The objective of the analysis is to highlight potential coding errors early in the development lifecycle.

The LDRA Tools automatically determine the complexity of the source code and provide metrics that give an indication of the maintainability of the code. A useful feature of LDRA is that it gives a visual picture of system complexity, and it has a re-factoring tool to assist with its reduction. It generates code assessment reports listing all of the files examined and providing metrics of the clarity, maintainability and testability of the code. Other LDRA tools may be used for code coverage analysis (Fig. 17.6).

Compliance to coding standards is important in producing readable code and in preventing error-prone coding styles. There are several tools available to check conformance to coding standards including the LDRA TBvision tool, which has reporting capabilities to show code quality as well as fault detection and avoidance measures. It provides intuitive functionality to view the results in various graphs and reports.

Some static code analysis tools (e.g. tools for formal methods) aim to prove properties about a particular program. This may include reasoning about program correctness or that of a program meeting its specification. These tools often provide support for assertions, and a precondition is the assertion placed before the code fragment, and this predicate is true before execution of the code. The post-condition is the assertion placed after the code fragment, and this predicate is true after the execution of the code.

	Percentage	Success Limit
▲ Productdatabase.cpp		
▲ Combined Coverage Run	Failed	
Statement Coverage	99	100
Branch/Decision Coverage	94	100
Modified Condition / Decision Coverage	75	100
▷ main		
▲ ProductDatabase		
▲ Combined Coverage Run	Passed	
Statement Coverage	100	100
Branch/Decision Coverage	100	100
Modified Condition / Decision Coverage	100	100
▲ resetCountedProducts		
▲ Combined Coverage Run	Passed	
Statement Coverage	100	100
Branch/Decision Coverage	100	100
Modified Condition / Decision Coverage	100	100
▲ countProduct		
▲ Combined Coverage Run	Failed	
Statement Coverage	97	100
Branch/Decision Coverage	86	100
Modified Condition / Decision Coverage	50	100

Fig. 17.6 LDRA code coverage analysis report

There are several open-source tools available for static code analysis, and these include the RATS tools which provide multi-language support for C, C++, Perl and PHP, and the PMD tool for Java. There are several commercial tools available, and these include the LDRA Testbed tool which provides support for C, C++ and Java. The fortify tool helps developers to identify security vulnerabilities in C, C++ and Java, and the Parasoft tool helps developers to identify coding issues that lead to security, reliability, performance and maintainability issues later.

17.7   Tools for Testing

Testing plays a key role in verifying that the software system satisfies the requirements and is fit for purpose. There are various tools to support testing such as test management tools, defect tracking tools, regression test automation tools and performance tools. The tools considered in this section include as follows:

- Test Director (HP Quality Center).
- Winrunner.
- Load Runner.

Test Director (now called HP Quality Center) is a web-based test management tool developed by HP Mercury.[6] It provides a consistent repeatable process for gathering requirements, planning and scheduling tests, analysing results and managing defects. It consists of four modules namely:

- Requirements.
- Test Plan.
- Test Lab.
- Defect management.

The Requirements module supports requirements management and traceability of the test cases to the requirements. The Test Plan module supports the creation and update of test cases. The Test Lab module supports execution of the test cases defined in the Test Plan module. The Defect Management module supports the logging of defects, and these defects can be linked back to the test cases that failed.

HP Quality Center supports a high level of collaboration and communication between the stakeholders. It allows the business analysts to define the application requirements and testing objectives. The test managers and testers may then design Test Plans, test cases and automated scripts. The testers then run the manual and

---

[6]Mercury is now part of HP.

Fig. 17.7 HP Quality Center

automated tests, report results and log the defects. The developers review and correct the logged defects. Project and test managers can create status reports and manage test resources. Test and product managers decide objectively whether the application is ready to be released.

The HP Quality Center™ tool (Fig. 17.7) standardizes and manages the entire test and quality process and is a web-based system for automated software quality management and testing. It employs dashboard technology to give visibility into the process.

Mercury developed the Winrunner tool that automatically captures, verifies and replays user interactions. It is mainly used to automate regression testing, which improves productivity and allows defects to be identified in a timely manner. This provides confidence that enhancements to the software have had no negative impact on the integrity of the system. The Winrunner tool has been replaced by HP Unified Functional Testing Software, which includes HP Quick Test Professional and HP Service Test.

Mercury developed the LoadRunner performance testing tool, which allows a software application to be tested with thousands of concurrent users to determine its performance under heavy loads. It allows the scalability of the software system to be determined, and whether it can support future predicted growth.

17.8   Review Questions

1. Why are tools used in software engineering?
2. How should a tool be selected?
3. What is the relationship between the process and the tool?
4. What tools would you recommend for project management?
5. Describe how you would go about selecting a tool for requirements development.
6. Describe various tools that are available for design and development.
7. What tools would you recommend for testing?
8. What tools would you recommend for configuration management?

17.9   Summary

The objective of this chapter was to give a flavour of various tools available to support the organization in engineering software. These included tools for project management, configuration management, design and development, test management. The tools are chosen to support the process.

The project management tools included a discussion of the Cocomo Cost Model, which may be employed to estimate the cost and effort for a project, and the Microsoft Project tool, which is used extensively by project managers to schedule and track their projects. The Planview Portfolio Management Tool was also discussed, and this tool allows an organization to manage a portfolio of projects.

The tools to support requirements development and management included IBM Rational Doors, RequisitePro and Core. The Doors tool allows all stakeholders to actively participate in the requirements process and aims to optimize requirements communication, collaboration and verification.

The tools to support design and development included the IBM Rational Software Modeler tool, the Sparx Enterprise Architect tool and Integrated Developer Environments to support software developers. The Rational Software Modeler® (RSM) is a UML-based visual modelling and design tool. Enterprise Architect is a UML analysis and design tool and provides traceability from requirements to design, testing and deployment. The tools discussed to support configuration management included PVCS and Clearcase.

The tools to support testing included Quality Center™, Winrunner and LoadRunner. HP Quality Center™ standardizes and manages the entire test process. It has modules for requirements management, test planning, Test Lab and defect management.

Tool selection is done in a controlled manner. First, the organization needs to determine its requirements for the tool. Various candidate tools are evaluated, and a decision on the proposed tool is made. Next, the tool is piloted to ensure that it meets the needs of the organization, and feedback from the pilot may lead to changes or customizations of the tool. Finally, the end-users are trained on the use of the tool, and it is rolled out throughout the organization.

Reference

1. B. Boehm, *Software Engineering Economics* (Prentice Hall, New Jersey, 1981)

Agile Methodology

18

Abstract

This chapter discusses the Agile methodology which is a popular lightweight approach to software development. Agile provides opportunities to assess the direction of a project throughout the development lifecycle, and ongoing changes to requirements are considered normal in the Agile world. It has a strong collaborative style of working, and it advocates adaptive planning and evolutionary development.

Keywords

Sprints · Stand-up meeting · Scrum · Stories · Refactoring · Pair programming · Test-driven development · Continuous integration

18.1 Introduction

Agile is a popular lightweight software development methodology that provides opportunities to assess the direction of a project throughout the development lifecycle. There has been a growth in interest in lightweight software development methodologies since the 1990s, and these include approaches such as rapid application development (RAD), dynamic systems development method (DSDM) and extreme programming (XP). These approaches are referred to collectively as agile methods.

Every aspect of Agile development such as requirements and design is continuously revisited during the development, and the direction of the project is regularly evaluated. Agile focuses on rapid and frequent delivery of partial solutions developed in an iterative and incremental manner. Each partial solution is evaluated by the product owner, and the feedback is used to determine the next steps for the

© Springer International Publishing AG 2017
G. O'Regan, *Concise Guide to Software Engineering*, Undergraduate Topics in Computer Science, DOI 10.1007/978-3-319-57750-0_18

project. Agile claims to be more responsive to customer needs than traditional methods such as the waterfall model, and its adherents believe that it results in:

- higher quality
- higher productivity
- faster time to market
- improved customer satisfaction.

It advocates adaptive planning, evolutionary development, early development, continuous improvement and a rapid response to change. The term *"agile"* was coined by Kent Beck and others in the Agile Manifesto in 2001 [1]. The traditional waterfall model is similar to a wide and slow-moving value stream, and halfway through the project 100% of the requirements are typically 50% done. However, 50% of the requirements are typically 100% done halfway through an agile project.

Agile has a strong collaborative style of working, and ongoing changes to requirements are considered normal in the Agile world. It argues that it is more realistic to change requirements regularly throughout the project, rather than attempting to define all of the requirements at the start of the project (as in the waterfall methodology). Agile includes controls to manage changes to the requirements, and good communication and early regular feedback is an essential part of the process.

A user story may be a new feature or a modification to an existing feature. The feature is reduced to the minimum scope that can deliver business value, and a feature may give rise to several stories. Stories often build upon other stories, and the entire software development lifecycle is employed for the implementation of each story. Stories are either done or not done (i.e. there is no such thing as 50% done), and the story is complete only when it passes its acceptance tests.

Scrum is an Agile method for managing iterative development, and it consists of an outline planning phase for the project, followed by a set of sprint cycles (where each cycle develops an increment). *Sprint planning* is performed before the start of the iteration, and stories are assigned to the iteration to fill the available time. Each Scrum sprint is of a fixed length (usually 2–4 weeks), and it develops an increment of the system.

The estimates for each story and their priority are determined, and the prioritized stories are assigned to the iteration. A short (usually 15 min) morning stand-up meeting is held daily during the iteration, and it is attended by the Scrum master, the project manager[1] and the project team. It discusses the progress made the previous day, problem reporting and tracking, and the work planned for the day ahead. A separate meeting is held for issues that require more detailed discussion.

Once the iteration is complete, the latest product increment is demonstrated to a review audience including the product owner. This is to receive feedback and to identify new requirements. The team also conducts a retrospective meeting to

---

[1]Agile teams are self-organizing, and small teams (team size <20 people) do not usually have a project manager role, and the Scrum master performs some light project management tasks.

identify what went well and what went poorly during the iteration, as part of continuous improvement for future iterations.

The planning for the next sprint then commences. The Scrum master is a facilitator who arranges the daily meetings and ensures that the Scrum process is followed. The role involves removing roadblocks so that the team can achieve their goals, and communicating with other stakeholders. Agile employs pair programming and a collaborative style of working with the philosophy that two heads are better than one. This allows multiple perspectives in decision-making which provides a broader understanding of the issues.

Software testing is very important in verifying that the software is fit for purpose, and Agile generally employs automated testing for unit, acceptance, performance and integration testing. Agile employs *test-driven development* with tests written before the code. The developers write code to make a test pass with ideally developers only coding against failing tests. This approach forces the developer to write testable code, as well as ensuring that the requirements are testable. Tests are run frequently with the goal of catching programming errors early. They are generally run on a separate build server to ensure that all the dependencies are checked. Tests are rerun before making a release.

Refactoring is employed in Agile as a design and coding practice. The objective is to change how the software is written without changing what it does. Refactoring is a tool for evolutionary design where the design is regularly evaluated, and improvements are implemented as they are identified. It helps in improving the maintainability and readability of the code and in reducing complexity. The automated test suite is essential in demonstrating that the integrity of the software is maintained following refactoring.

Continuous integration allows the system to be built with every change. Early and regular integration allows early feedback to be provided, and it also allows all of the automated tests to be run, thereby identifying problems earlier. The main philosophy and features of Agile are:

- Working software is more useful than presenting documents
- Direct interaction preferred over documentation
- Change is accepted as a normal part of life in the Agile world
- Customer involved throughout the project
- Demonstrate value early
- Feedback and adaptation employed in decision-making
- Aim is to achieve a narrow fast-flowing value stream
- User stories and sprints are employed
- A project is divided into iterations
- An iteration has a fixed length (i.e. time boxing is employed)
- Entire software development lifecycle is employed for implementation of the story
- Stories are either done or not done (no such thing as 50% done)
- Iterative and incremental development is employed
- Emphasis on quality

- Stand-up meetings held daily
- Rapid conversion of requirements into working functionality
- Delivery is made as early as possible.
- Maintenance is seen as part of the development process
- Refactoring and evolutionary design employed
- Continuous integration is employed
- Short cycle times
- Plan regularly
- Early decision-making.

Stories are prioritized based on a number of factors including:

- Business value of story
- Mitigation of risk
- Dependencies on other stories.

18.2 Scrum Methodology

Scrum is a framework for managing an Agile software development project. It is not a prescriptive methodology as such, and it relies on a self-organizing, cross-functional team to take the feature from idea to implementation. The cross-functional team includes the *product owner* who represents the interest of the users and ensures that the right product is built; the *Scrum master* is the coach for the team and helps the team to understand the Scrum process and to perform at the highest level, as well as performing some light project management activities such as project tracking, and the *team* itself who decide on which person should work on which tasks and so on.

The Scrum methodology breaks the software development for the project into a series of sprints, where each sprint is of fixed time duration of 2–4 weeks. There is a planning meeting at the start of the sprint where the team members determine the number of items/tasks that they can commit to, and then create a sprint backlog (*to do list*) of the tasks to be performed during the sprint. The Scrum team takes a small set of features from idea to coded and tested functionality that is integrated into the evolving product.

The team attends a daily stand-up meeting (usually of 15-min duration) where the progress of the previous day is discussed, as well as any obstacles to progress. The new functionality is demonstrated to the product owner and any other relevant stakeholders at the end of the sprint, and this may result in changes to the delivered functionality or the addition of new items to the product backlog. There is a sprint retrospective meeting to reflect on the sprint and to identify improvement opportunities.

The main deliverable produced using the Scrum framework is the *product itself*, and Scrum expects to build a properly tested product increment (in a shippable state) at the end of each sprint. The *product backlog* is another deliverable, and it is maintained and prioritized by the product owner. It is a complete list of the functionality (user stories) to be added to the product, and there is also the *sprint backlog* which is the list of functionality to be implemented in the sprint. Other deliverables are the *sprint burnout* and *release burnout* charts, which show the amount of work remaining in a sprint or release, and indicate the extent to which the sprint or release is on schedule.

The Scrum Master is the expert on the Agile process and acts as a coach to the team, thereby helping the team to achieve a high level of performance. The role differs from that of a project manager, as the Scrum Master does not assign tasks to individuals or provide day-to-day direction to the team. However, the Scrum master typically performs some light project management tasks.

Many of the traditional project manager responsibilities such as task assignment and day-to-day project decisions revert back to the team, and the responsibility for the scope and schedule trade-off goes to the product owner. The product owner creates and communicates a solid vision of the product and shares the vision through the product backlog. Larger Agile projects (team size > 20) will often have a dedicated project manager role.

18.3 User Stories

A *user story* is a short simple description of a feature written from the viewpoint of the user of the system. They are often written on index cards or sticky notes and arranged on walls or tables to facilitate discussion. This approach facilitates the discussion of the functionality rather than the written text.

A user story can be written at varying levels of detail, and a large detailed user story is known as an epic. An epic story is often too large to be implemented in one sprint, and such a story is often split into several smaller user stories.

It is the product owner's responsibility to ensure that a product backlog of user stories exist, but the product owner is not required to write all stories. In fact, anyone can write a user story, and each team member usually writes a user story during an Agile project. User stories are written throughout an Agile project, with a user story-writing workshop held at the beginning of the project. This leads to the product backlog that describes the functionality to be added during the project. Some of these will be epics, and these will need to be decomposed into smaller stories that will fit into the time boxed sprint. New user stories may be written at any time and added to the product backlog.

There is no requirements document as such in Agile, and the product backlog (i.e. the prioritized list of functionality of the product to be developed) is closest to the idea of a requirements document for a traditional project. However, the written part of a user story in Agile is incomplete until the discussion of that story takes place. It is often useful to think of the written part of a story as a pointer to the real requirement, such as a diagram showing a workflow or the formula for a calculation.

18.4   Estimation in Agile

Planning poker is a popular consensus-based estimation technique often used in Agile, and it is used to estimate the effort required to implement a user story. The planning session starts with the product owner reading the user story or describing a feature to the estimators.

Each estimator holds a deck of planning poker cards with values like 0, 1, 2, 3, 5, 8, 13, 20, 40 and 100, where the values represent the units in which the team estimates. The estimators discuss the feature with the product owner, and when the discussion is fully complete and all questions answered, each estimator privately selects a card to reflect his or her estimate.

All cards are then revealed, and if all values are the same then that value is chosen as the estimate. Otherwise, the estimators discuss their estimates with the rationale for the highest and lowest discussed in detail. Each estimator then reselects an estimate card, and the process continues until consensus is achieved, or if consensus cannot be achieved the estimation of the particular item is deferred until more information is available.

The initial estimation session usually takes place after the initial product backlog is written. This session may take a number of days, and it is used to create the initial estimates of the size and scope of the project. Further estimation and planning sessions take place regularly during the project as user stories are added to the product backlog, and these will typically take place towards the end of the current sprint.

The advantage of the estimation process employed is that it brings multiple expert opinions from the cross-functional team together, and the experts justify their estimates in the detailed discussion. This helps to improve the estimation accuracy in the project.

18.5   Test-Driven Development

Test-driven development (TDD) is a software development process often employed in Agile. It was developed by Kent Beck and others as part of XP, and the developers focus on testing the requirements before writing the code. The application is written with testability in mind, and the developers must consider how to test the application in advance. Further, it ensures that test cases for every feature are written, and writing tests early help in gaining a deeper understanding of the requirements.

TDD is based on the transition of the requirements into a set of test cases, and the software is then written to pass the test cases. Another words, the TDD of a new feature begins with writing a suite of test cases based on the requirements for the feature, and the code for the feature is written to pass the test cases. This is a paradigm shift from traditional software engineering where the unit tests are written and executed after the code is written.

The tests are written for the new feature, and initially all tests fail as no code has been written, and so the first step is to write some code that enables the new test cases to pass. This new code may be imperfect (it will be improved later), but this is acceptable at this time as the only purpose is to pass the new test cases. The next step is to ensure that the new feature works with the existing features, and this involves executing all new and existing test cases.

This may involve modification of the source code to enable all of the tests to pass and to ensure that all features work correctly together. The final step is refactoring the code, and this involves cleaning up and restructuring the code, and improving its structure and readability. The test cases are rerun during the refactoring to ensure that the functionality is not altered in any way. The process repeats with the addition of each new feature.

Continuous integration allows the system to be built with every change, and this allows early feedback to be provided. It also allows all of the automated tests to be run, thereby ensuring that the new feature works with the existing functionality, and identifying problems earlier.

18.6   Pair Programming

Pair programming is an agile technique where two programmers work together at one computer. The author of the code is termed the *driver*, and the other programmer is termed the *observer* (or *navigator*), and is responsible for reviewing each line of written code. The observer also considers the strategic direction of the coding and proposes improvement suggestions and potential problems that may need to be addressed. The driver can focus on the implementation of the current task and use the observer as a safety net. The two programmers switch roles regularly during the development of the new functionality.

Pair programming requires more programming effort to develop code compared to programmers working individually. However, the resulting code is of higher quality, with fewer defects and a reduction in the cost of maintenance. Further, pair programming enables a better design solution to be created as more design alternatives are considered.

This is since two programmers are bringing different experiences to the problem, and they may have different ways of solving the problem. This leads them to explore a larger number of ways of solving the problem than an individual programmer. Finally, pair programming is good for knowledge sharing and learning, and it allows knowledge to be shared on programming practice and design and allows knowledge about the system to be shared throughout the team.

18.7 Review Questions

1. What is Agile?
2. How does Agile differ from the waterfall model?
3. What is a user story?
4. Explain how estimation is done in Agile.
5. What is test-driven development?
6. Describe the Scrum methodology and the role of the Scrum Master.
7. Explain pair programming and describe its advantages.

18.8 Summary

This chapter gave a brief introduction to Agile, which is a popular lightweight software development methodology. Agile advocates adaptive planning, evolutionary development, early development, continuous improvement and a rapid response to change. The traditional waterfall model is similar to a wide and slow-moving value stream, and halfway through the project 100% of the requirements are typically 50% done. However, 50% of the requirements are typically 100% done halfway through an agile project.

Agile has a strong collaborative style of working, and ongoing changes to requirements are considered normal in the Agile world. It includes controls to manage changes to the requirements, and good communication and early regular feedback is an essential part of the process.

A story may be a new feature or a modification to an existing feature. It is reduced to the minimum scope that can deliver business value, and a feature may give rise to several stories. Stories often build upon other stories, and the entire software development lifecycle is employed for the implementation of each story. Stories are either done or not done, and the story is complete only when it passes its acceptance tests.

The Scrum approach is an Agile method for managing iterative development, and it consists of an outline planning phase for the project followed by a set of sprint cycles (where each cycle develops an increment). Each Scrum sprint is of a fixed length (usually 2–4 weeks), and it develops an increment of the system.

The estimates for each story and their priority are determined, and the prioritized stories are assigned to the iteration. A short (usually 15 min) morning stand-up meeting is held daily during the iteration and attended by the project manager and the project team. It discusses the progress made the previous day, problem reporting and tracking, and the work planned for the day ahead.

Once the iteration is complete, the latest product increment is demonstrated to a review audience including the product owner. This is to receive feedback and to identify new requirements. The team also conducts a retrospective meeting to identify what went well and what went poorly during the iteration, as part of continuous improvement for future sprints.

Reference

1. K. Beck et al., Manifesto for Agile Software Development. Agile Alliance (2001), http://agilemanifesto.org/

A Miscellany of Innovation

19

Abstract

This chapter discusses innovation in the software field including miscellaneous topics such as distributed systems, service-oriented architecture (SOA), software as a service (SaaS), cloud computing and embedded systems. We discuss the need for innovation in software engineering and discuss some recent innovations including aspect-oriented software engineering (AOSE).

Keywords

Distributed system · Service-oriented architecture · Software as a service · Cloud computing · Aspect-oriented software engineering · Embedded systems · Innovation in software engineering

19.1 Introduction

The objective of this chapter is to give a flavour of several topics that have become relevant to the software engineering field in recent times. The software field is highly innovative and continually evolving, and this has led to the development of many new technologies and systems. This includes distributed systems, service-oriented architecture (SOA), software as a service (SaaS), cloud computing, embedded systems. Software engineering needs to continually respond to the emerging technology trends with innovative solutions and methodologies to support the latest developments.

A distributed system is a collection of computers that appears to be a single system, and many large computer systems used today are distributed systems. A distributed system allows hardware and software resources to be shared, and it

© Springer International Publishing AG 2017

G. O'Regan, *Concise Guide to Software Engineering*, Undergraduate Topics in Computer Science, DOI 10.1007/978-3-319-57750-0_19

supports concurrency with multiple processors running on different computers on the network.

SOA is a way of developing a distributed system consisting of stand-alone web services that may be executing on distributed computers in different geographical regions. SaaS allows software to be hosted remotely on a server (or servers), and the user is able to access the software over the Internet through a web browser. Cloud computing is a type of Internet-based computing that provides computing resources and various other services on demand.

An embedded system is a computer system within a larger electrical or mechanical system, and it is *embedded* as part of a complete system that includes hardware and mechanical parts. An embedded system is usually designed to do a specific task rather than as a general purpose device, and it may be subject to real-time performance constraints.

Many innovative software engineering practices have been developed since the birth of software engineering. We discuss aspect-oriented software engineering (AOSE), which is based on the principle of separation of concerns. It states that software should be organized so that each program element does exactly one thing and one thing only. AOSE has been applied to requirements engineering, software design and programming, with the goal is to make it easier to maintain and reuse the software.

19.2   Distributed Systems

A distributed system (Fig. 19.1) is a collection of computers, interconnected via a network, which is capable of collaborating on a task. It appears to be a single integrated computing system to the user, and most large computer systems today are distributed systems. The components (or nodes) of a distributed system are located on networked computers and interact to achieve a common goal.

Fig. 19.1 A distributed system

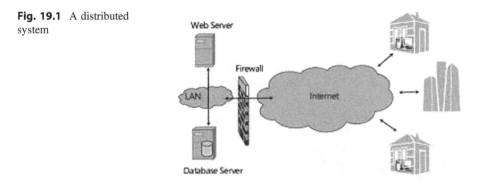

The communication and coordination of action is via message passing. A distributed system is not centrally controlled, and as a result, the individual computers may behave differently at different times, and each computer has a limited and incomplete view of the system.

A distributed system allows hardware and software resources (e.g. printers and files) to be shared, and information may be shared between people and processes located in distant geographical regions. It supports concurrency with multiple processors running on different computers on the network. The processors in a distributed system run concurrently in parallel, and each computer is running on its own local operating system.

A distributed system is designed to tolerate failures on individual computers, and the system is designed to be reliable and to continue service when a node fails. Another words, a distributed system needs to be designed to be fault tolerant, and it must remain available even if there are hardware, software or network failures. This requires recovery and redundancy features such as the duplication of information on several computers to be built in. The fault-tolerant design allows continuity of service (possibly a degraded service) when failures occur.

The design of distributed systems is more complex than a centralized system, as there may be complex interactions between its components and the system infrastructure. The performance of the distributed system is dependent on the network bandwidth and load, as well as on the speed of the computers that are on the network. This differs from a centralized system, which is dependent on the speed of a single processor. The performance and response time of a distributed system may vary (and be unpredictable) depending on the network load and network bandwidth, and so the response time may vary from user to user.

The nodes in a distributed system are often independent systems with no central control, and the network connecting the nodes is a complex system in its own right, which is not controlled by the systems using the network. There are many applications of distributed system in the telecommunication domain, such as fixed line, mobile and wireless networks, company intranets, the Internet and the World Wide Web. Next, we describe SOA and how it is used in distributed systems.

19.3   Service-Oriented Architecture

The objective of this section is to give a brief introduction to SOA, which is a way of developing a distributed system using stand-alone web services executing on distributed computers in different geographical regions. It is an approach to create an architecture based upon the use of services, where a service may carry out some small functions such as producing data or validating a customer.

A web service is a computational or information resource that may be used by another program, and it allows a service provider to provide a service to an application (*service requestor*) that wishes to use the service. The web service may be accessed remotely and is acted upon independently. The *service provider* is

Fig. 19.2 Service-oriented architecture

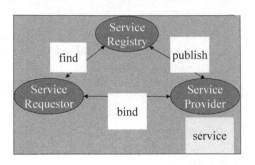

responsible for designing and implementing the services and specifying the interface to the service.

The service is platform and implementation language independent, and it is designed and implemented by the service provider with the interface to the service specified. Information about the service is published in an accessible registry, and service clients (requestor) are able to locate the service provider and link their application with the specific service and communicate with it. The idea of a SOA is illustrated in Fig. 19.2.

There are a number of standards that support communication between services, as well as standards for service interface definition. These are discussed in [1].

19.4   Software as a Service

The idea of SaaS is that the software may be hosted remotely on a server (or servers), and access provided to it over the Internet through a web browser. The functionality is provided at the remote server with client access provided through the web browser.

The cost model for traditional software is made up of an upfront cost for a perpetual licence and optional ongoing support fees. SaaS is a software licensing and delivery model where the software is licensed to the user on a subscription basis. The software provider owns and provides the service, whereas the software organization that is using the service will pay a subscription for its use. Occasionally, the software is free to use with funding for the service provided through the use of advertisements, or there may be a free basic service provided with charges applied for the more advanced version.

A key benefit of SaaS is that the cost of hosting and management of the service is transferred to the service provider, with the provider responsible for resolving defects and installing upgrades of the software. Consequently, the initial set-up costs for users is significantly less than for traditional software.

The disadvantages to the user are that data has to be transferred at the speed of the network, and the transfer of a large amount of data may take a lot of time. The subscription charges may be monthly or annual, with extra charges possibly due depending on the amount of data transferred.

19.5 Cloud Computing

Cloud computing is a type of Internet-based computing that provides computing processing resources on demand. It provides access to a shared pool of configurable computing resources such as networks, servers and applications on demand, and such resources may be provided and released with minimal effort. It provides users and organizations with capabilities to store and process their data in third-party data centres that may be in distant geographical locations.

A key advantage of cloud computing is that it allows companies to avoid large upfront infrastructure costs such as purchasing hardware and servers, and it also allows organizations to focus on their core business. Further, it allows companies to get their applications operational in a shorter period of time, as well as providing an efficient way for companies to adjust resources to deal with fluctuating demand. Companies can scale up as computing needs increase and scale down as demand decreases. Cloud providers generally use a "pay as you go" model (Fig. 19.3).

Among the well-known cloud computing platforms are Amazon's Elastic Compute Cloud, Microsoft's Azure and Oracle's cloud. The main enabling technology for cloud computing is virtualization, which separates a physical computing device into one or more virtual devices. Each of the virtual devices may be easily used and managed to perform computing tasks, and this leads to the creation of a scalable system of multiple independent computing devices that allows the idle physical resources to be allocated and used more effectively.

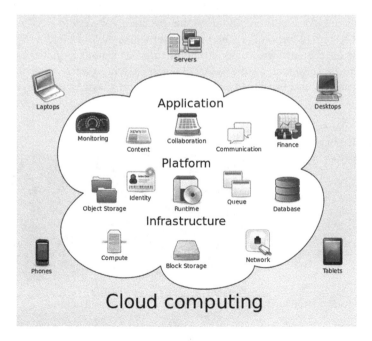

Fig. 19.3 Cloud computing. Creative commons

Cloud computing providers offer their services according to different models. These include infrastructure as a service (IaaS) where computing infrastructure such as virtual machines and other resources are provided as a service to subscribers. Platform as a service (PaaS) provides capability to the consumer to deploy infrastructure related or application related that are supported by the provider onto the cloud. PaaS vendors offer a development platform to application developers. SaaS provides capability to the consumer to use the provider's applications running on a cloud infrastructure through a web browser or a program interface. Cloud providers manage the infrastructure and platforms that run the applications.

19.6   Embedded Systems

An embedded system is a computer system within a larger electrical or mechanical system that is usually subject to real-time constraints. The computer system is *embedded* as part of a complete system that includes hardware and mechanical parts. Embedded systems vary from personal devices such as MP3 players and mobile phones, to household devices such as dishwashers and cookers, to the automotive sector and to traffic lights. An embedded system is usually designed to do a specific task rather than as a general purpose device, and it may be subject to real-time performance constraints (Fig. 19.4).

Some embedded systems are termed *reactive systems* as they react to events that occur in their environment, and so their design is often based on a stimulus–response model. An event (or condition) that occurs in the system environment that causes the system to respond in some way is termed a stimulus, and a response is a signal sent by the software to its environment. For example, in the automotive sector, there are sensors in a car that detect when the temperature in the engine goes too high, and the response may be an audio alarm and visual warning to the driver.

Fig. 19.4 Example of an embedded system

One of the earliest embedded systems was the guidance computer developed for the Minuteman II missile [2] in the mid-1960s. Embedded systems are ubiquitous today, and they control many devices that are in common use such as microwave ovens, washing machines, coffee makers, clocks, DVD players, mobile phones and televisions.

Embedded systems became more popular following the introduction of the microprocessor in the early 1970s, as cheap microprocessors were able to fulfil the same role as a large number of components. The vast majority of microprocessors produced today are used as components of embedded systems.

19.7 Software Engineering and Innovation

The software field is highly innovative, and many new technologies and systems have been developed. We have discussed a sample of these innovations in this chapter, and the software engineering field needs to continually respond to these emerging technology trends with innovative solutions and methodologies to support the latest developments.

There have been many innovations in software engineering since its birth in the late 1960s. These include the waterfall and spiral lifecycle models, the Rational Unified Process and iterative development, the Agile methodology, software inspections and reviews, software testing and test-driven development, information hiding, object-oriented design and development, formal methods and UML, software process improvement, the CMM, CMMI and ISO SPICE.

There is also the need to focus on best practice in software engineering, as well as emerging technologies from various research programs. Piloting or technology transfer of innovative technology is an important part of continuous improvement. We discuss AOSE to illustrate innovation in software engineering.

19.7.1 Aspect-Oriented Software Engineering

The objective of this section is to give a brief introduction to AOSE, which is a recent innovation in software engineering based on the principle of separation of concerns. This principle states that software should be organized so that each program element does exactly one thing and one thing only. It is an important way to think about and structure software systems and makes it easier to maintain and reuse the software. AOSE may be applied to requirements engineering, software design and programming.

Concerns reflect system requirements, and examples of concerns are specific functionality, performance requirements, security requirements and so on. In most systems, the mapping between the requirements (concerns) and components is not one to one, and this means that the implementation of a change to the requirements may involve changes to more than one component. AOSE is an approach that aims to address this problem, and it is based on the idea of an aspect, which is a program abstraction that encapsulates functionality based on the separation of concerns. Programs that have been designed with the principle of separation of concerns have clear traceability to the requirements.

The principle of separation of concerns is a key principle in software engineering and requires that the software be organized in such a way that each element in the program (e.g. class and procedure) does exactly one thing. Another words, it is a design principle that separates a computer program into distinct sections such that each section addresses a separate concern.

A modular program implements the principle of separation of concerns through information hiding, where access to the module is through a well-defined interface with the information inside the module hidden. The value of the principle of separation of concerns is that individual sections of programs may be reused or modified independently without needing to be familiar with or modifying other sections of the program.

19.8   Review Questions

1. What is a distributed system?
2. What is service-oriented architecture?
3. What is software as a service?
4. What is cloud computing?
5. What is embedded software engineering?
6. Describe the various models that are used in cloud computing.
7. What is aspect-oriented software engineering?

19.9   Summary

This chapter gave a brief introduction to distributed systems, SOA, SaaS, cloud computing, embedded systems and AOSE.

A distributed system is a collection of interconnected computers that appears to be a single system. SOA is a way of developing a distributed system consisting of stand-alone web service executing on distributed computers in different geographical regions. SaaS allows software to be hosted remotely on a server (or servers), and access is provided to it over the Internet through a web browser. Cloud computing is a type of Internet-based computing that provides computing resources and various other services on demand.

An embedded system is a computer system within a larger electrical or mechanical system, and it is usually designed to do a specific task rather than as a general purpose device, and it may be subject to real-time performance constraints.

AOSE is based on the principle of separation of concerns, and it has been applied to requirements engineering, software design and programming, with the goal is to make it easier to maintain and reuse the software.

References

1. I. Sommerville, *Software Engineering*, 9th edn. (Pearson, Boston, 2011)
2. G. O'Regan, *Introduction to the History of Computing* (Springer, Switzerland, 2016)

Epilogue

20

Abstract

This chapter is the concluding chapter in which we summarize the journey that we have travelled in this book.

Keywords

Future of Software Engineering

We embarked on a long journey in this book and set ourselves the objective of providing a concise introduction to the software engineering field to students and practitioners. The book was based on the author's experience at leading industrial companies, and it covered both theory and practice. The objective was to give the reader a grasp of the fundamentals of the software engineering field, as well as guidance on how to apply the theory in an industrial environment.

Customers today have very high expectations on quality and expect high-quality software to be consistently delivered on time and on budget. The focus on quality requires that sound software engineering practices be employed to enable quality software to be consistently produced. Further, it is an accepted view in the software quality field that the quality of the delivered software is closely related to the quality of the underlying processes used to build the software and on adherence to them.

Many processes are employed in the design and development of software, and companies need to determine the extent to which the underlying processes used to design, develop, test and manage software projects are fit for purpose. The process will need to be continuously improved, and often, model-based improvement using a framework such as the Capability Maturity Model Integration (CMMI) is employed. There is also the need to focus on best practice in software engineering, as well as emerging technologies from various research programmes. Piloting or technology transfer of innovative technology is an important part of continuous improvement. Companies need to focus on customer satisfaction and software quality, and they need to ensure that the desired quality is built into the software product.

© Springer International Publishing AG 2017   317
G. O'Regan, *Concise Guide to Software Engineering*, Undergraduate Topics
in Computer Science, DOI 10.1007/978-3-319-57750-0_20

We discussed project planning and tracking, software lifecycles, software inspections and testing, configuration management, software quality assurance, etc. The CMMI was discussed, and it provides a framework that assists organizations in software process improvement. The appraisal of an organization against the CMMI allows the organization to determine the current capability or maturity of selected software processes and to prioritize improvements. It reveals strengths and weaknesses of the management and engineering processes in the organization. The output from the appraisal is used to formulate an improvement plan, which is then tracked to completion.

We provided an introduction to project management and discussed project estimation; project planning and scheduling, project monitoring and control, risk management and managing project quality.

We discussed requirements engineering including activities such as requirements gathering, requirements elicitation, requirements analysis, requirements management, and requirements verification and validation.

We then discussed design and development, including the high-level architectural design, the low-level design of individual programmes, and software development and reuse. The views of Hoare and Parnas on software design were discussed, and we discussed function-oriented design and object-oriented design. We discussed software development topics such as software reuse, customized-off-the-shelf software (COTS), and open-source software development.

We then moved on to discuss configuration management and discussed the concept of a baseline. Configuration management is concerned with identifying those deliverables that are subject to change control and controlling changes to them.

We discussed software inspections including Fagan inspections, as well as the less formal review and walk-through methodologies. Software testing was then discussed, including the various types of testing that may be carried out, and we discussed test planning, test case definition, test tracking, test metrics, test reporting and testing in an e-commerce environment.

We then discussed the selection and management of a software supplier and described how candidate suppliers may be formally evaluated, selected and managed during the project.

We discussed software quality assurance and the importance of process quality, and the discussion included audits and described how they are carried out. We then discussed metrics and problem-solving, including the balanced score card and GQM, as well as presenting a collection of sample metrics for an organization.

We then discussed software reliability and dependability and covered topics such as software reliability and software reliability models; the Cleanroom methodology; system availability; safety and security critical systems, and dependency engineering.

We discussed formal methods, which are often employed in the safety critical and security critical fields. These consist of a set of mathematical techniques to specify and derive a programme from its specification. Formal methods may be employed to rigorously state the requirements of the proposed system; they may be employed to derive a programme from its mathematical specification; and they provide a rigorous proof that the implemented programme satisfies its specification.

We discussed the Z specification language, which was developed at the Programming Research Group at Oxford University in the early 1980s. Z specifications are mathematical and the use of mathematics ensures precision and allows inconsistencies and gaps in the specification to be identified. Theorem provers may be employed to demonstrate that the software implementation meets its specification.

We then discussed the unified modelling language (UML), which is a visual modelling language for software systems, and it is used to present several views of the system architecture. We presented various UML diagrams such as use case diagrams, sequence diagrams and activity diagrams.

We then discussed the important field of software process improvement, discussed the idea of a software process and discussed the benefits that may be gained from software process improvement.

We gave an overview of the CMMI model, and discussed its five maturity levels and their constituent process areas. We discussed both the staged and continuous representations of the CMMI.

We then discussed a selection of tools to support various software engineering activities, including tools to support project management, requirements engineering, configuration management, design and development activities and software testing.

We discussed the Agile methodology which is a popular lightweight approach to software development. Agile has a strong collaborative style of working, and it advocates adaptive planning and evolutionary development,

We then discussed some innovative developments in the computer field, such as distributed systems, service-oriented architecture, software as a service, cloud computing and embedded systems. This led to a discussion of the many innovations in the software engineering and the need for continuous innovation.

20.1 The Future of Software Engineering

Software engineering has come a long way since the 1950s and 1960s, when it was accepted that the completed software would always contain lots of defects and that the coding should be done as quickly as possible, to enable these defects to be quickly identified and corrected.

The software crisis in the late 1960s highlighted problems with budget and schedule overruns, as well as problems with the quality and reliability of the delivered software. This led to the birth of software engineering as a discipline in its own right and the realization that programming is quite distinct from science and mathematics.

The software engineering field is highly innovative and many new technologies and systems have been developed over the decades. These include object-oriented design and development; formal methods and UML; the waterfall and spiral models; software inspections and software testing; software process improvement and the CMMI; and the Agile methodology.

Software engineering will continue to be fundamental to the success of projects. There is not a one size that fits all: some companies (e.g. in the safety critical or security critical fields) are likely to focus on formal methods and software process maturity models such as the CMMI. For other areas, the lightweight Agile methodology may be the appropriate software development methodology.

Companies are likely to measure the cost of poor quality in the future, as driving down the cost of poor quality will become more important. Software components and the verification of software components are likely to become important, in order to speed up software development and to shorten time to market. Software reuse and open-source software development are likely to grow in popularity, and continuous innovation will continue in the software engineering field.

Glossary

AMN Abstract Machine Notation

AOSE Aspect Oriented Software Engineering

ATM Automated Teller Machine

BCS British Computer Society

BRS Business Requirements Specification

BSC Balanced Scorecard

CAR Causal Analysis and Resolution

CBA IPI CMM Based Assessment Internal Process Improvement

CCB Change Control Board

CCS Calculus Communicating Systems

CICS Customer Information Control System

CM Configuration Management

CMM® Capability Maturity Model

CMMI® Capability Maturity Model Integration

COCOMO Constructive Cost Model

COPQ Cost of Poor Quality

COTS Customized Off-the-Shelf

CR Change Request

CSP Communicating Sequential Processes

DAR Decision Analysis and Resolution

DMAIC Define, Measure, Analyse, Improve, Control

DMADV Define, Measure, Analyse, Design, Verify

© Springer International Publishing AG 2017
G. O'Regan, *Concise Guide to Software Engineering*, Undergraduate Topics
in Computer Science, DOI 10.1007/978-3-319-57750-0

DOORS Dynamic Object-Oriented Requirements System

DSDM Dynamic Systems Development Method

EAF Effort Adjustment Factor

ESA European Space Agency

ESI European Software Institute

FSF Free Software Foundation

FSM Finite State Machine

GG Generic Goal

GP Generic Practice

GQM Goal, Question, Metric

GUI Graphical User Interface

HP Hewlett-Packard

HR Human Resources

HTM Hyper-Text Mark-up Language

IaaS Infrastructure as a Service

IBM International Business Machines

IDE Integrated Development Environment

IEC International Electro technical Commission

IEEE Institute of Electrical and Electronic Engineers

IPM Integrated Project Management

ISEB Information System Examination Board

ISO International Standards Organization

JAD Joint Application Development

JVM Java Virtual Machine

KLOC Thousand Lines of Code

LCL Lower Control Limit

LDRA Liverpool Data Research Associates

LPF Logic of Partial Functions

LOC Lines of Code

MA Measurement and Analysis

MOD Ministry of Defence

MTBF Mean Time Between Failure

MTTF Mean Time to Failure

MTTR Mean Time to Repair

NATO North Atlantic Treaty Organization

OCL Object Constraint Language

ODC Orthogonal Defect Classification

OID Organization Innovation and Deployment

OMT Object Modelling Technique

OOD Object-oriented Design

OOSE Object-Oriented Software Engineering

OPD Organization Process Definition

OPF Organization Process Focus

OPP Organization Process Performance

OT Organization Training

PaaS Platform as a Service

PCE Phase Containment Effectiveness

P-CM People Capability Maturity Model

PI Product Integration

PL/1 Programming Language

PMBOK Project Management Book of Knowledge

PMI Project Management Institute

PMC Project Monitoring and Control

PMP Project Management Professional

PP Project Planning

PPM Project Portfolio Management

PPQA Process and Product Quality Assurance

Prince Projects In a Controlled Environment

PSP Personal Software Process

PVCS Polytron Version Control System

QPM Quantitative Project Management

RAD Rapid Application Development

RAG Red, Amber, Green

RCA Root Cause Analysis

RD Requirements Development

REQM Requirements Management

RFP Request for Proposal

ROI Return on Investment

RPM Rational Portfolio Manager

RSM Rational Software Modeller

RSKM Risk Management

RUP Rational Unified Process

SaaS Software as a Service

SAM Supplier Agreement Management

SCAMPI Standard CMMI Appraisal Method for Process, Improvement

SCM Software Configuration Management

SEI Software Engineering Institute

SEPG Software Engineering Process Group

SG Specific Goal

SLA Service Level Agreement

SLOC Source lines of code

SOA Service Oriented Architecture

SOW Statement of Work

SP Specific Practice

SPC Statistical Process Control

SPI Software Process Improvement

SPICE Software Process Improvement Capability dEtermination

SQA Software Quality Assurance

SRS System Requirements Specification

SSADM Structured Systems Analysis and Design Method

TDD Test Driven Development

TS Technical Solution

TSP Team Software Process

UAT User Acceptance Testing

UCL Upper Control Limit

UK United Kingdom

UML Unified Modelling Language

URS User Requirements Specification

VAL Validation

VDM Vienna Development Method

VDM⁺ Irish School of VDM

VER Verification

VOB Version Object Base

VSS Visual Source Safe

XP Extreme Programming

Y2K Year 2000

References

1. ARC:06 Appraisal Requirements for CMMI V1.2. (ARC V1.2). SCAMPI Upgrade Team. TR CMU/SEI-2006-TR-011, August, 2006
2. I. Bhandari, A case study of software process improvement during development. IEEE Trans. Softw. Eng. **19**(12)
3. M.B. Chrissis, M. Conrad, S. Shrum, *CMMI for Development. Guidelines for Process Integration and Product Improvement*, 3rd edn. SEI Series in Software Engineering (Addison Wesley, Boston, 2011)
4. W. Edwards Deming, *Out of Crisis* (M.I.T. Press, Cambridge, 1986)
5. W. Humphry, *Managing the Software Process* (Addison Wesley, Boston, 1989)
6. J, Juran, *Juran's Quality Handbook* (McGraw Hill, New York, 1951)
7. Ministry of Defence, 00-55 (PART 2) *I* Issue 1, The Procurement of Safety Critical software in Defence Equipment, PART 2: Guidance. Interim Defence Standard, UK, 1991
8. F. O'Hara, Peer reviews—the key to cost effective quality. European SEPG, Amsterdam, 1998
9. Standard CMMI Appraisal Method for Process Improvement. CMU/SEI-2006-HB-002. V1.2, August 2006
10. CMMI Executive Overview. Presentation by the SEI. Software Engineering Institute, 2006
11. CMMI Impact. Presentation by Anita Carleton. Software Engineering Institute, August 2009

© Springer International Publishing AG 2017   327
G. O'Regan, *Concise Guide to Software Engineering*, Undergraduate Topics
in Computer Science, DOI 10.1007/978-3-319-57750-0

Index

© Springer International Publishing AG 2017
G. O'Regan, *Concise Guide to Software Engineering*, Undergraduate Topics
in Computer Science, DOI 10.1007/978-3-319-57750-0

CPSIA information can be obtained
at www.ICGtesting.com
Printed in the USA
LVHW061451050219
606472LV00003B/65/P

9 783319 577494